Violent Origins

Violent Origins

WALTER BURKERT, RENÉ GIRARD, and
JONATHAN Z. SMITH on

Ritual Killing and Cultural Formation

EDITED BY ROBERT G. HAMERTON-KELLY,
WITH AN INTRODUCTION BY BURTON MACK AND
A COMMENTARY BY RENATO ROSALDO

Stanford University Press · Stanford, California

Stanford University Press
Stanford, California
© 1987 by the Board of Trustees of the
Leland Stanford Junior University
Printed in the United States of America
Original printing 1987
Last figure below indicates year of this printing:
97 96 95 94 93 92 91 90 89 88

CIP data appear at the end of the book

Preface

> Violence is the heart and secret soul of the Sacred.
>
> René Girard, *Violence and the Sacred*

> More can be said for the thesis that all orders and forms of author-ity in human society are founded on institutionalized violence. . . . Thus, blood and violence lurk fascinatingly at the very heart of religion.
>
> Walter Burkert, *Homo Necans*

RENÉ GIRARD AND WALTER BURKERT present analyses of human culture and its origins that focus on the role of violence. It is not only the timeliness of such a focus that commands serious attention, but also its success in elucidating the evidence of past and present cultures. Their proposals, especially in the field of religion, seem to offer a "general theory" of the origin and meaning of ritual and myth. Girard claims this explicitly, Burkert implicitly. Such an "out of season" claim could not fail to arouse the interest of those of us working in the field of religion, and so we resolved to arrange a con-versation among Girard, and Burkert, and a third party who could bring a critical acumen to bear on the conversation. That third party was Jonathan Z. Smith. The architect of the project was Bur-ton Mack, who conceived the event, issued the invitations, and set the agenda.

The result of that conversation, held at Pajaro Dunes, near Santa Cruz, California, in the fall of 1983, is this remarkable record. In papers that were prepared and circulated months before we met, Girard presents the most extensive exposition of his theory to date in English; Burkert provides *retractiones* of *Homo Necans* imme-diately prior to its publication in English; and Jonathan Smith contributes a view of sacrifice that needs neither Girard's nor Burkert's theories. Burton Mack provided an exposition of the thought of each for the sake of the others and identified areas of agreement and disagreement. Mack's paper is the "Call" for conversation, and the others wrote in response to his presentation of the issues and formulation of the questions. His paper in this volume has been abridged to serve as an introduction.

The special value of this volume is the conversation as such, the *vivae voces* of working scholars engaged with one another's theories over a period of three days. This is a rare document, because such searching discussion among leading intellectuals is, alas, so rare. Here, however, we have the record of a real dialogue, and can see how the challenges are made and met and how the principals move and maneuver. We are also privileged to have the commentary of a working anthropologist, Renato Rosaldo, which gives the impressions of an "outsider."

I believe that the edited transcriptions make unusually good sense and demonstrate a continuity of thought that is not often found in such documents, given the vagaries of the living voice. They do not have the tightness of a written text, to be sure, and should be taken for what they are: the living voice of debate in progress. There is an open-endedness to the volume, therefore, and the reader is invited to participate in the debate. No minds are changed; there are no "conversions" recorded; but the issues are clearly delineated, and we witness how the principals defend their methods and conclusions.

The origin of violence in human beings is difficult to explain, and its role in human culture hard to assess dispassionately. In 1932 the American Psychological Association decided by a vote of 346 to 10 that violence was the result of nurture rather than nature, an expedient that seems to illustrate the desperate situation of the social sciences in the face of this issue. Since then sociobiology has come on the scene, and its findings, judiciously summarized by Melvin Konner in his book *The Tangled Wing* (1982), confirm what common sense might have guessed, that both biology and culture play their part. The one thing that cannot be denied is that violence is ubiquitous and tenacious and must be accounted for if we are to understand humanity.

Two of the principals in these discussions make violence the center of their explanations, and to that extent open up an approach to an understanding of human nature and culture that faces facts from which more squeamish theorists turn away. Their theories attempt to account for phenomena that are usually glossed over, and they enable us to understand hitherto obscure texts.

The conference was sponsored by the Institute for Antiquity and Christianity at the Claremont Graduate School, Claremont, California, the Stanford Newman Institute, and the Stanford Memorial Church. Edith Bridges typed the manuscript more than once, and the editors of Stanford Press were especially helpful. To all these I express my thanks.

Stanford, California   R.G.H-K.
1986

Contents

Participants

CESÁREO BANDERA is University Distinguished Professor of Spanish Literature and Chair of the Department of Romance Languages at the University of North Carolina, Chapel Hill. He is the author of *Mímesis conflictiva: Ficción literaria y violencia en Cervantes y Calderón* (1974) and other publications.

WALTER BURKERT is Professor of Classical Philology at the University of Zurich. He is the author of *Structure and History in Greek Mythology and Ritual* (1980) and *Homo Necans: The Anthropology of Ancient Greek Sacrificial Ritual and Myth* (1983).

TERRELL BUTLER is Associate Professor of Comparative Literature at Brigham Young University. His book *History and Crisis* is in press, as is his edited volume *Myth, Literature and the Bible*, a collection of papers presented at the international symposium he organized in November 1984.

MATEI CALINESCU is Professor of Comparative Literature at Indiana University at Bloomington. One of his major scholarly interests is the study of cultural and social modernity. Among his publications on this subject is *Faces of Modernity: Avant-Garde, Decadence, Kitsch* (1977).

LANGDON ELSBREE is Professor of English and Chair at Claremont McKenna College. He is a co-author of *The Heath Handbook of Composition* and the author of *The Rituals of Life: Patterns in Narratives* (1982). He has also written on the dance in Jane Austen, George Eliot, Thomas Hardy, and D. H. Lawrence.

RENÉ GIRARD is the Andrew B. Hammond Professor of French Language, Literature and Civilization at Stanford University. Notable among his works are *Deceit, Desire, and the Novel: Self and Other in Literary Structure* (1965), *Violence and the Sacred* (1977), and *Le Bouc émissaire* (1982). His latest work is *La Route antique des hommes pervers* (1985).

ROBERT HAMERTON-KELLY, Dean of the Chapel and Consulting Professor of Religious Studies and Lecturer in Classics at Stanford University from 1972 to 1986, is the author of *Pre-Existence, Wisdom, and the Son of Man* (1973), *God the Father* (1979), and *Sprung Time* (1980) and the editor of *Philomatheis: Studies and Essays in the Humanities in Memory of Philip Merlan* (1971, with Robert B. Palmer) and *Jews, Greeks and Christians: Essays in Honor of William David Davies* (1976, with Robin Scroggs).

ROBERT JEWETT is Professor of New Testament Interpretation at Garrett-Evangelical Theological Seminary and the author of eight books, including *The Captain America Complex: The Dilemma of Zealous Nationalism* (1973), *Christian Tolerance: Paul's Message to the Modern Church* (1982), and *The Thessalonian Correspondence: Pauline Rhetoric and Millenarian Piety* (1987).

JOHN LAWRENCE is Professor of Philosophy at Morningside College. In addition to "Violence," a monograph published in 1970, he has written *The American Monomyth* (1977, with Robert Jewett), *Fair Use and Free Inquiry* (1980, with Bernard Timberg), and *The Electronic Scholar* (1984).

BURTON L. MACK is Professor of New Testament Studies at the School of Theology at Claremont. He is the author of three books, including *Wisdom and the Hebrew Epic* (1985), and numerous articles. He also serves on several editorial boards with primary responsibility for studies in Hellenistic Judaism and early Christianity.

RENATO ROSALDO is Professor of Anthropology at Stanford University. He is the author of *Ilongot Headhunting, 1883-1974: A Study in Society and History*. He has written articles on history, narrative, and ethnographic discourse, and on subjects in the field of Chicano studies.

JONATHAN Z. SMITH is the Robert O. Anderson Distinguished Service Professor in the Humanities and a member of the Committee on the History of Culture at the University of Chicago. He is the author of *Map Is Not Territory: Studies in the History of Religions* (1978) and *Imagining Religion: From Babylon to Jonestown* (1982).

FRITS STAAL is Professor of Philosophy and of South Asian Languages at the University of California at Berkeley. Among his publications are *Advaita and Neoplatonism* (1961), *Exploring Mysticism* (1975), *The Science of Ritual* (1982), and *AGNI: The Vedic Ritual of the Fire Altar* (2 vols., 1983).

Violent Origins

BURTON MACK

Introduction: Religion and Ritual

I

The history of discourse on religion has consistently preferred myth to ritual as the focus of its primary questions and concerns. It is true that ritual has always been recognized as a major datum of religion, but the earlier studies of religion did not explore the behavioral, motivational, and social life of religious actions and rites. They were, instead, preoccupied with the question of the origin of belief in the gods, and the relation of mythic mentality to human intellect. Rituals were handled as myths were, that is, as expressions of belief in and encounter with divine powers or entities. The question that exercised scholars was how to account for the origin and plausibility of mythic beliefs and notions, and rituals were regarded mainly as "responses" to these "myths."

The most significant of the classical studies of ritual, in our opinion, are those that moved away from this older orientation to religion as ideation and belief. Lines can be drawn that run from W. Robertson Smith to Henri Hubert, Marcel Mauss, and Emile Durkheim on the one hand, and to Sigmund Freud on the other. This scholarship discovered the relation of religious ritual to basic human patterns of behavior and to basic human social structures, but ritual theory was not immediately advanced by this discovery. What had first to happen, apparently, was the conceptualization and implementation of the emergent human sciences: sociology, psychology, and ethnography. Hubert and Mauss, for example, expanded the dramatic aspects of W. Robertson Smith's theory of ritual and explored ritual's social function. Especially important in this regard was the new sociology of reciprocity that they developed along with Durkheim. Nevertheless, they still understood the rationale for the religious content of ritual in terms of the older notion of the Sacred and its mystique. Killing was required because the gods were totally "other" and dangerous, and because contact with them required a transformation as radical as that between life and death. The purpose of the encounter was the well-known *do ut des*.[1]

This view of ritual has been the respectable theory among historians and phenomenologists of religion for more than seventy years. Its influence can be traced quite easily in the history of scholarship because there have been so few revisions of it. Geo Widengren's *Religionsphänomenologie* may serve as an example of its currency. In his discussion of sacrifice (1969: 280), he expressly states that he still finds the views of Hubert and Mauss most helpful as a definition of sacrificial ritual.

The phenomenology of religion emerged in the 1920's, and with it the attempt to articulate religion as a discrete system with its own rationale, in distinction from the functionalism developing in the various human sciences. Rudolf Otto's "Sacred" was reified as the objective reality with which *homo religiosus* had to do, and it was eventually ontologized. Thus the privileged position of being before manifestation, or logos before praxis, or myth before ritual was revived programmatically and taken up into the very definition of religion itself. The essence of religion was the *Sacred*, together with its modes of *Manifestation* and the forms of human *Response* to it. Ritual was interesting mainly as a symbolic expression of and "participation" in the Sacred; ritual sacrifice was mainly an embarrassment. One seeks in vain, for instance, for a critical discussion or theory of ritual killing in the works of Mircea Eliade. The orientation of this period of endeavor in the science of religion was to myth.

Adolf Jensen was an exception. In *Mythos und Kult bei Naturvölkern* (1951), he set forth a thesis about the origin of ritual killing among paleocultivators, which though still beholden to the priority of myth over ritual pointed to new theories. Jensen saw that the notion of "offering" was inadequate to account for the origin of sacrifice and explained it as the rationalization of later cultural stages.

[1]The formula of exchange, "I give in order that you may give," is frequently used to sum up older theories of ritual that viewed sacrifice as an offering to the gods.

He found in the myths and rituals of paleocultivators a simpler yet more profound explanation. Sacrifice celebrates and channels "killing" as the act of taking life (food) in order to live. This was a new notion for religious studies. Religion had to do with activity caused by basic human needs. Perceived as problematic, these activities were rationalized by myth, patterned by ritual, and integrated into the order of society. Jensen's work raised a storm of scholarly criticism and debate. Many of his assumptions (methodological, ethnological, and historical) can no longer be shared, but this does not detract from his achievement. He succeeded in shaking the foundations of the traditional "offering" theory, and he succeeded in making plausible an alternative approach to the study of religion: the investigation of the derivation of religious phenomena from ordinary human experience, especially in its social mode.

Victor Turner's work, published during the 1960's, followed Jensen's lead. His understanding of ritual as a process firmly embedded in the ongoing life of a complex society demonstrated the value of a careful description of social contexts for the construction of a theory of ritual. René Girard's *Mensonge romantique et vérité romanesque* (1961) and Walter Burkert's "Greek Tragedy and Sacrificial Ritual" (1966) were also contributors to this new line of approach. During this period, Jonathan Z. Smith was laying the foundations for his own approach in a series of lectures at the University of Chicago. Two of these were published in 1970 and 1971 ("The Influence of Symbols on Social Change" and "*Adde Parvum Parvo Magnus Acervus Erit*"). Then, in 1972, both Girard's *La Violence et le sacré* and Burkert's *Homo Necans* appeared, each presenting a major new theory of religion based on the phenomenon of sacrifice. Smith's emerging theory was sharpened in the Claremont Lectures of 1974, which included his "A Pearl of Great Price," "Map Is Not Territory," and "The Bare Facts of Ritual" (1976, 1978b, 1980). With these studies, ritual came into view as a phenomenon of primary significance for the definition of religion.

These theorists take a rigorous analytical approach, unencumbered by the "offering" theory, and break with the dicta traditionally accepted in the phenomenology and history of religions. In each case, new points of departure have been found, new perspectives won, and new methods developed. Each appears to have worked independently of the others, but they share a surprising and striking attitude both of restlessness with more traditional views and of eagerness to offer some alternative explanation of religion. Before attempting to describe each theory separately, we will do well to ask what they have in common.

At first, it might appear that Girard, Burkert, and Smith would have little in common. Certainly their fields of scholarly endeavor, and their respective points of entrée into the question of ritual and theory of religion, are different. Burkert is first of all a classicist, then a historian of Greek religion; Smith is a historian of the history of religions with special expertise in Hellenistic religions; and Girard is a literary critic versed in the history and theory of the human sciences. What perspectives might they share?

The first thing to be said is that all three understand religion as a social phenomenon and wish to clarify the role of religion in the formation of society and culture. Each is an empiricist, seeking to give an account of religious behavior in terms provided by the human sciences; none invokes the mystique of the Sacred in order to explain the attractiveness of religion. For all, religion arises in relation to some human activity fundamental to social life, and for each of them, religion in all its manifestations is essentially a human construction.

The struggle between the "human sciences" approach and the established "history and phenomenology of religion" position can be followed in the congress volumes of the International Association for the History of Religions after 1970. It is clear that sociologists and cultural anthropologists have begun to chart a course that is extremely uncomfortable for traditional morphologists. Traditional scholars hold that, though interesting, these new perspectives can hardly be said to account for all that religion really is. At issue are not merely the forms and structure of the Sacred, whether mandala or plot, but the very priority of the notion of the Sacred itself.

Followers of Eliade draw the battle line around the "irreducibility of the Sacred." By this they mean that only those who begin with the notion of the Sacred, defining religion in terms of "manifestations" of the Sacred and the human responses to it, belong to the phenomenological tradition; those who question this assumption, seeking to account for religion in terms of human responses to human situations, run the risk of committing the "reductionist fallacy." Eliade himself generously attempts to interpret the "tension" that has developed between the two approaches as a creative dialogue between "phenomenologists" and "historians"; however, it is clear that he sees the danger as lying with the "historicists," who may fail to grasp the essence of religion as "total claim," and who thus produce theories of religion on the basis of inauthentic, functionalist views of this or that human science (1969: 35-36).

Burkert sees this situation as a crisis for traditional views of "the human" in general. He refers to the "Copernican Revolution" that, as he understands it, took place in the ethological discovery of the primacy of rites over linguistic communications. He is the only one of the three to appeal repeatedly to ethological evidence in support of reconstructions of primitive ritual, and the question of the value of this evidence for theories of religion will no doubt need to be discussed; but he does speak for the others in his assessment of what it will mean for the study of religion if a strictly empirical-anthropological approach is taken.

The phenomenologists will see the theories presented here as "reductionistic," but they need to be careful before settling upon that judgment. They should at least note the full range of data, disciplines, and methods that informs the approach. Simple reductions to a single "cause" are not made; rather, extremely complex manifestations of social activity are usually taken into account. Each investigator seeks what might be called a cultural-anthropological construct—a theoretical schema of the human situation, and its modes of being perceived and engaged—that can make sense of the full range of human institutions, including religion. None appeals directly to structuralist theory, but the constructs sought by each of them are plausible alternatives to the cultural grammars proposed by the structuralists. It is, in fact, a most significant compatibility that all three theories combine structuralist perspectives with functionalist concerns (a combination viewed with grave suspicion in the American tradition of the anthropological sciences), and seek to include some accounting of "process" or "history" as well.

This restless exegesis, then, is a second mark of similarity among the three. Texts are basic, but the human constructs they seek are thought to lie "outside" the texts. None of the investigators appeals to poststructuralist categories such as Jacques Derrida's "*différance*," the notion of "intertextuality," or Michel Foucault's "*épistème*," but each treats texts as needing to be ranked on a scale of displacement, or human construction (interpretation), from the way things basically or actually go. Smith works with the "incongruity" between what is actually known, felt, and acknowledged (e.g., the hunt) on the one hand, and what the myth-ritual depicts as the perfect scenario on the other; for Burkert, a fundamental displacement must occur in order to resolve basic biological and sociological conflicts with religious symbolism; and Girard's thesis is simply that religion is, by definition, evasion—that is, avoidance of an unacceptable truth.

We may want to question this view of texts and data, this desire to find a point of departure within articulated cultural traditions on the one hand, combined with a fundamental skepticism about its referential adequacy on the other. What actually counts as data for the study of religion? Why are texts not enough? And what is the reason for the difference perceived between observable social constructions and their "religious" rationalizations? That each investigator sets out to explore this difference between social history and cultural tradition, a difference that demands a contextual and intertextual exegesis, is clear. What is not clear is how and why this is understood to be necessary, and what difference it might make for a theory of religion.

II

René Girard's Theory of Violence

In 1972, Girard published *La Violence et le sacré*, an essay that proposes a startling new theory of religion.[2] Violence, according to Girard, is endemic to human society, and there is no solution to this problem except for the answer that religion gives. Since that answer is given in rituals of killing and their rationalizations as "sacrifice," the solution religion provides is also an act of violence. Violence, then, is the manifestation of the Sacred in its dual mode of (1) the

---

[2]Throughout the discussion, I refer to the English translation, published in 1977 under the title *Violence and the Sacred*.

terror of uncontrolled killing, and (2) controlled rituals of sacrifice. Girard's book was written to give an account of how this could be, and to present a critique of the mythic mentality that underlies the solution religion offers.

His theory is outlined in bold strokes in the first ten pages of the book, fleshed out to a working hypothesis in the next three chapters, then refined as he broadens its scope of application to a full range of religious phenomena in debate with scholarly traditions. It is a striking essay. The straightforward proposal at the beginning sets the stage for a series of reflections that expands the notion of sacrifice to apply to ever larger arenas of human activity. Each of these expansions catches up questions the reader already will have asked, questions by which the force of the argument might have been avoided. The entire range of the humanities and the human sciences eventually comes under review. Competing theories are addressed and set aside, and finally the phenomenon of sacrifice is seen at center stage of the whole human drama, determining all of its enactments. "Sacrifice is the most crucial and fundamental of rites," according to Girard, and "it is also the most commonplace" (1977: 300). All systems that give structure to human society have been generated from it: language, kinship systems, taboos, codes of etiquette, patterns of exchange, rites, and civil institutions. Thus a theory of sacrifice has produced a comprehensive account of human social formation, religion, and culture.

There are a number of basic notions in Girard's thesis with which we may begin. They are extremely complex notions, interrelated and developed to form an interlocking conception of the process by which social formation occurs. These notions include "sacrifice," the "surrogate-victim mechanism," "mimetic desire," and the "sacrificial crisis."

For Girard, rituals of sacrifice are enigmas to be explored. The commonly accepted ideas of "sacrifice," intended as clarifications of the meaning of sacrificial rituals, belong, he says, to the level of mythic rationalization. If we want to go beyond this, it is important to notice what it is that happens in rituals of sacrifice, and to ask why mythic rationalizations have been given. What happens, of course, is a killing. Girard is impressed with the incidence and centrality of ritual killing in the most diverse forms of human culture.

Since ritual is, by definition, a reenactment of a "prior event," it must be investigated under two aspects: (1) the way in which ritual "represents" or "substitutes for" the "prior event" and (2) the way in which both the ritual and prior event interpret the act of killing. In Girard's view, the "prior event" that all ritual killings rationalize and represent in various "substitutions" is a collective murder, an act of mob violence. "Sacrifice" then becomes a term that can be used to refer to the complex phenomenon of the collective killing of a human victim, its mythic rationalization, and its ritualization.

To understand how a collective murder could stand at the beginning of human culture, how an act of violence could possibly define both the problem and the solution for social formation, Girard suggests the following scenario. Humans have no braking mechanism for intraspecific aggression. This means that rivalries and conflicts, once unleashed, cannot stop short of manslaughter. Violence, therefore, is endemic. Since the only answer to murder is another murder, cycles of reciprocal retaliation create unending series of revenge killings. To bring the series to an end, a "final" killing is necessary. The final killing is achieved in the "mechanism of the surrogate victim." From within the group, one person is separated out as victim. The selection is arbitrary and spontaneous, though there are requisites. The victim must be recognizable as a surrogate for the guilty party (or parties, and ultimately for the group itself); he must be vulnerable, unable to retaliate, without champions to continue the vengeful violence; and there must be unanimity within the group that he is the one at fault. When this unanimity is achieved the victim is treated as a criminal, killed, and expelled. This brings the violence to an end. The group has redirected its aggressions and its members are now able to cooperate.

Why is violence endemic in the first place? What is the cause of the rivalry and conflict that set the vicious cycle in motion? For this question, Girard also has an answer—namely, the "mechanism of mimetic desire," which he presents in another scenario similar to that given for the surrogate-victim mechanism. The notion itself is rather easy to grasp when first pointed out. Desire is usually thought to be focused on desirable objects whose value is inherent; in reality, however, the value of the desired object is a result of the fact that someone else desires it. Thus desire is learned, by imitating the other, and soon becomes not primarily a desire for the object, but a desire to be like the other. Not knowing this, the imitator assumes that he does well to value the object of desire, only to discover that the closer he comes to its acquisition, the greater becomes the hostility of and rejection by the one imitated. This creates what Girard calls the "double bind" in the relationship. The one imitated has said, in effect, "Be like me: value the object." But when the imitator reaches out to take it, rivalry occurs, and the one imitated says, "Do not be like me. It's mine." Veneration and rejection, mimesis and difference, are therefore experienced together in tension. The disclosure of rivalry then transforms the image of the model into that of one's "monstrous double." It is this problem that is the motivator and frustrator of human interaction.

When a society fails to address the problem of inherent rivalry by means of apotropaic rituals, the phenomenon of the "monstrous double" emerges in the form of "sacrificial crisis." Violence is the end result of this process and the mark of the crisis. Violence can indicate the breakdown of conventional ritual systems, but it also brings into play that which generates religion and culture in the first place. It is "generative" or collective violence that can transform the "monstrous double" into a savior. It does this by erasing all memories of rivalry and rejection, allowing only the beneficial effects of the "sacrificial" death to be remembered. It is this creative confusion (i.e., the necessary redirection of aggressions and the consequent displacement of guilt) that triggers the many linguistic, conceptual, and symbolic systems on which society is based. This displacement of guilt also accounts for the necessity of the delusion that determines religious mentality. To acknowledge the deed as arbitrary and the victim as surrogate would plunge the group back into the terror of reciprocal violence. Only by retaining a fictional or mythic account of the event can the community avoid the truth about itself, which would destroy it. The mythic account casts the victim as savior and the event of his death as sacrifice. Rituals of sacrifice are instituted to substitute for the real thing. Thus the circle closes.

The force of Girard's tightly woven analysis of the violent roots of religion is stunning. We need to ask how he has come to this theory, and what can be done to test it; but before we proceed to these questions, it will be helpful to point out a certain difficulty in its conception. I refer to the fact that each of the key notions can be used to describe functions that occur at different "levels" of social interaction. Three such levels can be distinguished: (1) the surface level of observable behavior; (2) a "hidden" level of unconscious motivation, where the dynamics of the mechanisms ultimately reside; and (3) the "generative" event, which Girard can imagine both as a "first time" and as a universal "moment," and which we can call the "originary" level.

Care must be taken while reading Girard to make the necessary distinctions between these levels of reference when technical terminology is used and its conceptuality is developed. The term ritual, for instance, is fairly consistently used to refer to what we can observe at the level of social history; in contrast, the term sacrifice, though it can be used to refer to actual rites, refers ultimately to the structuring mechanism of the hidden level, and appears to be an important term for the description of the originary event as well. This conceptual problem is compounded by the need to describe the key notions in dramatic or narrative discourse. Narrative is required in order to visualize the dynamic aspects of the events, mechanisms, and processes to which the key notions refer. The description of these moments can hardly be achieved without engaging in narrative sequencing, even though a chronological elongation of the process may not be intended. If Girard were not concerned about social history and change (which he is), and if he had not insisted on placing the "originary sacrifice" at the beginning of human history (which he does), we might be able to understand the three levels in terms of a structuralist phenomenology. Then the dynamic aspects of the mechanisms operant at each level could be understood as generative in respect to the next highest level, and a narrative description of this generative process could be understood essentially in synchronic terms. But Girard's concern for social and cultural history makes it extremely difficult to read him in terms of such a phenomenology. He wants, after all, to account for the entire sweep of human history in relation both to its origins and to its eventualities.

The several scenarios thus describe a single drama that has been played out "since" the beginning and "from" the beginning, at different levels of dynamic interaction and with various degrees of consciousness about the full extent of the script. Girard would like to convince us that this is so, and suggests that we should be able to see the drama being acted out in social history; but the element of concealment is also constitutive of the processes at every level, especially that of social history. This creates a problem. For the daily round, mimetic desire is continually operant, but only at the psychosocial level, and it is hardly recognized by those involved. In times of social crisis, the surrogate-victim mechanism can be observed to surface, but only by those looking on as spectators. Those who are caught in its vicious cycle, both killers and victims, do not know what they are doing. At the level of cultural institutions and rationalizations—ritual systems, for example—the mythic mentality prevails, concealing the motivational mechanisms by design; and at the originary level, the dramatic moment erases the horrible truth even as the event occurs. So where do we look to see the enactment according to the original script? The data appear not to be available. Cultural artifacts are structured so as to hide the mechanisms of violence, and the mechanisms are designed so as to conceal even themselves. A disclosure is required, but what veil can be lifted? How, in fact, has Girard himself made the discovery?

Girard is a literary critic well versed in contemporary French thought and well read in Western literatures, from the Greek and Hebrew classics to the modern novel. I have said that his theory of religion is startling, but equally surprising is the manner of its derivation. It is won in the course of a critical reading of literature. The history of religions is dotted, to be sure, with major theoretical contributions from scholars outside the field; but to know that is hardly to be prepared for Girard. Here the major thesis and argumentation derive from an analysis of literary texts not normally understood to be religious documents, and where appeal is made to religious phenomena and texts familiar to the historian of religions, they are treated no differently than other literatures. Girard moves easily from culture to culture, epoch to epoch, text to text, novel to myth, with a single assumption about language and a single method for its critical reading. The multiplicities of cultural and historical context are acknowledged in certain broad generalizations, but Girard sees no need to qualify his readings severely by considering historical particularities. Neither does he allow linguistic typologies of generic classifications of literature to stand in the way of comparative readings across the broad sweep of human literary activity. It is Girard's method, then, that many will find most astonishing. He is a literary critic who has dared to propose a theory of religion on the basis of his criticism. To understand how he has discovered the surrogate-victim mechanism that societies both manifest and conceal, we need to ask how he uncovers it in his reading of literature—literature that is, of course, a cultural production.

Girard does not offer us a programmatic statement on criticism. What he does do is point us immediately to texts and engage us in a reading of them. But as the study progresses, an earlier statement about "the pieties of classical humanists" (1977: 1) expands into a polemic against a naïve and fearful, self-deprecating approach to literature on the part of critics. These critics assume that literature is inconsequential for the serious business in which the human sciences are engaged. Girard's view is that literature is the very entrance into the inner sanctum of the human drama. We need to know where he found the key to that door.

We may not be able to explore this question satisfactorily. *Violence and the Sacred* is written as an essay in the style of scholarly allusion. Readers are challenged to detect for themselves dependencies on and divergence from Girard's precursors, his partners in debate. Those of us who are schooled in the scribal traditions of biblical, classical, and historical research, with their footnotes and *Forschungsberichte*, must therefore proceed cautiously and with humility; but there are some clues, and these we should follow.

The first is to notice that Chapter 6 of *Violence and the Sacred*, "From Mimetic Desire to the Monstrous Double," is crucial for the argument. There Girard grounds his theory of the surrogate-victim mechanism. At this point, his thesis is complete, and his exegeses of the major literary texts, especially the Greek tragedies, are finished. From this point on, he turns to engage Freud and Lévi-Strauss, "exegetes" themselves, in order to place his theory in its scholarly context before giving us his conclusions. From the discussion of Freud, we learn that it is the notion of mimetic desire that is at issue, and from the discussion of Lévi-Strauss, we learn that it is the significance of the monstrous double that concerns Girard. Thus Chapter 6 is where we must begin, and there, in a footnote (1977: 146, n. 1), Girard has left us a trace. He refers to an earlier work of his (*Deceit, Desire, and the Novel;* 1965) to support his statement that "only the major dramatists and novelists have partly understood and explored this form of rivalry [i.e., mimetic desire]." Such a clue should not go uninvestigated, though we cannot be sure it will lead us to the scene of the crime.

Deceit, Desire, and the Novel is Girard's study of Stendhal, Proust, and Dostoyevski. In the novels of these authors, Girard finds the curious phenomenon that he will call "mimetic desire." In case after case in the novels under consideration, Girard is able to show that this mechanism is at work. It is their exploration of this form of rivalry that makes these authors important. They are "great" because they understand mimetic desire, yet they have only "partly understood." It is Girard who has seen what they are up to and described the mechanism that is at work. This means that, though literature is the place where mimetic desire is explored, the mechanism itself has been fully seen and disclosed by the critic.

Where did Girard get this notion of mimetic desire? Mimesis is a term with a long tradition in criticism, and critics will have to judge just how novel Girard's interpretation is; but it is probably safe to say that what he makes of it, in relation to the notion of desire, is not won entirely from this tradition. The concept of desire points, rather, to central issues in the history of French thought, from Rousseau through the Durkheim-Bergson opposition and the Sartre–Lévi-Strauss alternatives, in quest of the ground of human social existence. Scholars of this intellectual tradition will have to tell us just how important the notion of desire has been for it, and how Girard is to be situated in relation to it; but his combination of desire and mimesis appears to be what sets Girard apart and gives him a mechanism with which to construct an entirely new social theory.

Girard shares with Sartre a concern to find the linkage between desire and "being." (One should note that in Chap. 6 it is "being" that is at stake in the rivalry; 1977: 146). However, Girard differs radically from Sartre's individualism by finding the linkage in mimesis, that is, in a necessarily social mechanism. He shares with

Lévi-Strauss both a critique of Durkheim's metaphysic of a transcendental society and a concern to anchor social constructs in the
actual experiences of social individuals; but he differs from Lévi-
Strauss in two significant regards: for Girard, the structuring mechanism is not the capacity to organize phenomena conceptually (by
the correlation of two systems of differences), as in Lévi-Strauss's
"savage mind" (1966); nor is that capacity to be located in the unconscious rational mind. Instead, he proposes that a radically ten-
sive and dynamic mechanism of rivalry is what determines social
behavior, and that this—though capable of being consciously acknowledged, and thus not to be located solely in the unconscious—
must be partially ignored for cooperative ventures to take place.
Thus Girard dares a most uncomfortable solution to the French
question; but did the courage for this come from France?

Girard devotes two chapters to a discussion of Freud. There he all
but tells us that Freud was his model, and that he achieved his theory of mimetic desire in the struggle to understand Freud. There we
see, as well, that the mechanism of rivalry in Girard's construct
bears a striking similarity to Freud's notion of the Oedipus complex; but as the exegetical analysis of Freud unfolds, the apparent
similarities are developed in such a way as to produce irreconcilable
differences. Instead of the father, we are given any model-rival; instead of the mother, any object valued by the model; instead of the
unconscious, there is mythic mentality. Thus the Oedipal order (desire for the object leads to rivalry with the model) is radically in-
verted to that of mimetic desire (imitation of the model-rival leads
to desire for the object). Only the child is left of the original figures
in Freud's "family romance," and the child now becomes the "dis-
ciple." Thus though Freud is important as the first to see conflict as
that which determines the socializing mechanism, and though he
explored its relations to the problem of desire, he did not fully understand the function of mimesis. And though he was the first to
discover that all ritual practices "have their origins in an actual
murder" (1977: 201), he did not see the mechanism of the surrogate
victim. Girard is too gracious to make the next move, dismissing
Freud. Instead, he explores the "traces of the mimetic conception"
that are "scattered through Freud's work" (1977: 169), and he de-

fends *Totem and Taboo* as far as he can, claiming that his own theory is simply a "synthesis of the two Freudian theories on the origin of incest prohibitions" (i.e., Oedipus and originary murder; 1977: 218). Both of the Freudian constructs have, however, been severely criticized and revised.

We may now understand Girard in an even larger intellectual context than that of his debate with Freud. He has not proposed a strictly psychoanalytic theory of religion, as his difference from Freud and his polemic against the Freudians shows. Rather, he has offered an alternative that, though worked out in an exegetical debate with Freud, can hardly be understood as derived from that debate. The two crucial notions—mimetic rivalry and the surrogate victim—point in another direction. That other direction seems to lead into the exciting ferment of contemporary French thought (e.g., the Lacan circle) where psychoanalytic theory is being explored as a possible foundation for a new (non-Oedipal) theory of social formation. In this exploration, the figures in Freud's Oedipal equation (father-mother-son) have been replaced by other configurations of human interaction, much as Girard has done. Girard has combined such a reading of Freud with his own reflections on the dynamics of desire and mimesis, and has thus constructed his mechanism of "mimetic desire." His reflections have been produced, apparently, in the course of his work as a critic, both of literature and of Freud's works, informed by the philosophical problems exercising the French quest for social theory. However, mimetic desire is not yet the mechanism of the surrogate victim, great novels not yet myths, and social dynamics not yet ritual institutions. If Girard begins with literature, he moves quickly to a consideration of religious phenomena. How has that jump been made?

Girard's notion of the surrogate-victim mechanism builds on his theory of mimetic desire, but it cannot be derived from it. Hence we need to ask how Girard managed to move from his discovery of mimetic desire in *Deceit, Desire, and the Novel* to his theory of violence, victimage, and sacrifice in *Violence and the Sacred*. He does not tell us how these thoughts occurred to him, but his argumentation provides some clues.

Chapter 6 of *Violence* moves from a discussion of Euripides's

Bacchae to mimetic desire and back again. In the course of the argumentation, the notion of mimetic desire is combined with that of the surrogate-victim mechanism to form a single construct:

Whenever he [the disciple] sees himself closest to the supreme goal, he comes into violent conflict with a rival. By a mental shortcut that is both eminently logical and self-defeating, he convinces himself that the violence itself is the most distinctive attribute of this supreme goal! Ever afterward, violence and desire will be linked in his mind, and the presence of violence will invariably waken desire . . . .

Mimetic desire is simply a term more comprehensive than *violence* for religious pollution. As the catalyst for the sacrificial crisis, it would eventually destroy the entire community if the surrogate victim were not at hand to halt the process and the ritualized mimesis were not at hand to keep the conflictual mimesis from beginning afresh (1977: 148).

Thus an explanation of the notion of mimetic desire has taken place. It has taken place in the context of a reading of the *Bacchae*, and the expanded notion now includes the phenomena of ritual, sacrifice, and the surrogate victim.

I strongly suspect that the *Bacchae* provided the bridge for Girard's move from literature to the myths and rituals of religion. It is a literary text that Girard counts among the great writings because it explores mimetic desire, but in this case the background is different from that of the novels read earlier. Girard speaks repeatedly of the "myth" that Euripides has studied. Euripides's genius is that he has all but exposed the horrible truth of collective violence, which the myth by design had concealed; and with the myth comes ritual, and religion. Once in view, the entire field of the history of religions suddenly unfolds, complete with its rich archive of texts. Girard shows that he has read them, and in the reading, two themes constantly recur.

One is that *myth* can be defined as a precritical literature that views violence only in retrospect, from the perspective of the salvific resolution. The other is that *ritual* can be defined as a substitution for some prior event; it functions in society "to keep the conflictual mimesis from beginning afresh." The key notions are *concealment* (in the case of myth) and *substitution* (in the case of ritual). Both notions can be correlated with the mimetic-desire mechanism: that which myth conceals corresponds to Freud's unconscious, and to

Girard's "nonconscious" level at which mimetic desire functions; and ritual substitution correlates with certain aspects of Freud's Oedipal drama, and of Girard's mimetic-desire mechanism.

Religious myths and rituals introduce embellishments, however, and these embellishments appear to have supplied important pieces for Girard's puzzle. Myths conceal the endemic rivalry of mimetic desire—that rivalry that generates the conditions for the violence—but myths do not conceal the nature of the ensuing violent climax; indeed, they relate the very act of killing to which rivalry and conflict lead. By combining the two literatures (novels with mimetic plots and myths of killing), Girard produces the full dramatic sequence. Each needs the other as its complement. Taken together, literature and myth show that mimetic rivalry leads to the monstrous double and the killing, and that it does so in such a way as to effect their erasure in the subsequent reflection on the event. Euripides's dramatic text is important because it shows this relationship between literature and myth. Myths of killing give us another kind of text; the curious metamorphoses of the victim in myths—now monster, now savior—explicate aspects of the mechanism of mimetic desire (e.g., the double bind). In some ways, myths are closer to the truth than literature, because they tell about the killing, but in other ways they are farther from the truth, because they erase the mimetic phase of the drama and view the victim as a god. Thus myths are the texts most proximate to the crucial, climactic event of the drama, but without great literature to interpret them and expose what they conceal, we never would have known this.

Rituals also introduce embellishments. Even after we know that mimetic desire can lead to rivalry, and that rivalry can lead to killing, we do not know that a surrogate victim might suffice. Ritual provides the example because it functions by making substitutions, according to Girard, and in the case of ritual sacrifice, it is the victim who is substituted. Thus the notion of the surrogate victim. Added to the mechanism of mimetic desire, which leads to the killing of the monstrous double, ritual sacrifice introduces the final swerve: the one who ends up being killed is not the rival, but a substituted victim.

Ritual, however, is a social institution. Once it is in view, read in the light of the notion of mimetic desire, questions arise that can lead to nothing less than a universal theory of religion and social formation. The task now is to discover that victim and that event for which rituals of sacrifice are substitutes.

As observed by the historian or ethnographer, rituals are "displaced" from the normal round of social activity. Maskings, roles, symbols, special times and places—all attest to the distance of ritual events from social processes. And because rituals are performed "as if not for the first time," scholars have spoken of reenactments, repetitions, and the like. It is this curious quality of ritual—embedded in the life of a society, yet separated from its own references in respect to both place and time—that enables Girard to expand his interpretation in the direction of a history of cultures. He notes ritual's elaborate symbolism, the failure of participants and scholars to understand it, and its strange conjunction of imaginative substitutions and actual performance. He points out that ritual is repetitive, that the mode of resolution is vicarious, and that it claims to be a mimetic reenactment of a prior event.

The prior event for all rituals of killing, according to Girard, must have been an actual killing of consequence for the society. Only such an event could account for the elaborate symbolisms that revolve around the moment of sacrifice. None of the usual explanations can account for this, but myths of killing provide the evidence for the way in which the mythic mentality comes to view the collective killing as salvific, and Girard's theory of myth and literature explains why the cover-up occurs. Accordingly, an actual event must have been at the beginning of the ritual tradition. It must have been at the beginning, period. The prior event must have been the first collective murder.

We need to pause here and take note of this unexpected thesis. Girard argues for it most directly in Chapter 8 of *Violence and the Sacred*, which is on *Totem and Taboo*. He is still in debate with Freud, but now the issue is not Freud's failure to understand mimetic desire, but his failure to understand the surrogate-victim mechanism. Girard is intrigued with Freud's thesis of a primal, collective murder. To imagine such a scene clarifies the origins of the psychosocial dynamics he has theorized. He appears to accept Freud's arguments for positing the first time as an actual event. I suspect, however, that Girard regards these arguments only as supportive of his own line of reasoning, which begins, rather, with ritual theory. In any case, he takes up the issue expressly in order to revise Freud's scenario in the direction of the surrogate-victim mechanism:

The sacrificial act is too rich in concrete details to be only a simulation of something that never actually occurred. This assertion can be made without contradicting my previous statement that the act is a simulated performance designed to offer a substitute satisfaction. Sacrifice takes the place of an act that nobody under normal cultural conditions would dare or even desire to commit; it is this aspect that Freud, wholly intent on the *origins* of sacrifice, paradoxically failed to perceive. [He] failed to unearth the surrogate victim (1977: 201).

One sees that Girard knows about the critique that Lévi-Strauss makes of Freud's original murder—namely, that it rides on a "vicious circle deriving the social state from events which presuppose it" (1977: 193). That is why Girard contends it was "an act nobody under normal cultural conditions would dare or even desire to commit"; nevertheless, his substitution of "the surrogate victim" for Freud's father does not negate Lévi-Strauss's critique. Both the mechanism of mimetic desire and that of the surrogate victim presuppose a social context within which to get started, yet Girard uses both mechanisms to imagine the originary event. He appears to be influenced in the description of this event by the *Bacchae*, because he mentions repeatedly the hysteria involved in reaching unanimity, the complete arbitrariness of the selection of the first vulnerable victim "at hand," and the unexpected subsidence of violence caused by the victim's death and expulsion. Only thus can the event be imagined that myth relates and ritual enacts. Girard does call the first murder accidental; he does speak of it happening only once; and he does regard it as a horrible, therefore unthinkable discovery. He must, however, posit it—this unique, originary moment—because it alone can make sense of its subsequent mythic concealments and ritual substitutions, as he understands them.

Thus Girard has found it possible to make a common set of all the texts there are. By so doing, the myths, tragedies, and great novels of the Western tradition can be read in the light of one another. A dramatic construct emerges, its partial concealments rationalized by a socialized Oedipal equation; and with the inclusion of the religious texts, Girard is compelled to locate the originary event at the beginning of social history as well as in the depths of the matrices that continually generate social behavior. This can only mean that the study of myth and ritual introduced the problem of history for Girard. He is concerned, after all, to give an account of social formation. His mechanisms do impinge on the way in which both human behavior and social institutions are patterned and function. The dynamics generated at the nonconscious level do break the surface, and those surface events should be readable as manifestations of mimetic desire.

Where can we see the full drama manifest, without the constraints that the mythic mentality provides? Only at the beginning, it seems, in the raw, or during times of sacrificial crisis. For the rest of social history, the primal act is ritualized, and as Girard explains the relation of a ritual event to this first collective murder, he must have recourse to the language of memory (though it is partial), repetition (though inexact), and reenactment (though only as "attempts"). This is where the language of mimesis appears to break down (i.e., at the level of social history), and the reader is left wondering how human history, with such a dark, dramatic origin, has been energized for so long by cultivating concealments of it.

Girard begins with texts; he also ends with them. And as his theory of mimetic desire expands into a theory of religion and culture, the significance of his texts is enlarged. Texts are in touch with the mechanisms and events that generate social structures and their history. In one sense, all texts are fair game; but in another, there is a ranking of text-types that we should notice.

Myths are distinguished from literature; "great literature" is marked off from other literature; and criticism is assigned a special function of its own. Myths are more closely related to the rationalizations that occur in primitive religions. They can be used, then, to investigate mythic mentality that has interpreted the surrogate-victim mechanism as that which achieves order and peace for the society. However, because myths view the "sacrifice" only from the perspective of its final resolution, and conceal by design the collective violence that generates it, they appear to be less valuable for Girard's enterprise of disclosure than the works of great literature. It is in any case noteworthy that Girard's use of mythic material supports an argument based primarily on the interpretation of literature. In his exegesis of the *Bacchae*, for instance, he refers repeatedly to "the myth" that lies behind it, but nowhere reconstructs it as a text to be analyzed in its own right. Great literature, in contrast—the Greek tragedies, Shakespeare, and the "major" novelists—explores the mythic mentality and discloses aspects of the mechanism that myth conceals. These, then, are of most importance for Girard's work as a critic. And the critic's role? His task is more daring still. He it is who can expose the mechanism for what it is—namely, the generative matrix of social existence.

There is, in all of this, a theory of the social function of myth, literature, and criticism that is the penultimate surprise of Girard's work. As he develops it, a tripartite historical reconstruction occurs as well. Myth is most appropriate to the primitive forms of religion and society; literature occurs in societies that find it possible to develop legal systems to serve the religious function; and the kind of criticism Girard calls for is most appropriate for our own time, when what he calls the "sacrificial crisis" has belatedly emerged even within the societies of law.

The correlation of literary types with epochs of human history emerges in the concluding chapters of *Violence and the Sacred*. Girard does not dwell on the momentous shift that must have occurred from primitive societies to societies governed by judicial systems, but he does elaborate the way in which legal systems substitute for sacrificial systems as an answer to the problem of violence, and he ends his book with some reflections on the current crisis in Western societies. We must take note of these reflections, for they contain the final, surprising twist in Girard's already astounding thesis.

Western culture has succeeded in prolonging the climax of a sacrificial crisis for some inexplicable reason, but as confidence in its judicial system erodes and cynicism with regard to the ideal of justice increases, the crisis manifests itself in overt violence at every level of social existence. It is therefore an appropriate time, according to Girard, for the critic fully to disclose the surrogate-victim mechanism behind all social institutions. This will force us to acknowledge the truth about our inherent violence.

Girard does not tell us in *Violence and the Sacred* how that dis-

closure can work to resolve the crisis, or where the courage comes
from to propose it, though that is what Girard himself has dared.
In his *Des Choses cachées depuis la fondation du monde* (1978),
however, one begins to see the beginnings of the rationale for such
a disclosure, and the source of the courage he has found. Here Girard argues that the literary foundation of the Judeo-Christian
tradition, the Bible, is marked by a radical disclosure of the surrogate-victim mechanism. The Bible knows about sacrifice and the
sacrificial crisis. But its stories are not told to conceal violence or to
reconstitute the surrogate-victim mechanism mythically. Rather,
they reveal the guilt and responsibility of the doer, and cast the victim as innocent. This reversal, not of plot but of characterization,
presents the reader/listener with another pattern of resolution: in
the knowledge of the truth about all concerned, and the rejection of
the mythic solution with its victim and delusion, one may "yield"
instead of demanding "full rights."

This view of the biblical tradition is apparently the basis on which
Girard dares a disclosure of the surrogate-victim mechanism at the
end of *Violence and the Sacred*, a twist indicated only briefly here
and there. With it, another large set of questions is raised as we attempt to integrate the two works, but only one question can be discussed now.

If the biblical texts propose a resolution to the sacrificial crisis
different from that proposed by myth and ritual, whence comes the
power to actualize that alternative? The power, apparently, resides
in the capacity of these texts to rob the myth of its fictions and disclose the truth of the human situation. Yet this is precisely the critic's task as well, "to expose to the light of reason the role played by
violence in human society" (1977: 318). It is this curious correlation between the functions of the biblical texts and the critic's task
with which Girard leaves us. We must ask whether and how they
may differ, and whether the biblical texts need, then, the critic, or
the critic the biblical texts. We might also want to ask whence the
confidence that such a text, or such a criticism, could really make a
difference in our world.

Walter Burkert's Theory of the Hunt

Walter Burkert is a historian of Greek religion who shares some
of the common scholarly assessments of the importance of the clas-

sical tradition for Western intellectual and cultural history. Because of this heritage, and because of the interpretation of religion achieved by Greek culture itself, Greek religion assumes a "unique position" for the scholar: "Among the most ancient forms of religion, it is still the most comprehensible and the one that can be observed from the greatest number of perspectives" (1983: xxii). The question, however, is whether either the Greeks or we have understood it properly. Two considerations seem to have played a role in creating for Burkert a certain hesitation.

Burkert observes that even during the highest period of classical culture, religious traditions and practices that appear to be pre-Greek in origin, perhaps even prehistoric, continued in force (e.g., the tripod, the name *tragodia*, the pervasiveness of the sacrificial theme in Greek festivals). To understand such anomalies, that which was "no longer understood," even by the Greeks, one requires a theory of ritual and religion that can account for the anomaly's function in terms that do not require that it be "understood." In dealing with the phenomenon, Burkert seeks to combine a strictly historical approach with a functional view of religion (1983: xxiii).

Traditional theories of religion have not provided much help in explaining the persistence of archaic religious practices. Burkert has not addressed this issue directly, however (i.e., entered into debate with the scholarship on a theory of religion), but his own theoretical position is clear. He objects that traditional scholarly approaches to religion assume a rationalistic anthropology and interpret religion as a function of conceptual needs and capacities. The evidence for this is the consistency with which scholars have focused their investigations on myths, symbols, ideas, and beliefs; and have proposed theories about religion that understand it as a primitive mode of offering explanations for the world.

Such an approach fails to account for the persistence of religion as ritual or for religion's quality of seriousness even after it has become an anomaly. (For Burkert, the appeal to "tradition" is important as a rationalization for the necessary transmission and continuity of social structures, but it cannot explain the basic function of the rite itself.) Burkert turns, therefore, to the human sciences and to the study of human behavior in order to understand ritual in relation to patterns of activity basic to social life. With this move, he introduces a different anthropology, one that does not assume a definition of "the human" primarily in terms of rationality, and he adopts a perspective for the exploration of religion as a social construction. Burkert's goal is to combine this approach with historical methods in order to investigate the primary (and abiding) function of religious ritual. Specifically, he wants to account for the persistence of those archaic survivals of religion in Greek culture, by tracing them back to pre-Greek stages of human cultural formation—as far back as he can go.

Two clues are given at the outset. One is the pervasive anomaly of sacrifice, a form of ritual that seems to accompany all the major manifestations of religion in Greek culture, whether in festivals, seats of oracles, games, cults, mysteries, funerary rites, state ceremonies, or mythologies and drama. The other is the observation made by Karl Meuli, who (in 1946) pointed out that certain aspects of Greek sacrificial practice, especially the care and handling of the bones of animal victims, were similar to the practice of Paleolithic hunters. With these as points of departure, Burkert begins an amazing study and reconstruction of Paleolithic hunting culture, and develops a theory of ritual and religion with which he can return to a thorough investigation of his classical Greek texts. A comprehensive statement of this theory is given in the first eighty-two pages of *Homo Necans* (1983).[3]

For Burkert, the decisive moment for human hunters was the kill. He understands the hunt to have required patience, planning, and group cooperation typical of the large carnivores (e.g., cats, wolves) but activities for which the prehominid apes were not socially (Burkert would say "ritually") prepared. The problem had to do with the inadequacy of older patterns of intraspecific aggression, which now had to be subliminated and redirected if the hunting party was to succeed. The full range of survival strategies had to be realigned, including behavior related to territory, feeding, pairing, and reproduction. As might be expected, the primary tensions occurred in terms of two sets of relationships: male-male and male-female. Males had to learn to cooperate among themselves in the quest for game and its distribution. They also had to learn new be-

---

[3]References to *Homo Necans* are to the English translation, published in 1983. However, the study is based on the German edition (1972) and a few technical terms in German have been retained in the discussion.

havioral patterns with respect to females. The problem was compounded by the role differentiation that occurred between male and female, the male now being responsible for the provision of food, and hence required to leave the female during the hunt. Thus the intraspecific aggression related to pairing and sexuality had to be rechanneled, as did that related to territory and feeding habits. Aggression found its outlet by being projected on the prey, and this projection both heightened the significance of the hunt and the kill and provided the focal point for its ritualization, from which new patterns of behavior then emerged. This could happen because the hunt was the main source of food and was thus the primary activity around which the new hominid society had to revolve.

Behavioral codes resulted ("rituals," in ethological parlance) that controlled cooperative planning, departures, and the coordination of the hunt. The approach to the hunt was ritualized so as to balance and retain motivational and psychological tensions stemming from the new social formations in the interest of the objective of the hunt. The kill was the climax that released those tensions and focused attention on the prey as the living creature that had to be killed in order to provide food for those who killed it. It was the complexity of the motivational (psychological) factors culminating in this single act that made the kill the focal point around which all the new patterns of social behavior (ritual) would be coordinated. As a focal event charged with such multiple motivation, the kill also triggered a new process of perception and reflection. This process, according to Burkert, created myth.

By redirecting aggression onto the prey, a complex set of motivations and images was superimposed on it. The prey remained fundamentally food to be taken, but as the object upon which intraspecific aggressions were superimposed, it was anthropomorphized. Supported by the observation of physical similarities between prey and human predator, the contrastive aspects of its characterization (both animal and human) invited yet other sets of contrasting images by association: now male, now female; now wild, now domestic; now prey, now predator, the prey was charged with a dynamic role layered with significance in an event that took on a dramatic aspect. And because the encounter was an action that had a radical consequence, the images of contrast could take a dialectical form:

enemy/friend; taking life/giving life; death/life. Thus such a focus of attention on the object of the kill could trigger a most unusual and creative process of reflection. The prey could even become the occasion for imagining the "Master of Animals," and the hunt could become a ritual encounter with that "master."

At this point, one might expect Burkert to make the usual appeal to language as the distinctively human(izing) capacity, or to linguistics as the way to explore how the juxtapositions of images function (as metonymies, analogies, metaphors, and symbols), but he resists this, in keeping with his thesis on the priority of ritual over myth. He proceeds, instead, simply to describe how the hunting ritual gave rise to the full range of articulations that we understand to be mythic or symbolic, articulations characteristic of religion. The naming of the "Master of Animals," the songs and "prayers" that address the prey, the gestures surrounding the kill, the care of the bones, the narration of the ritualized hunt as a sequence of events (myth), and the eventual articulation of social codes and honors, including honors due the Master of Animals ("worship")—all are found to be generated by the complex experience of the act of killing. Thus a theory of the ritualization of the hunt becomes a theory of the origin of religion.

I have emphasized the "anthropomorphization" that Burkert says occurs, in order to show that his theory can account for the emergence of myth, and thus offer an explanation of that phenomenon traditionally held to be definitional for religion. However, Burkert's own emphasis would not fall here. He is much more concerned to explicate the dramatic significance of the action itself. His view of religion is grounded in an assessment of the effectiveness of the kill in transforming patterns of motivation and behavior. He speaks of the "shock" of seeing that one has killed, taken life, spilled blood. He notes the "hesitation" before the kill ritualized in recent hunting cultures. He points to the rather pervasive phenomenon of disclaimers of responsibility for the act in these rituals (*Unschuldskomödie*). And he interprets all of this motivationally as horror and guilt, which in turn require resolution.

This means that the superimpositon of aggressions on the primary motivation of the quest for food creates an awareness of the significance of the kill that is found to be shocking. The act of killing does not immediately resolve the problem of conflicting motivations by some simple mechanism of balancing out aggressions. On the contrary, the new awareness actually compounds the motivational conflict by making the action itself highly problematic. Burkert seems to think it is this awareness that is the mark of human consciousness.

The "shock" created by the killing of such a highly charged prey is resolved by means of the ritualization of the hunt. The ritual does not erase the anxiety, but it does channel it creatively. The ritualized hunt begins with preparations at "home" for the encounter with the Master of Animals in the wild. The hunt itself is conducted as a dramatization (1983: 15-29) that orders the party, controls the approach, and heightens the anxiety and exhilaration of the kill. It also determines that the meat procured be distributed "for the others," especially the women and children at "home." Burkert understands this to be motivated by the desire to make amends (or "compensation," *Wiedergutmachung*) for the act of killing. It is this inversion of the motivational direction, now to give (back or away) what was taken, that is the great humanizing achievement of the ritualization. Thus ritual is an enactment that is charged with (1) motivational incitement, (2) horror, and (3) its inversion into joy and celebration.

It can now be seen that ritual killing functions as a dramatization of an activity around which society can be structured for the satisfaction of basic survival needs. Ritual killing guarantees the proper enactment of that activity on which the group depends. It can also become a dramatic paradigm for structuring all aspects of social life in which encounter must be transformed into a moment of exchange. Indeed, it is precisely because of that capacity to resolve motivational conflicts by rechanneling behavioral patterns that sacrificial ritual continues to be the definitive and central religious enactment in systems of religion and culture long after the hunting stage is left behind.

As other cultural systems evolve, this basically dramatic ritual pattern continues in force. Its power to persist is clarified when the significance of that moment—the taking of life and its resolution in the distribution of the "gifts"—is seen as fundamental to human existence and social formation. Sacrifice articulates a moment of transaction and transformation so basic to any social exchange that its cultivation is required. Thus rituals of sacrifice continue to be performed on those occasions when social orders are in need of rearrangement or reestablishment: initiations, seasonal transitions with implications for changes in patterns of public activity, the beginning of great undertakings. The "sense" of sacrifice, therefore, is just the ritualization of a social pattern of transactional behavior. Burkert emphasizes that it is precisely as pattern that rituals of sacrifice give rise to other articulations as well. The myth of the hero, Greek drama, the royal hunt, and the entire range of specialized and occasional rites in later societies—all can be traced back to the basic script of the ritualized hunt.

Burkert's reconstruction has been achieved by means of research that is exceedingly wide-ranging. The evidence for a pattern common to hunting ritual and sacrificial ritual required the investigation of every stage of human social formation from Paleolithic times through the classical high culture of the Greeks. What Burkert seeks to demonstrate is the persistence of a pattern of behavior perceived as a structural system, but this system is not understood as a set of symbols by which the world is ordered, things classified, and relationships understood. It is more like a script or scenario that plots a sequence of significant moments on the occasion of fundamental human endeavors, experiences, or transactions.

The disciplines called for, therefore, encompass the range of the human and historical sciences. Archaeology and anthropology are especially important for reconstructing the Paleolithic configuration. Ethnography and cultural anthropology are called for to correlate evidence from recent contemporary hunting cultures. Philology and the historical sciences are basic to an exploration of immediately pre-Greek and cognate cultures from the period of writing. From these and other subdisciplines, extremely detailed information is sought and organized. The list of evidence accumulated is large and quite diverse in both type and content. Bits and snippets from archaeological findings are brought into relation with etymologies, myths, native and classical explanatory statements, ethnographical documents, scholarly judgments, and, above all, ethological data.

There appear to be three paradigms by which Burkert brings this material together into a single reconstruction of the ritual occasion as he sees it. The first is the model provided by Greek sacrificial ritual itself. Burkert does not discuss this model at first, in *Homo Necans*, but as the circles of investigation return repeatedly to the Greek evidence for testing, a reconstruction of the basic pattern behind all Greek rituals of sacrifice emerges. This basic pattern can then be used to control the interpretation of ever more fragmentary bits of evidence. Artifacts found to be functionally similar can be seen as comparable, and their alignments can thus allow one to trace the evidence in ever larger arenas of cultural times and locations. This aspect of Burkert's approach to the reconstruction of the ritual of sacrifice will be difficult to question. He has managed to integrate an immense amount of data in the course of his work, and his detailed discussions, especially of philological and archaeological evidence, are persuasive.

The second paradigm Burkert calls on is a narrative description of the hunt as performed in primitive hunting societies. This narrative pattern is reconstructed partly by analogy with Greek rituals of sacrifice, partly by appeal to Paleolithic evidence for ritual observances, and partly by an imaginative narration of primitive hunting activity itself. This procedure is different from that used to reconstruct the archaic Greek rituals, and it is open to serious question. Its plausibility rests on two assumptions: (1) the "hunting hypothesis," and (2) the ritual interpretation of Paleolithic/Mesolithic evidence for curious behavior related to hunting, such as the condition and position in which skulls and thighbones have been found.

Burkert has accepted the hunting hypothesis in order to explain the ritualization of the hunt, but the evidence available for a ritualization of the hunt during the Paleolithic period is very skimpy, and such evidence as there is, is amenable to other explanations. The hunting hypothesis is now in serious trouble among paleoanthropologists. There does appear to be evidence for the hunting of mammoths, but it is not at all clear, even in this case, that hunting was a chief source of food. Burkert has emphasized the necessity of the hunt as that activity on which survival depended for the exceedingly long reaches of primitive culture; but the picture painted by current studies in primitive cultural anthropology is that gathering was at least as important as hunting, and perhaps more significant as the normal means of getting food. As for the "noble" hunt, there now appears to be evidence that primitive man was a scavenger much of the time.

The third paradigm of importance for Burkert's theory is taken from ethology. Certain patterns of ritualized behavior observable in animals have provided a kind of substratum with which both the hunt and the Greek sacrifices might be aligned. If Karl Meuli's work provided the clue and set the agenda for Burkert's program of historical research, it was Konrad Lorenz's book *On Aggression* (1966) that provided the basis for Burkert's interpretation of ritual and religion in behavioristic terms. Burkert's indebtedness to ethology in general, and to Lorenz in particular, is clear already in his 1966 essay. It made possible the fully developed theory of ritual presented in *Homo Necans*, and it became the point of departure for a correlate theory of myth in the Sather Lectures of 1977 (published in 1979 as *Structure and History in Greek Mythology and Ritual*).

The importance of ethology for Burkert's reconstruction and interpretation of sacrificial ritual is expressly acknowledged in each of his works. It can be assessed by listing those mechanisms of ritualization for which ethological theory is seen to provide the primary explanation. These include the notion that only a small number of actions are basic to biological survival, and that it is these actions that are ritualized. Two are of primary importance: the hunt for food and pairing for reproduction. Burkert is impressed with the fact that the rituals of hunting cultures manifest a complex interrelationship of just these two action-mechanisms. He does not discuss in the same way two other basic ethological patterns, namely, the marking and protection of territory and intragroup rivalry to establish "pecking order"; but it is clear that these also inform his understanding of, for instance, the formation of the hunting party and the notion of territory, with its "inside" (home place) and "outside" (the wild), as basic to the structure of a hunting culture. Ethology does provide striking analogies for Burkert's contention that basic patterns of human behavior are relatable to basic survival needs.

A second appeal to ethology is made to explain the phenomenon of ritualization itself. Burkert is impressed with studies showing that certain patterns of behavior (e.g., the triumph ceremony among the greylag geese) continue to function as important gestures of communication in social encounters even after the original stimulus for the gesture is no longer the occasion (Lorenz 1966, Chap. 11). Thus the pattern of behavior comes to serve another function, is displaced. It is, in fact, this discovery of displaced ritualized behavior as communicative among animals that, for Burkert, established the priority of ritual over myth (language, symbolism) and ushered in the "Copernican Revolution" in the human sciences (1983: 27).[4]

A third point of dependence is the notion of aggression and the assessment of its importance as a basic behavioral-motivational mechanism. For Burkert, aggressive behavior is both the primary energy and the basic problem in human survival and social formation. As we have seen, his understanding of ritual is determined precisely by this problem and its need for resolution. Aggression became a special problem when its intraspecific (pairing and territorial?) function frustrated the necessary formation of the hunting party as hominids became carnivores, male-female roles were differentiated, and pairing had to be regularized. Thus Burkert initially describes the solutions that humans achieved to this problem as variant and more complex forms of ritualized behavior (e.g., the hunt itself as ritual; initiation into the male hunting party; the kill as ritualized redirection of aggression; the return and distribution of food; the keeping of sexual pairing codes within the group).

As he describes the complex of conflicting motivations that require resolution if the new social formation is to succeed, it is clear that some appeal to psychological categories is necessary for Burkert's thesis as well. Accordingly, he shifts from ethological to psychological categories. The redirection of aggression is understood as "projection." Initiation rituals indicate that a new kind of learning and transmission of lore is at work, utilizing the child's urge to imitate (*Nachahmungstrieb*). Sexual codes require "sublimation"; codes of distribution are made possible by "continence" and the desire to make amends (*Wiedergutmachung*) for the act of killing. Some shift from ethological to psychological categories may be appropriate to a behavioristic model, of course, but Burkert is not as clear about his indebtedness to a particular school of psychology as he is about his indebtedness to Lorenz in ethology, and one has the

[4]The reference to the "Copernican Revolution" in the German edition (1972: 37) was deleted in the English translation.

impression that Burkert's psychology is more eclectic. Its function for his argument may therefore be more tentative, experimental, and illustrative than theoretically fundamental. Thus the problem is how to understand the legitimacy of a behavioristic model of motivation when used to reconstruct the "originary" formation of ritual and human society. If the ethology of ritualization is not adequate to account for the strange new human pattern, how are we to understand the emergence of these psychological mechanisms? And, given the data at our disposal for the reconstruction of the primitive ritual "text" (archaeological and ethnographic data), how can the presence of these motivational factors be established?

There is, however, an even more serious question to be raised in this regard. To explain the shocking aspect of the experience of the kill, Burkert has had recourse to a language of motivation that does not derive easily either from his ethological or from his behavioristic theories of ritual motivation. He speaks of the "human aversion to killing and the feeling of guilt and remorse caused by the shedding of blood" as "represented in Greek sacrificial rites" (1966: 106). When explicating the Paleolithic ritual, he refers to the "shock" and anxiety that result from disturbing a basic "biological life-preserving inhibition" (1983: 21). These are clearly religious notions. It appears that Burkert has interjected them into his already complex combination of motivational categories derived from ethology and behavioristic psychology. One might ask, therefore, whether the language of guilt can be justified as an interpretation of the motivational aspects of the ritual he reconstructs. Indeed, this is the most intriguing and potentially constructive aspect of his theory; it is also the most troublesome and potentially questionable thesis he proposes.

Jonathan Z. Smith's Theory of Rationalization

Jonathan Z. Smith is a historian of the history of religions who has special expertise in Hellenistic religions. His work is available to us in a substantial set of essays, many of which have been collected in his two books, *Map Is Not Territory* (1978) and *Imagining Religion* (1982). With Smith, the essay has become the vehicle for a particular style of investigation. It is probing and programmatic, exploring crucial junctures in the history of the discipline. He is in quest of methodological clarity and sound theoretical foundations.

The typical essay is organized around four components: (1) a text is placed in view to provide an exegetical challenge; (2) a commonly accepted interpretation of the text is reviewed; (3) an alternative reading is given, based on strictly historical methods of textual reconstruction and placement; and (4) conclusions are drawn for questions of method and theory in the study of religion.

Taken as a set, Smith's essays offer the most comprehensive rethinking of the discipline in our generation. The texts selected for analysis turn out to be programmatic in and of themselves. They are "typical" religious texts for a particular culture, or at least have been held to be so, and they are, by and large, the very texts that have served earlier scholars as points of departure for constructing theories of religion. They are thus the "canonical" texts of the discipline, and their reinterpretation will prove to be critical for questions of method in the discipline. They tend, therefore, to be myths and ritual texts from primitive cultures, to which, however, Smith frequently juxtaposes a second text from the Hellenistic or Greco-Roman age.

In the course of his work, Smith has addressed the major theorists, schools, and enduring issues in the history of the history of religions.[5] In every case, theories are confronted with texts, the texts are placed in their own historical contexts, and the theories are reassessed as to their adequacy and plausibility. The approach is thus analytical, inductive, and critical in form, although the intention is thoroughly constructive.

The rigor begins with the historical-critical method. For Smith, the historian of religions should be at least a historian. This determines his own approach to his texts and to their placement in historical contexts. Reconstructions of the text, which must account for variant versions and the history of its transmission, are critical. Historical placement is essential, and careful attention must be

[5]A partial survey includes Frazer ("When the Bough Breaks," in 1978a: 208-39); from Levy-Bruhl to Lévi-Strauss on the question of primitive mentality ("I Am a Parrot [Red]," in 1978a: 265-88); Jensen and the myth-ritual school ("A Pearl of Great Price and a Cargo of Yams," in 1982a: 90-101); and Eliade and the question of the Sacred ("The Wobbling Pivot," in 1978a: 88-103).

given to how a text was first noticed by the scholarly community and why it entered into the community's hermeneutical discourse. Only after performing these tasks has an analyst won the right to offer an alternative reading.

There is an implicit set of assumptions about scholarship, texts, social history, and religion that underlies this insistence that the study of religion acknowledge the historian's craft as its primary discipline. Both "religion" and the "study of religion" are understood to be engaged in the human endeavor to make sense of things. History is pursued initially as an empirical science, because all human enterprises, including religion, are understood to be ways that humans find to understand and thus to control experience. History, then, is not chosen as the primary discipline in order to champion either a particular philosophy of history or a view of religion based on a certain historical consciousness. Historical research is called for, at first, simply because it is the only way we know to "place" a text in human context and ask about the kind of sense it makes of its own time (i.e., its experience of the world).

To do that guards against facile readings of the text, which (1) begin with recognitions of its similarity to other texts and phenomena in its own or other cultural contexts, (2) move to identifications by type, and (3) end with conclusions about archetypes, in relation to which the text itself is then seen as paradigmatic (i.e., as the clearest manifestation). Smith sees this circular procedure as definitive for the morphological-phenomenological approach to the study of religion. This approach is ahistorical by design and thus, for Smith, inadequate. His insistence on the historical placement of a text within a specific social context is intended to frustrate this program.

But why two texts? Here we encounter the most unusual characteristic of Smith's own approach. Where the second text is Hellenistic, the device allows Smith to take up issues in his own special field of competence, but that cannot be the only reason for his two-text approach. If it were, his exegetical method would seem to contradict his purpose. How can one historically placed text, read in the light of its particular social circumstances, elucidate another text in another historical-cultural context? By taking up two texts, Smith has consistently placed himself before the crucial methodological question: how to combine morphological and historical approaches to religious phenomena—or how to compare disparate texts, times, and cultures. The reason for two texts, therefore, must involve a strategy.

Smith has specifically addressed himself to the problem of comparison in two essays: "*Adde Parvum Parvo Magnus Acervus Erit*" (1971) and "In Comparison a Magic Dwells" (1982). In the earlier essay, Smith analyzes the ways in which comparisons have been made in the study of (comparative) religions. He distinguishes four kinds. (1) The "ethnographic" model begins by noticing similarities and differences in the "other" culture vis-à-vis one's own culture, and proceeds to descriptive comparison on that basis. However, until it becomes possible to provide a systemic description of both cultures, as well as some historical-anthropological theory of culture to allow cross-cultural comparison, ethnographic comparisons remain isolated observations, frequently idiosyncratic, and unhelpful. (2) The "encyclopedic" tradition aims at collecting as many examples of a given phenomenon from as many cultures as possible, in order to compare them; but the principles of classification are based on surface associations of various kinds, and the contextless listings provide no clue to how or why one is to make the comparisons suggested. Both of these ways of making comparisons are ancient and unreflective. They work with a basic human penchant for seeing things in terms of similarities and differences, but their notion of analogy is not yet scientific.

For the "morphological" (3) and the "evolutionary" (4) methods, however, the natural sciences, especially comparative anatomy (of the eighteenth and nineteenth centuries), can be shown to have provided the model. These two approaches are interrelated. The morphological approach classifies items according to similarities and differences in formal or systemic structure. It presupposes a hierarchy from simple to complex structures (organisms), and thus can lead to the evolutionary approach that transfers the models of organic growth and evolutionary theory to the process of cultural "history." Though these approaches are to be seen as advances in the scientific study of religion, both, according to Smith, suffer from the same problem. The evolutionary approach, which compares the "earlier" with the "later" in the interest of charting "developments" through time, still works with the assumption and morphological description of a hierarchy of systems. (Thus the "simpler" is "earlier.") In this respect, it remains ahistorical—indebted still to the natural science model and inadequate for human cultural systems. The morphological approach reifies the hierarchy, looking for basic structures and/or archetypes, and refuses to take history into account. Hence Smith's critique is that the history of religions has failed to find a way to combine comparative methods with the historical disciplines.

In his later paper ("In Comparison a Magic Dwells"), delivered to the American Academy of Religion in 1979, Smith continues this investigation of comparative methodologies and adds several important observations. He notes that the "finding" of an analogy occurs only after the scholar (or anyone) has taken note of something new, peculiar, "unique," (i.e., "different"). It is difference, then, that initiates the process of recalling from memory or seeking something similar in order to make a comparison. This observation is not elaborated, but it provides us with a clue to the direction of Smith's thought. In any adequate comparative method, difference as well as similarity (the usual focus of the comparative methods) must be taken into account.

As he develops this essay, Smith summarizes his conclusions from the earlier study and goes on to investigate the problem of comparing "different" religions with one another. His conclusions, though not resolutions to the problem, are enlightening. The first is that "we have yet to develop . . . the integration of a complex notion of pattern and system with an equally complex notion of history" (1982b: 29). The second is that "comparison is, at base, never identity. Comparison requires the postulation of difference as the grounds of its being interesting (rather than tautological) and a methodical manipulation of difference, a playing across the 'gap' in the service of some useful end" (1982b: 35).

Smith does not say what the "useful end" might be for the historian of religion, or what the "complex notion" of religion and history might require for doing comparative studies. But if we read his exegetical essays with these statements in mind, we may dare to say what it is he has been up to. Two texts are placed in their respective historical contexts, related to their respective religious systems, and compared—this has been his manner of work. And the "useful end"? It can be nothing less than the quest for a comprehensive method of inquiry appropriate to a comprehensive theory of religion. This means that "history" is a "complex notion" after all. The historian of religion must be a historian not only to place his texts in contexts that may then be grasped structurally. He must be a historian also because of some "gap" that exists between texts and their contexts. It is this complex notion of the gap between different texts, and between texts and their contexts, that seems to lie at the heart of Smith's theoretical enterprise.

In 1970, Smith published a telling essay called "The Influence of Symbols on Social Change: A Place on Which to Stand."[6] In it, he juxtaposes two sets of texts, one from the cultures of the ancient Near East, the other from the Greco-Roman period. He has already announced his theme—a curious distinction between two attitudes toward space (the vast) that he has noted throughout human history. One is horror; the other is exhilaration ("enthusiasm"). Each of these attitudes corresponds, according to Smith, to a worldview: "A total world-view is implied and involved in assuming these postures, one that has to do with a culture's or an individual's symbolization of the cosmos and their place within it" (1978a: 131).

The attitude of horror of the vast belongs to a "bounded," or "closed," worldview that builds "walls" against the vastness outside the social order, and within which humans find a securely defined "home place." The cultures of the ancient Near East were "closed" and highly organized worlds of this type. Smith calls this the "locative" view of things, and speaks of one's "place" within it as a stance (view, acceptance of the hierarchical order) that sees orientation to order as well-being.

The attitude of "enthusiasm" for expanse belongs to an "open" system that regards limitations as oppressive and seeks to "break out" of the walls, to venture beyond. Religions of the Greco-Roman age shared such an "open" view. For each of them, the boundedness of the locative view had turned oppressive, danger and threat were the marks of social life, and man was defined "by the degree to which he [could] escape the patterns" (1978a: 139). From the older

---

[6]Citations are from the republished version (Smith 1978a: 129-46).

locative view to the later open view, "a radical revaluation of the cosmos occurred" (1978a: 138).

What makes this typology so interesting is that both worldviews (symbol systems) are spatial, or "locative." Smith uses the term locative only to refer to the closed order, but the only difference between the two worldviews is a "radical revaluation," that is, an inversion of values. The structures are the same. Smith can even talk comfortably about the myths or epics "characteristic" of each type. For the closed system, there is the "hero-that-failed" and the scribe who knows the patterns. For the open system, there is the "hero-that-succeeded" (in breaking out) and the savior who knows the escape routes. Smith goes on to elaborate both types with illustrations from other cultures and discussions of political and economic typologies that correspond. One begins to wonder about the change from one view to the other, about history, and about the events recounted in the narratives and myths.

Smith has announced in the title that he will discuss social change: "Social change is preeminently symbol or symbolic change. At the heart of the issue of change are the symbolic-social questions: What is the place on which I stand? What are my horizons? What are my limits?" (1978a: 143). The two attitudes are the two basic "stances" one can take with regard to these questions. Change, then, is simply to change "stances," trade "places," revaluate symbol systems: "To change stance is to totally alter one's symbols and to inhabit a different world" (1978a: 143).

If we ask what it is that can trigger such a change of stance, Smith replies: "Social change, symbolic change of the sort we have been describing, occurs when there is disjunction, when there is no longer a 'fit' within all the elements of this complex process" (1978a: 143). Again, we might have expected to hear something about history, but the "disjunction" of which Smith speaks is described mainly in terms of the coherence or lack of coherence of the symbol system itself. However, an important substitution has occurred. It is not the symbol system per se that breaks apart, but a "complex process" that cannot seem to "fit" all the pieces together. What is this process? And what are the "elements"?

Smith has been describing the process of human endeavor by reference to Ernst Cassirer ("work," "the system of human activities") and Peter Berger ("outpouring of human being into the world"), who see in it a definition of human existence. As Smith elaborates, this endeavor is both the "discovery" and the "creation" of the world; it is the process of ordering social life and signifying cultural systems. It is, ultimately, "symbolic activity" because man is "a symbol-producing animal." Presumably, the lack of the "fit" of things has something to do with the perception of the "world" itself as in need of ordering—or with the perception of the disjuncture between a given symbol system and the way things actually go in social experience—but there is as yet no reference to "history," either as the arena of disorder or as the process by which a new social order comes to be that then requires resymbolization.

Smith does mention history in the last paragraph, but in a curious way. Picking up his use of the term disjunction just cited, he notes that "each society has moments of ritualized disjunction," but goes on to say that they function within a stable order, whereas "change is required when such moments meld into history. When the world is perceived to be chaotic, reversed, liminal, filled with anomie" (1978a: 145-46). "History" is in view here, to be sure, as well as "disjunction" and the "complex process"—all terms that alert us to a set of questions Smith will explore more fully in later essays. But at this juncture in his thought, it is clear that he views *homo religiosus* as *homo symbolicus*, that a mythic worldview is a culture's symbol system, that "change" is "the discovery or creation of new modes of significance and order" (1978a: 144), and that ritual functions aid minor transitions (e.g., of status) within a stabilized society.

Smith may have emphasized the human capacity to create symbolic order on purpose. He wanted to demystify the notion of the transcendental Sacred as definitive for *homo religiosus*. He wanted to talk about "change" in some way other than "as stages in social (or individual) evolution or growth" (1978a: 143). And he wanted to establish an anthropological basis for comparing two sets of texts in the context of two contrasting cultural systems. It is important to see that he did this entirely on the morphologists' own "turf," though to do so, he was bound to stay with a purely formalistic conceptuality and press the language of process and change into purely structural terms. Smith knows that he is doing this, and that

it will appear problematic to his readers. At first, he offers a defense: "Place (whether in an open or closed structure) ought not to
be viewed as a static concept. It is through an understanding and
symbolization of place that a society or individual creates itself"
(1978a: 143).

We know what he means by "creation." We have already seen
that he makes the move quickly from "work" and human "activity"
to the "creation of world and significance" (i.e., symbol systems).
When Smith continues, then, to offer an argument for the nonstatic
notion of place, he must engage in the creative resignification of the
term itself, and this is the most arresting and intriguing statement
in his essay: "Without straining the point, this active sense is crys-
tallized in the expression 'to take place' as a synonym for 'to happen,' 'to occur,' 'to be'" (1978a: 143). We can see what Smith is
doing here, and should take the time required of us to see how far
we can go with him. He wants us to crystallize the active sense of
the verb (and thus all actions and events?) and regard locative placement as primary (thus assigning primacy to categories of territory,
space, and ordered systems).

Smith has achieved a critical revaluation of the morphological-
phenomenological notion of Sacred Order, a closed system of symbols in which to be at home means to accept the transcendental,
acknowledge epiphanies, and respond mimetically. He has done it
by inverting values and turning the world upside down, by replacing
the transcendental with the capacity of the human mind to create
and "take place." He seems already bothered, though, with the
problem of where to locate and how to understand the "disjunction"—that which can also be called the "gap." The question is, how
does he move to explore it?

In 1976, Smith published his critique of the myth-ritual school
and the Frobeniusschule ("A Pearl of Great Price and a Cargo of
Yams: A Study in Situational Incongruity").[7] That essay is of particular importance for us, because one of the two texts under discussion is the Hainuwele "mythologem," the text on which Adolf Jensen based his theory of the nonsacrificial origins of ritual killing.
Smith summarized Jensen's reading of the text as follows: "Jensen

[7]Citations are from the republished version (Smith 1982a: 90-101).

. . . understands the tale to describe the origins of death, sexuality, and cultivated food plants. The myth is a description of human existence as distinct from ancestral times—with the act of killing (creative murder) as the means of maintaining the present order" (1982a: 97). In this summary, which is substantially correct, Smith has announced his program. The critical terms are "origins," "distinct," and "present order."

Smith begins his investigation by noting that the scholarly history of transmission of "the" text is particularly troublesome. Jensen translates only one of many "versions," and it strikes Smith as a composite paraphrase. Despite his uneasiness, however, Smith bases his observations on Jensen's translation, as a sort of *textus receptus*.[8] As Smith reads the story, Hainuwele's murder is not at all the origin of sexuality, death, or paleocultivation. These are "presupposed" by the story, "not its results" (1982a: 97). He does acknowledge that the myth contains a few details that belong to a widespread "motif"—namely, "that Hainuwele was killed, buried, then dug up and dismembered, and that, from the pieces of her body which were reburied, tuberous plants grew" (1982a: 97). This corresponds to the way in which yams are actually cultivated, and the anthropomorphizing is easily understood when one knows that tropical yams can grow to approximately the same size as the human body.

What interests Smith about the story, however, are other details. The story relates that Hainuwele was "not like an ordinary person," for she excreted valuable articles. At the Maro festival, it was these "gifts" that she distributed instead of the traditional areca nuts and betel leaves, and it was because the people "thought this thing mysterious" and were "jealous" that they killed her. Smith calls these details incongruous and notes that the story emphasizes incongruity: "they thought this thing mysterious . . . and plotted to kill her" (1982a: 98). Exploring this, Smith finds that there is in fact a double incongruity. The first incongruity exists within the story itself: the "valuable" articles are excretions. The second exists between the

[8]Smith is gracious not to note that both English translations readily available, those of Mircea Eliade (1967: 18-70) and Joseph Campbell (1969: 173-76), diverge even from Jensen's German translation—the former by excising significant portions, the latter by moving interpretive statements up into the text of the story itself.

two cultures reflected in the story: all of the valuable articles are manufactured trade goods from outside Ceram!

The trade goods include Chinese porcelain dishes, metal knives, copper boxes, golden earrings, and great brass gongs. The identification of these goods allows Smith to date the tale. It cannot be earlier than the spice trade of the sixteenth and seventeenth centuries, and it is probably as late as the early twentieth century, when the Dutch intensified colonialist activities, attempting to reform the ancestral headhunting cults and impose a tax. To understand the pressure this exerted on Oceanic cultures, Smith cites Marcel Mauss's study on exchange (1925) and Kenelm Burridge's studies on exchange systems and cargo cults in Melanesia (1969, 1970). The introduction of foreign goods and money (a capitalistic exchange system) produced a crisis for the reciprocity exchange system. In the adjacent cultures of New Guinea and Melanesia, this crisis produced cargo cults. Smith concludes that the Hainuwele story reflects a "cargo situation" without a cargo cult (1982a: 98): "Using the phrase literally, the myth of Hainuwele is not a tale of the origin of death or of yams; it is a tale of the origin of 'filthy lucre,' of 'dirty money.'"

With a very few, deft moves, Smith has succeeded in presenting a radical critique of Jensen's reading of the privileged mythologem. The tale is not an "archaic" myth but a recent construction. That takes care of the nostalgia for the primitive, characteristic of evolutionary hypotheses. Moreover, it is not about the origin of Ceramese culture; it is about the "origin" of the social crisis. That takes care of the archetypal function of myth. And it is not to be described "in terms of repetition of the past," but "in terms of a difficult and incongruous present" (1982a: 101). That takes care of reenactment theories of ritual.

We should take note of the importance of the term incongruity for this revised reading. It is the term Smith has chosen to investigate the problematic "disjunction" mentioned in "The Influence of Symbols on Social Change" (1970). It is no longer problematic, at least for Smith, because he has turned it to good advantage. It is used in two contexts. There is both a textual and a social-historical incongruity. Their correlation provides entrée into the function of the text. Incongruity is now a tension within the structural system (text, culture), caused by a conflict with another culture outside itself.

What, then, is the function of this tale, if not mythic in Jensen's sense? As Smith sees it, "the Ceramese myth of Hainuwele does not solve the dilemma, overcome the incongruity, or resolve the tension. Rather, it results in thought. It is a testing of the adequacy and applicability of traditional patterns and categories to new situations and data in the hopes of achieving rectification" (1982a: 100-101).

Smith's assertion that the myth does not convey encoded meanings or enable resolutions, but "results in thought," is astonishing. We can, of course, understand the myth's logic as Smith explains it, given its new historical placement; but if that is myth's function, has cultural conflict turned *homo symbolicus* back into the old *homo sapiens*? Incongruity, though it is perceived as a clash of cultural symbol systems, articulated mythically, refers nevertheless to "a social and moral crisis," a problem to be solved "in thought"—namely, the problem of the integration of two disparate systems of cultural symbols.

According to Smith, the textual incongruity in the Hainuwele myth is created by taking an "archaic mythologem" and recasting it to include new social problems. Here he goes back to the "few details" of the myth that are "widespread" and says that a "mythic precedent" has been "applied" to the new situation (1982a: 100). Thus it is the juxtaposition of the "mythic precedent" with the indicators of European culture in the story that creates the text's incongruity and allows it to reflect the tension in the new cargo situation.

What strikes us as surprising, coming at the end of the argument, is that Smith is prepared to acknowledge an archaic mythologem of the killing of the *dema* (the anthropomorphic figures in myths of paleocultivators): "In primordial times, when Yam Woman, Sago Woman, or some other similar figure mysteriously produced a previously unknown form of food, the figure was killed, the food consumed, and thereby, acculturated" (1982a: 100). What if we were to accept Smith's critique of Jensen's reading of Hainuwele and were still left with this? Smith does not tell us what to do with it. But even shorn of (1) its function as a myth of origins, (2) its study in the interrelationship of sexuality, mortality, and paleocultivation, and (3) its overt ritual setting, the story is arresting. A (the?) basic foodstuff is symbolized anthropomorphically, and "finding" it (cultivating it?) and consuming it are narrated in terms of a killing. It is this association of "taking" food and killing that makes the "mythic precedent" work in the Hainuwele text. It is the "archaic model" that is applied. Clearly, we need to understand more about it.

In 1980, Smith published his 1974 Claremont lecture on "The Bare Facts of Ritual."[9] Its particular importance for us is twofold. In it, Smith takes up a ritual "text," and the ritual he chooses is a "primitive" ritual, the ritualized bear hunt. Therefore, his statements are especially relevant to our discussions. The essay is a study of two sets of texts, each of which contains two texts. All the texts are about ritual or ritualization, "one of the basic building blocks of religion" (1982a: 54). We are already wondering what the other block(s) might be.

The first two texts are taken from Franz Kafka and Plutarch. Each is a one-sentence story containing the report of an event and a response that interprets it:

Leopards break into the temple and drink the sacrificial chalices dry; this occurs repeatedly, again and again; finally it can be reckoned on beforehand and becomes a part of the ceremony (cited from Kafka in 1982a: 53).

At Athens, Lysimache, the priestess of Athene Polias, when asked for a drink by the mule drivers who had transported the sacred vessels, replied, "No, for I fear it will get into the ritual" (cited from Plutarch, ibid.).

As Smith elaborates the similarities and differences between these two stories, we recognize the (by now) standard set of categories. Place (or space) is the primary category for Smith, and two notions of space are distinguished. There is "bounded" space (the temple or sacred place is "marked-off space") and "open" space (outside the sacred space is the realm of the ordinary, accidental, and noisy). Signification is a matter of *placement* ("the ordinary . . . becomes significant, becomes sacred, simply by *being there*"; 1982a: 55). And both kinds of space are structures of systems that give things significance by being placed in relationship to other things: "There is nothing that is inherently sacred or profane. These are not substan-

---

[9]Citations are from the republished version (Smith 1982a: 53-65).

tive categories, but rather situational or relational categories, mobile boundaries which shift according to the map being employed. There is nothing that is in-itself sacred, only things sacred-in-relation-to" (1982a: 55).

Read in relation to "The Influence of Symbols on Social Change," however, one has the impression that the categories of space and order are being pressed to take up the question of the "gap" in a more direct way. Smith is still using locative terminology, but now the two orders of signification (worldviews) are no longer two contrasting cultural systems, but two different maps for the same territory. The "gap" or the "disjunctive" has been internalized—that is, located between two maps (sacred or profane), both of which function as systems for the placement of things within a single cultural context. The result is that any activity within the two-map territory may be either ordered or disjunctive, depending on whether it is viewed according to this or that map. Smith's terms for these two ways of viewing an event or activity are "accidental" (if profane) and "routinized" (if sacred).

We return now to the stories. But as we do, it is important to remember that in taking up the question of ritual and event, Smith has not given up his preference for spatial and formal categories. The two stories are the same in that an ordinary (accidental) activity (taking a drink) is under consideration for placement in the Sacred Order (for routinization). They differ, however, in that Kafka's story allows the activity to be ritualized, whereas Plutarch's story does not. Smith makes two points. The first is that the difference is a matter of choice: "Ritual is an exercise in the strategy of choice" (1982a: 56). Smith seems to prefer the choice made by the priestess in Plutarch's story. It is the one he elaborates by noting that signification depends on an economy of selection. If everything becomes ritualized, "the result will be either insanity or banality" (ibid.).

The other point is more unnerving and will prepare us for Smith's consideration of the bear-hunting ritual. He asks a "rabbinical" question: "What if the Leopards do not return? What if the mule drivers had taken their drink without asking anyone and then were discovered? What then?" (1982a: 57).

Smith does not give us the answer with respect to these stories. But the point has been scored about the curious disjunction between the accidental and the Sacred. Neither story presents us with this irreverent question. But that may be just the point. Nothing need happen *to the stories*, even though the accidental may prevail. And the ritualization? That is to be explored. For the moment, though, we learn from this contrast what a second "building block" of religion is: "Here we begin to sense the presence of another one of the fundamental building blocks of religion: its capacity for rationalization, especially as it concerns that ideological issue of relating that which we do to that which we say or think we do" (1982a: 57).

Smith turns now to a set of bear-hunting rituals from Paleo-Siberian peoples. The first ritual is the description of the hunt itself as a ritual. He follows the descriptions of A. I. Hallowell (1926) and E. Lot-Falck (1953), which are well-known classics and contain the familiar pattern from "Preparation" through "Leaving the Camp" and "Kill," with its etiquette and disclaimer, to the "Return" and distribution.

Can the actual hunt really have gone that way, Smith asks? The answer, of course, is no, on grounds of both common sense (a hunter refusing a kill because the bear has not played its role properly!) and ethnographic reports of the hunt (hunting actually occurs by all manner of stealth and capture). The hunt as ritual turns out to be a myth!

How, then, can the hunters themselves "believe" it, we must ask, if we refuse to see the "primitive" as having "some other sort of mind"? Smith holds that "there appears to be a gap, an incongruity between their ideological statements of how they ought to hunt and their actual behavior while hunting. It is far more important and interesting that they say this is the way they hunt than that they actually do. For now we are obligated to find out how *they* resolve this discrepancy" (1982a: 62).

Smith now cites the songs of the pygmies on the occasion of the elephant kill. He focuses on their disclaimer, addressed to the prey, which contains "an extraordinary set of rationalizations" but ends in a cry of victory. Smith summarizes in paraphrase: "(1) We did not mean to kill you, it was an accident. (2) We did not mean to kill you, you died a natural death. (3) We killed you in your own best interests. You may now return to your ancestral world to begin a better life. The final ejaculation may be paraphrased: 'To hell with all that! Wow! I did it!'" (1982a: 62).

The juxtaposition of disclaimer and victory cry establishes Smith's point about the pygmies being fully aware of the "gap." It also justifies seeing the disclaimer as a "rationalization": "It is here, as they face the gap, that any society's genius and creativity, as well as its ordinary and understandable humanity, is to be located in their skill at rationalization, accommodation, and adjustment" (1982a: 62).

The question now is, how have they achieved this rationalization? We have learned that rationalization is one of the building blocks of religion, and that it works in the gap between contingent actuality and sacred ritual, but the hunt itself cannot be the ritual because it has been disclosed as belonging to the realm of actuality. Where, then, is the ritual, and how has it made the rationalization possible?

At this point, Smith reminds us that there *is* such a thing as a bear ritual among the Paleo-Siberians. It is the second text of the set, the well-known bear festival:

A young, wild bear cub is taken alive, brought to a village, and caged. It is treated as an honored guest, with high courtesy and displays of affection, at times being adopted by a human family. After two or three years, the festival is held. The bear is roped and taken on a farewell walk through the village. It is made to dance and play and to walk on its hind legs. Then it is carefully tied down in a given position and ceremonially addressed. It is slain, usually by being shot in the heart at close range; sometimes, afterward, it is strangled. The body is then divided and eaten with ceremonial etiquette (the same rules that pertain to the consumption of game). Its soul is enjoined to return to its "Owner" and report how well it has been treated (1982a: 63-64).

We note immediately the signs of the Sacred: bounded space, repetition, patterned order. The ritual has been achieved by "domesticating" the wild bear cub and controlling the accidental variables of the actual hunt. What does that achieve?

Smith says that "the bear festival represents a perfect hunt." It assures a reciprocity between hunter and hunted that the actual hunt cannot achieve. During the actual hunt, the hunter "might hold the image of this perfect hunt in his mind." It is also possible that "he reflects on the difference between his actual killing and the perfection represented by the ceremonial killing." Thus it gives rise to the rationalizations: "The fact that the ceremony is held is eloquent testimony that the hunter knows full well that it [the perfect hunt] will not transpire, that he is not in control" (1982a: 64).

We are now at the end of a long journey. Smith has taken us from the grandeur of symbolic worldviews through cultural crimes and historical conflicts to looking at a bear cub in a cage and contemplating ordinary activity, its ritualization, and the function of ritual in helping to rationalize the ordinary again. He has retained his locative preference, his structuralist view of systems of similarities and differences, his method of comparison and contrast, his empiricism, and his rationalistic anthropology. We end up with "ordinary and understandable humanity [and the human's] skill at rationalization, accommodation, and adjustment." Even ritual turns out to be an aid to rationalization. Religion does not change anything at all; rather, it is a way of coping, creatively, with the contingent.

Smith's theory of religion is compelling, but it does leave some questions still unanswered. I begin with the "ought" and the notion of "perfection." Why should the hunt go perfectly in the first place? The only hints I can find are interesting but not completely satisfying. The first is a sort of "James Bond" performance aesthetic. According to this view, our fumbling performance in both practical and important affairs (the "Inspector Clouseau" performance) is not funny but embarrassing. Out of our better moments an aesthetic ideal of the smooth, clean shot emerges, which then becomes the "proper" way to do it; but could such an aesthetic sense account for the elaborate mechanisms that ritual and its symbols appear to be?

The other hint is given in Smith's use of the term control. The term appears to be innocent enough, but it is highly charged with older theories of religion (man against nature) and Western theologies (man over nature). Since Smith has carefully avoided the nature-culture problem (we await his essays on Rousseau and Lévi-Strauss), we cannot be sure what might be at stake here; but if man's desire to control is constitutive for Smith's anthropology, we need to see how he understands what happens to that desire in the rationalization of the contingent.

I also wonder about the killing of the bear as an "ordinary" event. Smith has told us that selection plays a role in ritualization. Why, then, is it the bear hunt that is ritualized? In Smith's system, we have only the "ordinary" and the "accidental" as categories to guide us. They do not help with the selection question. Is the selection of the bear hunt arbitrary, or is there some other reason for it? If the bear hunt is a particularly significant event for other reasons—say, because it is the basic source of food, or particularly dangerous and exciting, or crucial for social formation—it would be important to know those reasons and to factor them into the equation.

Smith does speak of "reciprocity" as an element that makes the perfect hunt perfect, and this, I think, must be explored. If reciprocity derives from a social contract, why is it transferred to the bear? And if it derives from encounter with the bear, can the perfect-kill theory account for it?

We press a bit here, because one of Smith's distinctions, in contrast to the other two theorists we are discussing, is his resistance to psychological explanations and his reluctance to address the question of motivation. One might have expected, for instance, that following his statement about how Paleo-Siberians thought they "ought" to hunt, Smith would have reflected on the reasons for thinking so in the first place. Instead, he introduces the question of how they solved the discrepancy (1982a: 62). But the question of why is crucial, because unless we know why the notions of perfect performance and reciprocity are important at the level of myth and ritual, we cannot know what it is about the actual hunt that calls for reciprocity and perfection. Smith sticks with the notion of incongruity as that which is problematic in every perception of a "gap," or "disjunction," or lack of "fit," between two symbol systems, "maps," or patterns of activity. The point is made forcefully, especially because he has stolen the thunder from the morphological reification of the Sacred by revaluating the categories of space, location, and order basic to the phenomenological approach.

We must now take seriously the human capacity and need for rationalization of the "accidental" even in the way in which ritual functions. But it is important to see how Smith has led us to this consideration. The foundations are already laid in the careful analyses of comparative methods in his earlier essays. Not satisfied with the comparative approach, which notes only the formal similarities between separate phenomena and constructs constitutive patterns on the basis of congruities, Smith called for clarity in our understanding of how comparisons actually are made and for rigor in our comparative approach to the history of religions. The recognition of "difference" was found to be prior to the quest for similarities in all comparative attempts at understanding: thus the mind of the scholar and the mind of the primitive are seen to function similarly with respect to incongruities and rationalizations. This is Smith's great contribution.

At the level of rationalization, however, we are still uninformed about why the ritual is created in the first place. Once it is there, the rationalizing function can be seen, but Smith has not given an adequate account of the reasons for its emergence. In the study of the Hainuwele myth, social conflict was indicated as the problem needing rationalization, but Smith has not followed this up, as far as I can see. And in the case of the "archaic mythologem"—a myth (myth-ritual?) phenomenon that also requires placement in some historical-social context in order to ask about what it might be rationalizing—Smith has again left us dangling.

Our questions, then, have to do with the nature of the problem that generates ritual. It seems that the perception of symmetrical incongruities is not a sufficient impulse, even though that perception, the capacity for ordering things, and the need for rationalization may be the ways in which the problem is addressed. Energizing the process, however, appears to be a matter of motivational conflicts and some awareness of them. Smith has not probed in this direction; he has not discussed rivalry, conflict, or violence as human problems with which religion may have to do. Nor has he discussed human encounter with the natural environment in such a way as to clarify why primitive myth and ritual appear to be so strongly focused on certain exchanges with the wild. We need to know, after all, about foraging, pairing, rearing, rivalry—all dynamic processes in the formation of a social group that inhabits a territory, constructs maps of it, and worries about incongruities.

We are left, then, with a formalistic view of religion that has succeeded in demystifying even the ritual of killing. In the course of our exploration, the categories of "disjunction," "gap," and "incongruity" have teased us into thinking that "history" (i.e., social change, cultural conflict, traditional group activity, or even hunting as an event) might become the "problem" in such a way as to require religion to take up history and propose a stance and pattern of encounter with it. But it appears that history is assigned to the "accidental," and that the only activity religion knows how to acknowledge is the routinized activity of ritual itself.

III

I have chosen to treat each theory as the author's writing (or reading) of a ritual script or scenario. Each of the three men has, in the course of theorizing, created a picture of some ritual event. These scenarios can be compared, noting significant differences in how they are cast, as a first step in phrasing further questions about the methods and designs used to construct them. To construct a scenario, some description of the scene, action, agent, and object, as well as some consideration of the purpose, is customary. These are the topics, in any case, for the rhetorical analysis of narrative description. They can be used to sharpen perspectives on particular aspects of the scenarios. At each point in the review, care will be taken to treat the rhetorical topics as windows that reveal the larger scape of religion and society in general that each theorist might have in view.

The use of a rhetorical schema is heuristic in one sense, intentionally provocative in another. Each theorist has worked primarily with texts, reconstructing his view of ritual from them, but each has rendered a different account, not only because the selection and type of texts were different in each case, but because the hermeneutics were different as well. This suggests different assumptions about the nature of human nature.

The scenarios described by each theorist are essentially narrative and rhetorical in nature. It has been customary in the scholarship to regard the narrative aspects of a ritual event as related in some way to the narrative structure of myth, frequently by suggesting that myth might provide the script for ritual enactments. None of the theories here assumes such a relationship. The tendency, rather, has been to grant privilege to ritual (or event) as the generator of symbols and myths. Yet the scenarios of the ritual event bear uncanny resemblance to the narrative structures of myths, even though the occurrence of narrative sequences and dramatistic resolutions has been accounted for in some other way. Girard's scenario appears to be quite dramatistic, in fact, and Burkert has expressly followed up on his theory of ritual with a reflection on the narrative structure of myth that may derive from it (1979). Only in the case of Smith may some injustice be done, therefore, by using topics of narrative description. He has not emphasized a narrative aspect, much less proposed a dramatic interpretation of his scenario, but he has emphasized its function for rationalization, a function that could well be explicated rhetorically. Thus I hope to have found an acceptable way to outline a set of topics for discussion. To the traditional topics just mentioned, I have added the notions of displacement and enactment, in order to entertain issues of a more contextual and integrative nature.

Rituals "take place," to use Smith's coinage, and the place they take can be described as a scene. The way in which the several scenes have been imagined appears to be an important consideration. Each theorist has described one scene, though three quite different pictures have emerged. Formally, there is some agreement, to be sure. Each has mentioned such things as the relation of the ritual to the larger social world, where the boundaries lie, what belongs in the picture, and so forth. In each case, the scenery within the ritual boundaries is complex enough to provide a sense of completeness, a scene adequate to the enactments. The world outside must somehow be in the picture also, a kind of peripheral background in relation to which the bounded world of the ritual derives its significance. These similarities are worth holding onto, although there are also significant differences in how each theorist has imagined and arranged his scenery.

Burkert imagines the larger context to consist of (1) a "home" camp, described mainly in terms of familial and tribal groups, and (2) a natural environment, understood to be wild in contrast to the home place and inhabited not by humans, but by animals. It is ritual that links the two spheres by turning the hunt into a pattern of action in which the encounters appropriate to each sphere are merged with their opposites in a complex set of imaginary associations. The climactic moment takes place away from home, in the wild out and into which the hunters must venture, but the social dynamics centered at the home base determine the venture from start to finish. Ritual emerges in the transection of the two orders or scenes (i.e., social group and natural environment). In the course of major reformulations of the social and environmental worlds in later agrarian and city cultures, the hunt is no longer significant as a primary means of food production, but the distinction between society as the sphere of domestication and the environment as the sphere of the untamed continues to set the imaginary stage for ritual sacrifice. In the later rituals of sacrifice, therefore, the enactments continue to explore the encounter of the human with the wild. They do this by reconstructing the primeval situation as the scene within which ritual killing is to be imagined as a socializing event. As Burkert works it out, it appears that sacrificial rituals in archaic and classical Greek societies functioned primarily at times of transition, rearrangement, or reconstitution of a given pattern for structuring social life. Yet those new social patterns do not appear to be reflected in the ritual scene in any fundamental way: the scene still reflects the primitive world. People step into it again in order to share once more its experience.

Smith also locates a home place within a natural environment as the larger context for the bear-hunting ritual, but the environment is not wild—it is simply the world within which accepted and customary activity takes place—and the hunt itself is not a ritual occasion. The ritual of the "hunt" takes place at home, in a setting that reflects the controlled environment of the social order more than the accidental nature of the activity of hunting. That is all. Smith argues that the ritual scene is fabricated, and that those who fabricate it know they have done so. Thus the ritual scene depicts an ideal scenario for a specific human activity; its purpose is not to explore a dramatic encounter between two separate spheres of determination (social world and natural environment), but to reflect knowingly on the way things actually go in the world of normal human enterprise.

Girard's scene is, in contrast, decidedly limited to the social sphere. Natural environment is not in view; human enterprise that engages the natural environment is not significant. Food gathering is only one of many "pre-texts" (1977: 219). Ritual depicts the social group at the moment of its own internal crisis and dramatic resolution. As a scenario, it does not reflect the social world of the everyday, to be sure, because the ritual reenacts a social dynamic that resides at the subsurface level of psychosocial dynamics. At this generative level, however, social process and the mythic world of ritual killing do coincide. Mythic traits in scenery and characterization at the observable level of ritual are the result of substitutionary revisions that have been determined by the incapacity to acknowledge full participation in the raw social dynamic and its eventualities. For Girard, ritual reflects only on the moment of conflict and its resolution that resides at the core of social formation.

Merely to set these three scenes alongside one another is to wonder whether the comparative task can be carried through in any systematic way. It is obvious that each theorist has cast his scene at a different point on a scale that runs from ethnographic description (or historical reconstruction on the model of ethnography) on the one end to imagistic depictions of social dynamics not at all intended as ethnographic description on the other. To ponder these three scenes and settings is to wonder, then, whether all three theorists are describing the same phenomenon, extrapolating from the same "text." We know, of course, that each has a different set of texts, a different problem, and a different way of going about his investigations, but the studies do crisscross around and about the phenomenon of ritual sacrifice (i.e., rites in which an animal is slain), and all three men recognize ritual sacrifice to have been a matter of performance in certain cultures.

The first problem for the reader is to account for the differences in the descriptive interpretations of ritual sacrifice. Are the differences in the scenarios due only to different construals of a commonly recognizable phenomenon, which could be described in social-historical terms that everyone could agree on? Or is it a matter of using different texts from the outset—texts that are different because their social-historical contexts are different? If so, do we not need to ask why those texts and contexts are different? If the ritual scene looks different in different social settings, the factors involved in those changes seem to be of some importance. Before proceeding to theories about the dynamics involved (whether compensation, desire, or rationalization), do we not need to get the pictures straight at the level of description alone? Burkert's reconstruction and Smith's scenario, for instance, do not agree, even though both are describing a hunting rite and culture. Would it not be important to adjudicate such an obvious and crucial difference?

The request to ponder the task of description is naïve in one sense, naughty in another. The naïveté is due, simply, to the desire on my part for a more ethnographic description to start with. Reading Victor Turner, for instance, and his full descriptions both of the ritual process and of the social world, or Roy Rappaport's careful documentation of some very practical functions for animal sacrifice in a contemporary primitive culture, the picture one learns to expect is exceedingly colorful, busy, and complex. One gets the impression that reflections and representations of the whole social world have been packed into the ritual scene by design, making of it a little microcosm. If that kind of ritual scene is what we are talking about, some agreement on what it looks like from an ethnographic point of view seems to be important. It is this fuller picture that fades from view in the construction of theories. Theories reduce to mechanism and equations. There can be no quarrel with the theoretical reductions, but now that we have three theories based on decidedly different reconstructions of the sacrificial scene, we can see that each omits much that seems significant for the others. Thus the scene and setting need elaboration in order to provide adequate data for testing each theory against the others.

The naughtiness is that the ethnographic approach comes with its own humanistic assumptions, and I know that. Smith comes closest to setting up his ritual-scene/social-world equation in keeping with the descriptive demands of an ethnographic approach, so he should have less difficulty with my query. Burkert also may not mind, for full and accurate description of the Greek rites is very important for him, though there is a sense in which he might agree with Girard that a full description of the social context may not be absolutely necessary. This is because both scholars understand the ritual event to reflect essentially and immediately not any contemporary pattern of social activity, but the primitive or even originary moment of social formation.

Hence the request for descriptive agreements may really be naïve. Perhaps it is not possible to agree on the description of a single or typical ritual event, or even on the value of trying to do so. At this point, then, the debate seems to break between a more phenomenological and a more ethnographic approach. The phenomenological approach would seek to get at the basic psychosocial process by imagining an originary scene. The ethnographic approach would seek to trace a ritual's relation to its immediately contingent context.

But then we would be in trouble, would we not? There must be some data common to both approaches, and the ritual texts of animal sacrifice seem to be those data. Is there not some way to start with these common texts, then discuss the bracketing of details found to be insignificant and the delineation of displacements that must have occurred? How do we decide what to leave out? Since sacrificial ritual has been fastened on merely as a point of departure for theories whose intent is to investigate the processes that generate human society, religion, and culture in general, should it not be the phenomenon by which those theories continue to be refined and tested? Ritual sacrifice is the only set of describable data that the three theories have in common, as far as I can tell, and it may be the only kind of hard data we have. Thus ritual sacrifice needs to stay at the center of the picture, even (and especially) when the horizon of interest opens out onto the whole world of human activity, social formation, and cultural construction. It is precisely the significance of the ritual event in relation to human activity in general that is at stake in any theory.

We might note, for instance, that there is no agreement about the way in which the natural environment has been painted into the picture. Burkert and Girard take positions that appear to be in direct opposition to each other on this matter; and Smith and Burkert disagree about how to describe the terrain (wild or not) and whether the ritual of the hunt takes place there or at home. It is easy to see that three different views of the significance of human activity with respect to the natural environment are in play, and that significance is a fundamental consideration for any anthropology. Indeed, the construal of the ritual scene and setting can make a big difference for the theory of religion. Do we not need to be certain of the (historically reconstructed) ethnographic setting in order to build arguments about the perceived texture of the natural world and its function or lack of function for ritual description?

The same is true for the relation of the ritual scene to the larger social world in view. For Burkert, there is no distinction between the ritual event and the actual event at the level of hunting culture where ritual originates. Only in the case of agrarian and city cultures must one begin to consider the displacement of the ritual from those patterns of activity that determine the general structure of the social life. In Smith's case, the distinction between ritual event and normal human activity is definitional. Ritual takes place according to a mental map that, while reflecting the actual territory inhabited, has "perfected" it imaginatively by superimposing the controls of the home environment; it is precisely the difference between the two spheres that is significant. And Girard speaks of two substitutions or displacements that determine the distance of institutionalized ritual from the social scene. In this case, however, the social scene in question is the subsurface level of social dynamics. The first substitution is the mythic avoidance of acknowledging the full truth about collective murder. This casts the characters differently. The second is the ritualized form of reenacting the mythic interpretation of the originary event. This casts the nature of the action differently.

So the way in which the actual world of social activity is "reflected" in the ritual scene is hardly a matter of cosmetics. As the setting is reflected in the ritual scene, so the function of the ritual has been theorized. Is there any way to make more precise just what it is about the phenomenon of ritual sacrifice, as observed, that calls for this or that move in the direction of this or that theory?

To the ritual scenario belongs the description of an action, which each theorist has taken note of as important, and this for at least three reasons. The first is that, should ritual turn out to be a primary form of religion, religion may turn out to be a particular mode of human behavior. Burkert, especially, has taken this position. The second is that, since ritual is understood to reflect (on) the social world, social life may need to be described in terms of patterns of social activity. All three scholars seem to suggest this possibility in one way or another at a very general level. The third reason for thinking the action particularly important is much more specific. Both Burkert and Girard have focused on the act of killing as distinctive, significant in its own right, and a clue to the very formation both of society and of religion. This means an exploration appears to be under way to determine that mode of activity, that perception of action, or that particular act that may be constitutive for human social and cultural formation.

For Burkert, the act is specifically that of killing prey. It is a necessary act in the sense that the acquisition of food is necessary. But it becomes problematic. The problematic aspects of killing are perceived in the course of complex associations that compound conflicts between socialization and the activity of hunting. The problems are resolved in the process of ritualization. Then, however, the act of killing becomes that action around which all social intercourse revolves ritually. Thus it is that killing becomes definitive for human being as social being (Burkert's *homo necans*).

Girard thinks that the first act of killing (i.e., the killing that makes a difference) was accidental, but that, though aberrational and violent, human society as we know it could not exist without it. Thus for Girard, too, the act of killing is definitional for human social being. He differs from Burkert, however, in the object and quality of the act, which is murder from the beginning. Only the collective killing of another human being gives the act its human significance. All other killings in social context, especially ritual killings of sacrifice, derive their meaning from this primal, extreme event.

Smith does not approach his ritual texts in such a way as to introduce questions about the significance of a particular kind of human activity. In the case of hunting and its ritualization, killing belongs to the hunt, and hunting belongs to the larger arena of normal activities. Killing is not the focal point for a type of ritual (i.e., "ritual killing"), nor are rituals that contain killings definitive in any way for social constructions. Smith has not put forth a theory of "sacrifice." Nevertheless, human activity in general—work, pursuits, and the construction of systems of technology and exchange—does appear to be what Smith is most concerned to describe and understand. Ritual killing must be related to what people are about in order to investigate its social significance.

Merely to have shifted the focus of investigation from myth to ritual, being to behavior, belief to enactment, may be the most challenging aspect of the new directions these studies represent. *No longer does an epiphanic object or being focus the picture for the religious imagination, providing a center around which a Sacred*

Order is organized by means of a system of symbols. Instead, an act (action, activity) has been noticed as a transaction of consequence, reflected on as patterned sequence, and cultivated in ritual as of prime importance.

Burkert, more than the others, has emphasized the significance of this shift for his work. He has proposed, in fact, the adequacy of ritualized behavior alone to generate and communicate social codes. If Burkert is right, we may have more than a shift in focus on our hands: we may be inviting consideration of a very complex process for which there is no adequate language, much less theory. Indeed, more seems to be involved than those behavioral dynamics that action and performance theory investigate. This is because the observance that makes a difference, according to both Burkert and Girard, is a moment in which motivation, action, awareness, and reflection are all combined in one. It is a mechanism in which one becomes aware (or evades awareness) of the consequence of what one is doing.

This seems to point to a special kind of consciousness, one that does not have "thing" and "selves" at its center. If Burkert and Girard are right about this, ritual studies may eventually help us better understand how societies imagine and structure human exchange. Ritual studies may also help us understand the role religion can play in the generation and support of notions and codes basic to societies as systems of exchange. The notion of "reciprocity," a marvelous fiction that appears to be fundamental for human transaction in many societies, might be related to the marvelous fiction of transaction that ritual seems to be, and so forth.

Tremendous pressure has been put on our linguistic and conceptual resources by this shift. For example, when Burkert and Girard describe the dramatic transaction as a moment of awareness, they point not to a change in the perception of the action and its performance, but to the change that occurs in the awareness and characterization of the victim. Thus language will need to be devised for the task, if indeed the action involved in ritual performance is as momentous as these two scholars say it is.

We are tempted to read Burkert and Girard together, seeking ways to combine the two theories in support of their common emphasis on the generative significance of the act of killing. Contemporary studies in aggression and violence set the climate for doing so, and data for the exploration of the theme unfold: killing in various types of ritual—as well as the theme of killing in diverse mythologies—is noticeable, does require explanation, and seems to invite comprehensive theories to account for what appears to be a heightened attentiveness and concern with killing in human cultures. The hunting hypothesis places the kill at the center of the exceedingly long reaches of the social formation that began when hominids became carnivores, and the discovery of intraspecific killing in apes has been taken as troubling documentation for the problem that hominid carnivores then had to solve. Burkert brings this discourse into focus by interpreting primitive hunting ritual; Girard interprets the myths of (ritual) killing and constructs a psychoanalytic rationale. Can these theses be combined?

Theoretically, Burkert might be able to accommodate Girard up to a point. He might do this because his own thesis includes intrasocietal conflict, especially in the formation of the hunting party. This conflict is resolved by being projected onto the prey. If homicide were named as the problem created by that conflict, some accounting for the significance of murder for social formation might be given. If projection is the means of resolution, as Burkert says it is, one does wonder why aggression would not have focused on a surrogate human being. But positing a human alternative to the prey, taken from the group, would produce a scenario something like Girard's, and that would threaten to cancel out Burkert's emphasis on the constructive aspect of the basic motivational nexus: the need for food. If the victim were taken from an "other" group, considerations would have to be given to intersocial recognitions and conflict as the contextual web that gets broken and repaired.[10] Thus Burkert's scenario of the ritualized hunt is a critical proposition for him. Only by beginning there can he make the point he wants to make—namely, that a "legitimate" killing gave rise to constructive compensations, that a weakness for violence, always threatening to destroy human society, does not lie behind it all.

[10]One of the more interesting observations to be made at this point is that the theories do not consider intergroup conflict. Only Smith has touched on cultural interference as a significant factor in the study of religion, and that was in relation to the rationalizing function of (the Hainuwele) myth, rather than to a ritual killing.

Girard, in contrast, has stated expressly that only a murder can account for sacrifice, that natural needs (e.g., for food) are not contributory, and that animal sacrifice is a secondary substitution derived from the primary experience of the collective killing of a human. He also thrusts the act back to the beginning, to the point where the "horde" is about to become human. He must do this to establish the priority of human sacrifice over animal sacrifice. For Girard, a kind of evolutionary theory is implicit, and if points can be made from historical data about the direction of substitution, he will make them. But his notion of the original murder is not really derived from historical considerations on the direction of substitutions, as is Burkert's. The first killing is posited as necessary on theoretical grounds. The unusual result of this is that "at the beginning" he must explicitly reject the "pre-texts" for the killing in the interest of his theory, and thus not address the evidence from prehistoric cultural anthropology or the hypothesis of the ritual killing of animals as an archaic institution. Hence there appears to be no way to combine the two theories: the two scenarios do not mix, and the two notions of an "act of killing" are construed quite differently. We simply are not talking about the same phenomenon, and this makes a both/and approach impossible.

"Sacrifice," according to Girard, "is the most crucial and fundamental of rites; it is also the most commonplace" (1977: 300). I take that statement to be telling. It is Girard's conclusion based on the archives of the history of religions. Burkert has not put it that way, because he limits his discourse to a study of those traditions that provide the prehistory to classical Greek culture. But within these limits, Burkert, too, would say, I think, that sacrifice is the common theme for myths and rituals. The question, then, is whether that judgment can be tested. Can the archives of the myths and rituals of killing bear the weight of a general theory about killing, sacrifice, and social formation? Is the phenomenon truly universal? Smith, we should note, has explained a classical text of ritual killing without recourse to the notion of sacrifice and without assuming the central significance of the action of killing for social formation. He also has called into question the scholarly consensus about a ritualized performance of the hunt itself.

So, issues for debate begin to line up around and about the primary data themselves. Can the data adjudicate the impasse? Is sacrificial ritual the central and universal phenomenon it has been assumed to be? Some cultures (including some preliterate cultures) and religions are not obviously oriented toward sacrifice as a religious notion or institution. Many rituals do not contain actions of killing, and many that do, do not seem to be focused on killing as the central moment. Burkert's and Girard's arguments for a general theory of religion seem to derive from the assumption that ritual sacrifice is a universal occurrence. What if that cannot be demonstrated?

It should be said that neither Burkert nor Girard is unaware of this problem, nor have they rested their cases on the archives of the history of religion. Each has found other ways to support his thesis. But each knows that plausibility is related to actual incidence, and each makes a point of asking the reader to imagine as real that incident of killing posited "at" and "from" or "since" the beginning. Moreover, each is dependent at some point in his argument on the evidence for ritual sacrifice that the history of religions makes available. Hence evidence is extremely important, and such evidence as there is needs to be marshaled and tested with care.

To explore religion as ritual means that a human agent comes into view. The study of religion becomes a study in anthropology. Great care has been taken to develop theories with a strictly social anthropology in mind. Indeed, none of the three investigators intends a discourse beholden to an individualistic view: Girard's mechanisms are relational and dynamic, if not collective; Burkert is emphatic in his appeal to ethology and the formation of the hunting party, familial unit, and social group; and Smith has a whole society in view when analyzing his texts.

It comes as some surprise, therefore, that in the course of describing ritual processes, a sizable number of notions tend to resurface that continue to carry individualistic connotations. Some of these derive from traditional views of human being based on philosophical and theological assumptions. Examples are the languages of desire, guilt, intention, repression, awareness, and compensation. Is it significant that these tend to occur when describing the processes of motivation and perception? They are clearly inadequate for the designation of strictly social functions that can be vaguely imagined as their correlates. Part of the problem may be that, in dealing with a ritual scenario, the role of the single agent (sacrificer) slips into place to determine the reconstructions. But the suspicion that older anthropologies might still be guiding the formation of categories is troubling.

It may be unfair even to raise this issue, because to suggest that it be discussed is to scuttle the agenda in favor of a dip into very murky waters indeed. But the hermeneutical Catch-22 should at least be acknowledged: the fact is, ritual sacrifice must serve as evidence for theories that seek to explain it. To know this is to know, also, that it makes some difference which assumptions, questions, discourses, and disciplines are brought to bear on the phenomenon. This observation might have some effect on our conversations, in that some correlations can be made between the basic anthropologies in play and the disciplines to which appeal is made for theoretical foundation. The spread runs from ethology (Burkert) through (social) psychology (Girard) to a rationalism that might be comfortable with Durkheim's sociology or Lévi-Strauss's ethnology (Smith). My request for a more ethnographic approach tips my own hand as well, I suppose. But it does seem that, insofar as sacrificial ritual is the evidence we need, as well as the phenomenon requiring explanation, we must hope for lots of texts on the table.

One would think that the object of the action, at least, could be named. One would hope, also, that the scenarios might come to some agreement at this point. Such naïveté. The bear, it seems, just will not hold still. Now tame, now wild; now itself, now an "other"; now animal, now man—the generative grids multiply and the phenomenon of the religious imagination is born before our very eyes. The problem is, no two theorists agree on how it happens or on what you end up with.

Much seems to hang on getting this matter straight. The combination of agent-action-object forms a little unit, and any change in any part of that unit could result in a different script. But the script depends mostly on how the object is seen. Regarded as tame(d) and as a source of food, there is not much drama to the ritual object, but regarded as a surrogate for a surrogate human being, all hell could break loose, as it were. Moreover, only if the object is an "other" of a certain beneficent kind can the notions for transaction, transformation, and reciprocity be appropriate for the action itself. It would be nice to be able to adjudicate even one of the many disagreements about how to understand the role of the victim in rituals of sacrifice. A painful and crucial impasse exists between Burkert's prey and Girard's human as contestants for the role of victim in the first event. But Girard's hypothesis of the one and only first time is, by definition, not amenable to demonstration, and with the hunting hypothesis called into question by paleontologists, it is difficult to argue for Burkert's claim as well. There must be something I have overlooked, however. Surely there is something more that could be said about this problem, some other construction of it that could open it up for discussion.

Pending that clarification, one observation might be dared about the phenomenon of recharacterization in general. Each theorist has noticed this phenomenon in one way or another. The ritual role does seem to involve some change in how the victim comes to be viewed. The terms that tend to be used are "anthropomorphizing" and "substitution." As we have seen, the analyses of this fictional moment for the imagination can lead to very complex phenomenologies. This is especially the case when the object comes to "represent" other imaginary figures as well (e.g., the "Master of Animals," or the "first" victim). Surrounding that moment of awareness or revisioning are said to be all of the etho-, socio-, psychological processes of motivational readjustment—associational compounding, seeing double, and so forth. But if we were to bracket these phenomenological tumbles for a moment, we would see that the language used to indicate the recharacterization normally refers to linguistic operations. Burkert and Girard do not regard the phenomenon of "naming" the victim as a linguistic achievement, preferring an explanation from the dramatic, experiential aspects of the encounter. But are not the phenomena of "anthropomorphizing," making "substitutions" (metaphorically), and producing "representations" really linguistic procedures? And are not the capacities for such linguistic-imaginative achievement usually regarded as not requiring dramatic encounter? I press here a bit because, with linguistic fictions as a possible way to understand the renaming of the victim (and the agent), a dramatic interpretation of the ritual event as a whole seems less necessary. The impression I get from reading the ethnographic literature is that it is precisely the moment of drama that seems to be lacking. Is there any way to gain more clarity about this? I note that those who interpret the moment as transformative also emphasize encounter and conflict as the motivational matrix. Smith, who does not regard ritual as dramatic, sees anthropomorphization merely as a (linguistic) fiction.

Placing ritual in a social-life calendar of special times, frequently understood to be times of transition or realignments within the structures of a society, has become the commonly accepted procedure in cultural anthropology. Function is then analyzed by noting changes in roles, projects, and seasons. The three theories under discussion have not considered the function of ritual from this perspective.

Burkert has integrated his thesis about the origins of ritual killing with this consensus, to be sure, by showing how the plot and themes of the hunt persist in the calendrical cycle of Greek sacrificial rituals. But he is mainly concerned to demonstrate the correlations that can be made between Greek sacrifices and the archaic hunting ritual, and to argue for the persistence of ritualized behavior formed in pre-Greek times. Insofar as the ritual continues to be effective, a kind of primitivism seems to be involved, a periodic reenactment of the age-old encounter. Yet it is not clear whether Burkert understands this ritualized encounter with the wild to be essential for the ordering of social life in the polis, or whether he sees it as an archaic relic that civilization could do without.

Girard speaks about the preventive aspect of ritual sacrifice, some effectiveness of its dimly reminiscent reenactment of the horrible event, as a social control against violence. But his emphasis on the "sacrificial crises" that societies can nevertheless experience shows that he does not regard ritual sacrifice as a sufficient solution to the problem he has in mind, even for primitive cultures. Surely that is why he has not been concerned to address the question of the function of ritual for the ordering of the social-life calendar. In the larger sweep of things, only a single, critical moment of conflict/resolution is important for him. Seen in this light, his theory of ritual is actually an account of ritual's inadequacy.

Smith's approach would appear not to have problems with the conventional consensus, but he has not made a point of the timing in his description of the ritual event. I think he would say that the timing is important, and that it would be helpful to know about it, but whether consideration of the occasion would change his picture significantly is not clear. As it stands now, the ritual occasion for Smith is hardly an event at all, is certainly not dramatic, and has nothing to do with social crises.

So again we have a spread along a spectrum, now arranged in terms of eventfulness: from routine activity through periodic occasions of social stress to sacrificial crises where cultural chaos threatens—these are the "times" that sacrificial rituals have been understood to mark. What would be wrong with a critical approach to careful consideration of the social-seasonal calendar? The issue is important because as soon as the question of timing is introduced, the function of the ritual occasion in relation to the past is up for discussion as well, in terms of prior rituals, social history, and tradition. Ritual happens "as if not for the first time." But does that mean that ritual "refers" to, repeats, or reenacts some "first time"? Girard seems to think so, positing the originary event as what a ritual occasion reenacts. Burkert argues for the primitive and persistent pattern of ritualized behavior, which is "continued" in a ritual repetition. And Smith seems to regard the normal, social activity that a ritual perfects as the only precursor-referent necessary. Should we not add a fourth—a ritual's own precursory occasion(s)? That would help with the question of the social function of ritual. Both the social history, as remembered, and the social patterns of activity that order the society in the present could be brought into contact with a ritual occasion for investigation in this way.

As the ancient rhetors knew, the really big question was the why of it all. Why is the action performed? Why such a thing as ritual killing? What can account for this strange performance, with its fictions, elaborations, and persistence, displaced as it is from the normal round of social life? One reads the theorists to satisfy a certain curiosity about these questions, and one's expectation is surely met. But the answers given are different, even discordant, as they touch on the difficult theme of human motivation in general. The why of the wiggle in all biological and human life is ultimately the issue, and that is where the basic disagreements ultimately seem to reside as well.

Burkert begins with the biological need for food, as we have seen. This is the basic purpose for the act of killing in the first place. It becomes problematic, however, in the context of the social formation of the hunting pack or party, which has to agree to kill only the prey. Further complications arise as all of the basic drives (related to food, pairing, turf, and dominance) clash and require readjustment. The mechanism that solves the problem is the projection of intraspecific aggression onto the prey. Thus social survival is added to biological survival as an interrelated complex of basic needs that determines the motivation for the kill in its ritualized form. Because of the projection, the prey is charged with complex anthropomorphic valences, and the act of killing the prey produces reflections on the consequence of the act, both for the prey and for the human agent. A disclosure occurs in the act of killing that creates an awareness not only of one's complicity in the relational nexus, but also of the consequences should the act of killing go wrong. Hence the first-level solution produces another problem at the level of awareness or reflection. The act is ritualized in keeping with these reflections, and thus the fiction of reciprocity and the practice of distribution emerge.

Burkert performs a dismantling and reconstruction of the complex phenomenon of societal behavior by placing the enigma of ritual sacrifice at its center. Ritual is then analyzed, accounting for the accretions of its several layers of functionality and fiction, back and down to the basic biological need for food. The axial matrix has been found around which all revolves in ever more complicated elaborations, though "need" remains as the primal and primary "motivation" at every level. There is the biological need for food, the ethnological need to work out group survival strategies, the need to project tensions outward as divergent roles conflict, and the need to create a fiction so the focus of the shared projection will function as it should. Why do people do it? They need to. Ritual is a solution to a biosocial set of needs requiring adjudication for survival. Ritual is the necessary texture of biosocial existence. That we no longer understand how it works is simply our own problem. So I read him.

Girard, in contrast, resists any reduction to biosocial needs as the motivational matrix for ritual sacrifice. The reason he must reject any exploration of the "instinctual" matrix for clarifying human motivation is stated expressly:

The notion of an instinct (or if one prefers, an impulse) that propels men toward violence or death—Freud's famous "death wish"—is no more than a last surrender to mythological thinking, a final manifestation of that ancient belief that human violence can be attributed to some outside influence—to gods, to Fate, to some force men can hardly be expected to control (1977: 145).

The basic drives (related to the "pre-texts") belong, apparently, to the instinctual level of motivation and cannot (should not) be seen as the cause of the distinctively human form of violence—namely, murder. Violence arises out of the intrahuman rivalry for Being, as made both problematic and possible by the mechanisms of mimetic desire and the surrogate victim.

The operation of these constructs at the level of human psychosocial development is what accounts for the act of murder that becomes ritualized. The "pre-texts" cannot be the object-ives because resolutions at the basic-need level would result in an ethological definition of human society. Something called human Being is at stake instead. Girard intends this focus on Being as a fundamentally constructive move. According to Girard, the bone of contention is worth the rivalry, and the ritualized form of its terrible resolution is humanizing in the sense that society is ordered. One suspects it is, above all, the horror of the thought of the terrible resolution that leads Girard to see the act of murder as happening only once in its nonritualized form of originary accident. Subsequent attempts to reproduce that event ritually, though necessary and effective (resulting in the strong statements about religion as the sine qua non of human social order), are judged by Girard to be way stations in a long process of demythification, which eventually must produce another solution: learning how to let each other "be." The basic problem, then, which in turn generates ritual killing as its solution, is the desire to take one's place as a human being among human beings.

It is desire, therefore, that motivates the complex machinations of the social arena, accounting for violence in all its many shades of manifestation, including ritual killing. Ultimately, that desire is an individual's desire to take his or her place, to "be." But what it means to "be" is learned by recognizing another human being. Desire takes the form of mimesis, a desire to be like the other. The "pretexts" have their place as pseudo-objects of desire until there are not enough to go around. Conflict then creates the double bind, and desire suffers a metamorphosis. Now Being can only be achieved by displacement, by the elimination of the other. Violence erupts, and the desire to be creates the final fiction. The deed was called for, invited by the "beneficent" other. And thus the script is given for the ritual, which displays the desired resolutions. Why do people do it? Desire. Ritual killing is the necessary, public justification and display of the many transformations involved in the psychosocial dynamics of a dark desire.

Smith resists the quest for motives. He does not discuss the question of why at all. He wants to describe what people do, and he wants to compare this with what people say they do. It is the difference between the two that he explores, not the motivation for activity in the first place. Thus it may not be fair to compare Smith's thesis about religion and rationalization with the theories of motivation that Burkert and Girard have proposed, because his thesis seeks to account for the function of religion without recourse to psychosocial considerations. Accordingly, we should take care not to translate his thoughts about thinking into disclosures of motivational mechanisms. And yet an analysis of motivation appears to be possible in Smith's case, also. It can even be delineated as a complex, purposive process, as has been possible for the other two theories. The key word may be "interest," a term that combines connotations of curiosity about, and investment in, a matter.

Humans, then, according to Smith, are those who take an interest in their life-world. To make life interesting, a limited number of things are selected for observation. "Observance" includes both the observation of things and attention to their handling, that is, trying out various "arrangements" and exploring their several interrelationships. An interesting world to live in is produced. Selecting some of the more interesting things for perfecting, one notices the difference one has made/can make. This, too, is found to be curious, of interest, and worth exploring, and so the play proceeds. Every investment of pointed observance is found to return its interest in kind. Why do people do it? Why do people perfect the hunt?

Smith himself does not say why. But I think he might say, "Out of interest."

Thus we have three theories and three motivations: need, desire, and interest. I have sought to trace the imaginative moments of scholarly thoughts and insights that succeeded in giving us these alternatives. I have wanted to find such differences as might exist among the three, such contours as might indicate a lack of fit, such common traits as might have been shared, some basis for constructive dialogue among them. I still hope, secretly, for little shifts in the direction of theoretical accommodations, but that cannot be the purpose of our conversations, lest we lose sight of the sharply profiled figures in some conjunction that is forced on them, and premature. But we might want to ask whether each of us sees the same configurations. If so, certain fundamental issues in ritual theory will have been clarified.

One

RENÉ GIRARD

Generative Scapegoating

I

In current usage, the word scapegoat has three frequently confused meanings that should be carefully distinguished: a biblical
meaning, an anthropological meaning, and a psychosocial meaning.

1. *The biblical meaning.* In the Mosaic ritual of the Day of Atonement (Lev. 16), the scapegoat is "that one of the two goats that was
chosen by lot to be sent alive into the wilderness, the sins of the
people having been symbolically laid upon it, while the other was
appointed to be sacrificed" (*Oxford English Dictionary*). The word
was apparently invented by William Tindale to render the "*caper
emissarius*" of the Vulgate, itself a mistranslation of the original Hebrew specifying that the goat is "destined to Azazel," who is the
demon of the wilderness. This error is relatively unimportant for the
interpretation of the ritual. "Scapegoat" is as good a term as any
other to designate, in the Leviticus ritual, the first of the two goats
and the function it is called on to perform.

2. *The anthropological meaning.* Beginning with the eighteenth
century, or before, analogies were perceived between the Leviticus
ritual and other rituals. In his book on India, for instance, Raynal
observed that "they have a scape-horse, analogous to the scape-goat
of the Jews."[1]

In the nineteenth and twentieth centuries, Frazer and others freely
utilized the term scapegoat in connection with a large number of
rituals. These rituals, they felt, were based on the belief that "guilt"
or "sufferings" could be transferred from some community to a rit-

---

[1] The English translation is quoted from the *Oxford English Dictionary*; the original French has *cheval émissaire, bouc émissaire*.

ually designated victim, often an animal but sometimes a human being, the Greek pharmakos, for instance.

For many years, the notion of "scapegoat" remained popular with a number of anthropologists who took for granted the existence of a distinctive category or subcategory of rituals they named "scapegoat rituals." In recent decades, most researchers have felt that no such category can be isolated and defined with any accuracy. The result is that most anthropologists now avoid any systematic use of "scapegoat," and the word has fallen into silent disrepute. It is reminiscent of an outmoded anthropology.

3. *The psychosocial meaning.* In popular novels, conversations, newspaper articles, and so on, the victim or victims of unjust violence or discrimination are called scapegoats, especially when they are blamed or punished not merely for the "sins" of others, as most dictionaries assert, but for tensions, conflicts, and difficulties of all kinds. In connection with "scapegoat" in this third sense, the English language has forged such words as "to scapegoat" and "scapegoating." In the present essay, I will use these words only when these psychosocial connotations are implied.

Scapegoating enables persecutors to elude problems that seem intractable. But scapegoating must not be regarded as a conscious activity, based on a conscious choice. The very fact that it can be manipulated by people who understand its operation—politicians, for instance—supposes a basic lack of awareness in the passive subjects of such manipulation. Scapegoating is not effective unless an element of delusion enters into it. Proof that we are all prone to that delusion is indirectly accessible through the following paradox: all of us can observe and denounce numerous examples of scapegoating we have personally observed, yet none of us can ever identify past and, above all, present instances of his or her own involvement in scapegoating.

Scapegoat delusion, we can already see, cannot be assimilated with the "unconscious" of the psychoanalyst, whatever its definition. Some kind of reciprocal suggestion seems to be at work in every form of scapegoating. A social dimension is always present. The victim is often in the singular and the persecutors in the plural. Even when the victims, too, are plural, they are less numerous than their persecutors and, as a result, more or less defenseless. The persecutors are a majority and their victims a minority.

Scapegoating in this sense implies a process of displacement or transference that is reminiscent of Freud. But even though it can have sexual connotations, it is not exclusively sexual, as in Freud, and even though it has a linguistic dimension, it is not purely linguistic, as in Frazer.

Decades before Freud began to speak about transference, Frazer used the term in connection with scapegoating. Unfortunately, he defined it in an excessively narrow fashion—in a completely misguided fashion, I feel, that empties it of its universal significance, even though (or perhaps because) it is curiously prophetic of the method advocated by linguistic structuralism:

The notion that we can transfer our guilt and sufferings to some other being who will bear them for us is familiar to the savage mind. It arises from a very obvious confusion between the physical and the mental, between the material and the immaterial. Because it is possible to shift a load of wood, stones, or what not, from our own back to the back of another, the savage fancies that it is equally possible to shift the burden of his pains and sorrows to another who will suffer them in his stead. Upon this idea he acts, and the result is an endless number of very unamiable devices for palming off upon someone else the trouble which a man shrinks from bearing himself. In short, the principle of vicarious suffering is commonly understood and practised by races who stand on a low level of social and intellectual culture (Frazer 1922: 624).

The scapegoat illusion of Frazer is predicated on a simplistic confusion between word and thing. The "rude savages" would wrongfully extend to the spiritual realm the physical significance of such words as carry, load, burden. The implication is that a correct understanding of these words should suffice to rid us of all nasty scapegoat practices. Modern English gentlemen do not make the mistake of confusing a physical burden with a mental one—except, perhaps, in the case of the famous "white man's burden." If we accept Frazer's definition, we will assume, as he does, that modern gentlemen are immune to scapegoating in any form.

This, at least, is the conclusion suggested by Frazer's linguistic theory. His rather simplistic interpretation of scapegoat rituals neatly confirmed his cultural prejudices against primitive societies and his concomitant belief in the absolute superiority of modern civilization. *The Golden Bough* shows no real understanding of "scapegoating" in the modern and popular usage, even though that usage antedates Frazer by several centuries. This silence could mean that (1) Frazer was not aware of any propensities to psychosocial scapegoating around him, or (2) he was aware of such tendencies but firmly believed in his linguistic-confusion theory of the scapegoat, which protected him from all subversive speculation concerning the possible similarities between "savage" scapegoating and "civilized" scapegoating.

Should we ourselves avoid that same speculation? Is there a relationship between primitive religion on the one hand, and the modern and popular usage of scapegoating on the other? Can the question make sense to anthropologists? Many, I am sure, would answer negatively. Anthropology, they would say, has outgrown this type of debate. If true, this is a great theoretical achievement. How did it come about? As far as I know, the issue has never been raised. Even and especially if we reject the Frazerian rationale for ritual "transference" (i.e., the confusion between a physical and a spiritual burden), can we deny that some victims, in rituals the world over, are expelled, persecuted, and killed for the sake of the entire community? Can we deny the "persecutory" aspect of certain rituals?

The question of the so-called scapegoat rituals is not settled. We no longer believe in the clear-cut category of former days. The grouping together of these rituals cannot be justified by the simplistic reasoning of Frazer. Have we ceased to feel, however—can we cease to feel—that these rituals belong together? The experience of their kinship is something that cannot be denied, and it remains inseparable in our minds from the idea of scapegoating, not as Frazer understood it, but as we ourselves understand it.

How could it be otherwise? Take the pharmakos ritual of the Greeks, for instance. With its victim a human being rather than an animal, and a human being collectively manhandled before he is killed, this ritual does not merely recall the collective persecution of psychosocial scapegoating: it *is* it. When we read about the pharmakos, we cannot help feeling that it and similar rituals must be the simultaneously crafty and naïve institutionalization of the type of spontaneous persecution we call scapegoating. The only difference is that the same phenomena that occur in our world underhandedly were then practiced deliberately and systematically, but not necessarily with a greater consciousness of what they really are.

The current meaning of "scapegoating" is not a mere figurative use of the more original and literal concept that occurs in the Leviticus ritual, as dictionaries assert; it is, rather, among other things, a rough-and-ready but coherent interpretation not of that ritual alone, but of all others that resemble it. The Leviticus ritual is only one and not even an exceptionally striking and enlightening example, compared, for instance, with the Greek pharmakos. The reasons for the popularity of the term scapegoat are rooted in our historical relationship to the Bible and have nothing to do with the specific features of any particular ritual.

Is there some value in this spontaneous interpretation? Our first inclination is to deny this possibility. The practice is too popular and unreflective, we feel, to have any scientific future. Frazer's interpretation was a failure, and it probably owed too much, rather than too little, to the popular insight I want to rehabilitate. From vulgar definitions, nothing but a cheap and vulgarized pseudoscience can emerge. But can we afford to reject an insight as irresistible as this scapegoating insight?

Do phenomena branded as scapegoating really occur? Often, of course, they are alleged to occur when in fact they do not. In our world, the position of a victim is eagerly sought, at least for propaganda purposes. No one, however, can seriously doubt the reality of scapegoating. Minorities are oppressed by majorities the world over, and many genuine modalities of collective persecution must be captured by the vocabulary of scapegoating, judging from the widespread though unsystematic use sociologists make of it.

Could these phenomena be completely unrelated to the so-called scapegoat rituals? Can anthropology dispense with phenomenal insights rooted in everyday life? Do we really possess other means of investigation? Is it not significant that the vocabulary of scapegoating occasionally creeps up even under the pens of those researchers most theoretically opposed to its past use?

Opposition to this past use is sound, I believe, but must not turn into a fetishistic avoidance of a word that could teach us many things if we carefully examined the implications of current, nonan-thropological usage. The Frazerian definition was an impoverished or embryonic version of the insight, right or wrong, that is shared, implicitly at least, by all reasonably perceptive people in our con-temporary world. A systematic investigation of this insight is in or-der, not in connection with ritual alone but in connection with all religious phenomena.

II

In order to be genuine, in order to exist as a social reality, as a stabilized viewpoint on some act of collective violence, scapegoat-ing must remain nonconscious. The persecutors do not realize that they chose their victim for inadequate reasons, or perhaps for no reason at all, more or less at random.

How can the choice of such a victim be perceived as anything but random or arbitrary? How can such a grossly irrational phenome-non pass for rational and legitimate? The answer is within our reach, I believe, but we must be careful. For the truth of scapegoat-ing, our subjective experience obviously does not suffice. As I re-marked earlier, this subjective experience hardly exists. We never catch ourselves in the act of scapegoating.

Objective observation is plentiful, but it will not do, either. It is *too* plentiful. Scapegoating by others, scapegoating for which we feel no sympathy, appears to us an evil so stupid, so senseless, and nevertheless so widespread that it arouses our indignation. We can-not perceive it as "sincere" and spontaneous. We cannot believe participants are really fooled by their own scapegoating, and we be-lieve in foul play. Our understanding is blurred. Those we regard as scapegoat-makers, we are tempted to turn into . . . our own scapegoats.

If we understand neither the scapegoating of others nor our own, where shall we turn? The secret of it all must lie in the paradox it-self, the paradox of this double impotence in the face of a phenom-enon we can never fully apprehend, either objectively or subjec-tively, but whose reality we cannot doubt. In our most perceptive moments, we suspect that we ourselves cannot be immune to the disease.

Why is our own participation in scapegoating so difficult to perceive and the participation of others so easy? To us, our fears and
prejudices never appear as such because they determine our vision
of people we despise, we fear, and against whom we discriminate.
Our avoidance of them, our psychological violence, like the physical
violence of a more brutal world, appears entirely justified by the
very nature and behavior of these people. The negative behavior
that we perceive as scapegoating in others we always perceive as
well founded when it is ours. Whether physical or psychological, the
violence directed at the victim appears to be justified—justified by
the responsibility of the scapegoat in bringing about some evil that
must be avenged, something bad or harmful that must be resisted
and suppressed.

Let us suppose, now, that a myth is an account of scapegoating
narrated from the viewpoint of the persecutors. Can this myth inform us that its scapegoat is really innocent, that he was chosen
more or less at random, or for reasons completely alien to the misdeed he supposedly committed? Can such a text advertise the scapegoat status of its own scapegoat? Certainly not. We can expect from
this myth only what we would expect from any account of a violent
deed provided by its perpetrators. We can expect the victim to be
seen as guilty and therefore to *be* mythically guilty. We can expect
the violence of the group to be condoned and justified. This violence
will be presented as a legitimate defense against a fearsome monster, as the just punishment of a guilty criminal.

In an enormous number of myths, we find a cluster of themes
that, despite the extremely diverse variations they can undergo, always remain compatible with the pattern I have in mind, the pattern
of a scapegoating delusion narrated from the standpoint of the deluded persecutors. My first example is a myth of the Yahuna
Indians:

From the great Water House, the Land of the Sun, there came, many years
ago, a little boy who sang so beautifully that many people flocked from
near and far to see and hear him; and the name of this boy was Milomaki.
But, when those who had heard him returned to their homes and ate fish,
they all died. Hence their relatives seized Milomaki, who meanwhile had
grown to manhood, and because he was so dangerous, having killed their
brothers, they cremated him on a great pyre. Nevertheless, the youth con-

tinued to sing beautifully to the end, and even while the flame was licking his body. . . . He died and was consumed by the flames, but his soul ascended to heaven while from his ashes there grew, that very day, a long, green blade, which became steadily bigger and bigger, spreading out, until the next day it was already a tall tree—the first paxiuba palm in the world (Koch-Grundberg 1910; cited in Campbell 1959: 292-93).

Milomaki is a victim of collective violence. He was cremated by the united relatives of the people whose death he supposedly caused. People who listened to his music and then ate fish died as a result. Apparently it was possible to listen to Milomaki and survive if one did not eat fish; it was also possible to eat fish and survive if one had no contact with Milomaki, but the combination of the two was mysteriously fatal. Why should this be? We are not told, but the amazingly selective nature of Milomaki's destructive power over the local population is presented as something unquestionable. All this is exactly as it should be if the myth were really an account of nonconscious scapegoating. Indeed, we would regard scapegoating as a good explanation for this story if we felt it had some relationship to a nonmythical reality, if the death of Milomaki were not accompanied by events too fantastic to believe—if the story were not a myth, in other words.

Deadly epidemics break out easily in a tropical climate, especially when hygiene is primitive. Accidental deaths could result from some bad fish eaten by some of the natives and not by others. It is unbelievable that the mere presence in a community of a young stranger with a talent for the flute, even a talent as uncanny as Milomaki's, might be responsible for such an epidemic. It is quite believable, however, that such a belief could arise, especially among primitive people in a state of panic. Such a belief would spread like wildfire and become so strong and unanimous that the community could only remember it as an established and unquestionable fact, even if there were no proof whatsoever.

The fantastic aspects of our myth are not all fantastic in the same manner. There may be a rational approach to the interpretation of at least some of them in a first phase, and maybe to more later. It is clear that Milomaki could be a "scapegoat," not in the obvious, deliberate, and flat-footed style of the old anthropology but in the nonconscious manner just defined: the manner of all majorities holding minorities responsible for whatever goes wrong in the community, and notably for outbreaks of contagious disease.

III

Is the possibility of a nonconscious scapegoating genesis present in other myths beside Milomaki's? Can it shed light on the organization of these myths? Let us examine a second myth, the best known of all Greek myths, perhaps, the myth of Oedipus.

Oedipus, like Milomaki, is responsible for an epidemic of plague. And we observe in both myths the same contrast between the first, highly favorable impression made by the hero, and the later discovery of a harmful influence. Milomaki charmed the Yahuna with his music; his Greek counterpart outsmarted the sphinx and freed Thebes from this monster. The Thebans were so impressed with Oedipus at first that they put him on the throne, but then the epidemic broke out that the new king proved unable to curb. After being synonymous with good luck, his presence alone spelled disaster.

Our two myths very much resemble the distorted remembrance a mob would have of its own hasty violence if it were absolutely confident it had acted justly. It is in the nature of mobs, of course, to have such confidence. The presentation of the "culprit's guilt" as an unquestionable fact, the complete lack of proof notwithstanding, provides a possible indication of unshaken faith in the perspective that triggered the violence.

In the Milomaki myth, we see an actual lynching mob spurred into action by a contagious belief in the hero's responsibility for what might or might not be an outbreak of food poisoning. In the Oedipus myth, there is no physical violence, there is no mob, the hero is not killed. But the king who replaces him banishes him from Thebes. The citizens are unanimous in their horrified rejection of Oedipus, and Creon acts in their collective name when he pronounces Oedipus's sentence.

Oedipus, therefore, is a victim not of the same physical violence as Milomaki, but of a legal violence that may ultimately rest on the same collective delusion as the Yahuna myth. Oedipus, too, could be a scapegoat, not in the sense of Leviticus, not in the Frazerian sense, but in the nonconscious and psychosocial sense to which we all spontaneously resort when we speak about political or racial witch-hunts.

The resemblance between Milomaki and Oedipus extends to other features of the two myths. Both hero-victims are strangers to the two communities they unknowingly endanger. Oedipus was born in Thebes, to be sure, but this fact is unknown, even to Oedipus himself, and he never lived in Thebes until he became a king. For all practical purposes, Oedipus, like Milomaki, is a visiting stranger.

A nonconscious scapegoat genesis can never appear explicitly and unambiguously in the myth that would result from it. If it did, it would not be effective, it would not be the real genesis of the text. There is nothing esoteric or mystical about this impossibility. Unjust persecutors will never picture themselves as unjust persecutors, but they will always think and act as unjust persecutors; they will always see their victims, and themselves and their actions, in the same stereotyped manner. No group addicted to scapegoating will knowingly publicize the fact. Its arbitrary scapegoats will be presented, if not as culprits deliberately bent on evil, at least as individuals unwittingly responsible for some disastrous event.

We cannot expect a scapegoat-generated myth to be explicit about the arbitrariness of its victim's choice. But there may be indirect clues, and the more numerous they are, the more probable the scapegoat genesis becomes. We can expect only indirect clues of the victim's innocence.

In both the Milomaki and the Oedipus myth, the identification of the hero as a visiting stranger may be such a clue; the contrast between the initial popularity of the visitor and the sudden about-face demonstrated by the collective violence that follows may be another. Both clues point in the same direction. In times of stress, people in groups tend to embrace almost anyone as a potential savior, especially someone totally unknown and thus easily endowed with a certain exotic prestige. If things do not rapidly improve, however, the new man's instant popularity is likely to turn into its opposite, and yesterday's idol becomes today's scapegoat. Taken in isolation, of course, the identification of the two heroes as "visiting strangers" means next to nothing. The same is true of their rapid changes of fortune. Yet these two details must be viewed as only two in a series of indirect clues that, taken together, cannot fail to mean a great deal.

Changes of fortune that appear astonishing from the individual's standpoint are, in reality, determined by the instability of the group and the heightened contagiousness of feeling that goes with it. Contemporary politics provide perpetual examples of these reversals, but many people are not fully aware that each episode is one more instance of the same basic phenomenon. The horrible crimes of the hero immediately come to mind when the Oedipus myth is mentioned. There is nothing comparable in the case of Milomaki. The great Freudian ado about parricide and incest might lead us to believe that the absence of these crimes in the Milomaki myth should make a real difference, but I don't think it does. In their basic outline, the two myths are very much alike, because the parricide and the incest in the Oedipus myth are not essential but secondary themes.

The Yahuna myth could very well include patricide and mother incest, or other, similar crimes, such as sister incest, adultery, or bestiality. Examples are numerous—so numerous and so diverse, as a matter of fact, that they cast doubt on the special significance Freud conferred on the two particular instances he so passionately espoused, the patricide and mother incest of Oedipus. Myths are remarkably eclectic in regard to the crimes of sex and violence attributed to their heroes.

The important question is not the absolute significance, if any, of these crimes, but their significance relative to the myths in which we find them and, above all, the function that goes with this significance in the overall system of the myth. The answer is not difficult. The answer lies in the word that must be used when we mean none of these actions in particular and all of them in general. That word is crime. These actions are all crimes from the standpoint of the myth itself, even if they are not labeled as such. They are invariably sanctioned by death, expulsion, ostracism, or some other form of punishment.

In many myths, these crimes of sex and/or violence within the family are the sole cause of the hero's punishment. Prajapati, for instance, the Indian god of sacrifice, has committed incest with one of his daughters, and the gods, his children, unanimously decide he must be put to death. Since Prajapati is the creator and father of all creatures, the possibility of some sexual union that would not involve incest is completely excluded, but that does not seem to count as an excuse. In the view of the other gods, his children, incest is such a horrible deed that it must be punished.

In many other myths, crimes of sex and violence do play a role in the overall definition of the hero as a troublemaker, but they are not his primary crime. They are adjuncts, so to speak, to some more fundamental misdeed. The hero is responsible for some great social, natural, or even cosmic disaster. And contrary to what the Freudian mystique suggests, this is the case with the Oedipus myth. The plague comes first; the crimes Oedipus commits against his next of kin serve primarily to bolster the argument in favor of making him responsible for spreading the disease.

This view sounds paradoxical to the literary critic and the psychologist, but it is routinely evident in an ethnological context. In primitive culture, the belief is extremely widespread that parricide, incest, bestiality, and other transgressions destructive of elementary forms of human kinship can bring about deadly epidemics. Contagious disease is not clearly distinguished, it seems, from acute internal discord. This type of transgression is punished with a view to forestalling possible disasters. If some epidemic breaks out first, logic demands that the reverse order be followed: some "culprit" must be discovered who caused the disease, and, in order to restore its health, the community must take appropriate sanctions. In the Oedipus myth, as in many others, the parricide and the incest have a function that no psychological mystique, Freudian or otherwise, should be allowed to obscure. These two crimes clinch the case against a man whose rapid social rise could easily make him a target of jealousy.

What kind of a logic is it that finds the cause of an epidemic in one man, but only after it was decided that this man had secretly murdered his father and committed incest with his mother? It is mythical logic, we are often told, and we should leave it at that. There is nothing more to say.

It is certainly not the logic of civilized and well-informed men. But is there nothing more to say? Such logic is imaginary, but not in the sense of a pastoral poem. It is outlandish, and yet there is a familiar ring to it. We would immediately recognize it if our minds were not paralyzed by the quasi-religious respect that still surrounds mythology. This respect is especially intense in the case of the Oedipus myth, which for many years has held the status of almost a Sacred Scripture in the world of our cultural sciences.

The causal link between family crimes and "the plague" belongs to the logic of mobs on the rampage. Whenever any of these crimes is mentioned in the midst of a mob—and some are likely to be mentioned whenever mobs congregate—the collective rage gathers strength and tends to focus on the first available or most visible object (perhaps, too, on some habitual object). The violent impulse becomes so intense that it silences all other considerations, and the mad logic we see here takes over, the logos of human groups in a state of disarray. The innumerable crimes of sex and violence in the myths of the entire world suggest that the mob and its logic play a role in the genesis of mythology, and the myths themselves seem to confirm that suggestion when they show us, as they often do, the collective expulsion or death of those who supposedly committed these crimes.

The Yahuna myth dispenses with crimes of sex and violence, and the reason is obvious: it does not need any. The community is of one mind in regard to Milomaki. There is nothing fishy about Milomaki's responsibility for the fish poisoning. No additional "proof" is required. In the Oedipus myth, the parricide and the incest function as an additional "proof." Between the vast dimension of the social disaster and the smallness of one individual, the Greek myth needs the mediation of crimes dreadful enough to magnify the evil-making potential of the hero.

There has been so much exegetical effervescence around Oedipus, from Sophocles to Freud, and so little around Milomaki, that the basic similarity and simplicity of the two myths escapes us. But we must not allow secondary differences to sidetrack our interpretation. At their core, the Oedipus myth and the Milomaki myth are the same. The same logic is at work in both cases, and it is the logic of the mob; and the logic of the mob is at one with the logic of nonconscious scapegoating in its most brutal form. The mob is highly visible in the Yahuna myth, but it is not completely invisible in the *Oedipus Rex* of Sophocles. At the end of the tragedy, the chorus tends to speak more and more like a mob in search of a victim.

Let us recall, at this juncture, the amazing number of myths concerning murders collectively planned and/or enacted by human or divine groups, usually for the most "urgent" and "legitimate" reasons, but sometimes, too, for no stated or apparent reason, except that *it must be so*. Entire clusters of myths, the Dionysus saga, for instance, happen to have as their common denominator one scene only, and it is a veritable lynching scene. In view of the theriomorphic nature of mythology, of its lack of differentiation, rather, between men and animals, it must be significant, too, that in all parts of the world, animals living in herds, schools, packs—all animals with gregarious habits, even if completely harmless to each other and to man—appear in the role of the murderous Walküre of Germanic mythology, which is always the same, at bottom, as the role of those who lynched Milomaki in the Yahuna myth.

This role can be held by animals everywhere: the horses and wild boars of Greek mythology, the kangaroos of Australia, the bison and buffalo of the American plain, or the water buffalo of India. Remember, in the first *Jungle Book*, the lynching of the evil tiger by the water buffalo, led by Mowgli; remember the almost innumerable scenes of collective violence in both the first and the second *Jungle Book*. Remember, also, the almost countless scenes of collective hunting, murder, or expulsion performed by animals against other animals or human beings in mythology, by human beings against other human beings or animals. My own inclination is to interpret these scenes as transpositions of the collective murder, rather than the collective murder as a transposition of the collective hunt. In that context, and without attempting to be exhaustive, I will mention the vultures and many other birds, in many parts of the world, and more particularly in the American myths studied by Lévi-Strauss; and also in these same myths, we may recall the deer, the fish, and several species of insects, including flies that buzz around a mythical corpse not without a violent purpose.

IV

At the time of the Black Death, foreigners were killed, and Jews were massacred, and a century or two later, "witches" were burned, for reasons strictly identical to the ones we found in our myths. All these unfortunates were the indirect victims of internal tensions brought about by epidemics of plague and other societal disasters for which their persecutors held them responsible. The imaginary crimes and real punishments of these victims are the crimes and punishments we find in mythology. Why should we have to believe, in the case of mythology only, that if the crimes are imaginary, the punishments and the victims themselves cannot be real?

Every sign points the other way. The texts that document historical atrocities—the judicial records of witch-hunts, for instance—offer the same fantastic charges as myths, the same indifference to concrete evidence, and the same unexamined and massive conviction that everything is true, a conviction often voiced, if not actually shared, by the scapegoats themselves. All the clues to the scapegoating of imperfectly assimilated people—outsiders of one type or another, the physically or otherwise handicapped—are present in these records, just as they are in mythology, as far as we can ascertain, and to us modern observers, they give away the true nature of what happened.

We do not doubt that some real persecution took place, triggered or facilitated by collective heresy. It struck innocent people, for complex psychosocial and historical reasons we cannot fully analyze, but the imperfection of our knowledge does not deter us from interpreting these documents as reliable evidence of some kind of collective madness that resulted in real events, in real "scapegoating."

Far from discrediting an entire document, the fantastic nature of the accusations increases the probability that it also contains solid information. These Jews and witches are not imaginary; they are real people, no doubt innocent people, who suffered unjust persecution. The more obviously false the stereotyped slander against them and the more distorted the vision of the persecutors, the more certain we feel that real collective violence lies behind the text—provided, of course, that the distortions due to scapegoating are interspersed with what we regard, not unjustifiably in such a context, as trustworthy indications of the violence that took place.

All these features are present in mythology, and here, too, some could be real precisely because others are unreal in the manner typical of persecutors everywhere. The attribution to Milomaki of the deaths by food poisoning is certainly fanciful, but not in a gratuitous and poetic sense; it is fanciful in a sense we would judge sinister in a historical context, because it increases the likelihood that a real victim was burned on a pyre. The perpetual recurrence of this typical combination of themes cannot be any more fortuitous in mythology than it was in the fifteenth century.

Our view of mythology remains dominated by a global true-or-false alternative that fails to attain the level of finesse that our handling of historical persecution attained centuries ago. We have learned to separate the wheat from the chaff in the statements of medieval and modern witnesses. We have learned to criticize their accounts in a highly selective fashion. But we have not learned in the case of mythology. Past attempts to root myths in reality have been so disappointing that we do not dare follow the scapegoating route in this case. We fear a relapse into the view of a religious age and its naïve assimilation of fanciful language with reality.

Far from reflecting greater methodological sophistication, the contemporary abandonment of reality is almost as naïve as the religious trust in the truth of the mythical message, but it is the reverse naïveté. The historian's handling of the scapegoating vision lies beyond these two opposite kinds of one-sidedness. The commonsense ability to rate certain statements as possibly true (Milomaki's pyre), not in spite of but because of the fact that other statements are obviously false (Milomaki's responsibility for food poisoning), is identical with the popular insight into scapegoating—the insight we automatically turn on when we confront a historical situation and automatically turn off when we interpret a mythical text.

Let me repeat once more that the scapegoat genesis requires an awareness of the nonconscious dimension of scapegoating. The one thing we must not expect from a scapegoat-generated myth is a recognition that the victim is a SCAPEGOAT in the ritual or Frazerian sense, or, in other words, a recognition that the choice of the victim is arbitrary, that the causal link between the victim and whatever disaster is ascribed to him is not real. We expect no such thing from medieval or modern persecutors. We understand that it would be completely absurd. On the contrary, this causal link will be regarded as a fact so well established and so certain that its validity will need no proof, and it will appear in the myth on an equal footing with all other data of the myth, some of which have a good chance of corresponding to real events.

Which mythical data could correspond to real events? First and foremost, the collective violence, of course, then such disasters as the food poisoning of the Yahuna myth and the plague of the Oedipus myth. These catastrophes may be real not merely because there is nothing impossible and fantastic in them, but because, if real, they would really intensify the (nonconscious) need for scapegoats that the myth as a whole seems to satisfy. Thus they could well have triggered the collective process that generated the Yahuna myth or the Oedipus myth.

It is possible, of course, that none of these plagues really occurred. It does not really matter. None of the clues I have discussed will ever enable us to reconstitute the real events behind the myth but, I repeat, it does not matter. The only thing that these clues permit us to ascertain is that some real violence must have taken place. This is insignificant from a historical viewpoint but of considerable significance in regard to the nature of mythology. The goal of this research is a generative principle, not a historical reconstitution. Anthropologists are right to regard the second goal as unattainable.

When we are asked to describe the type of belief that triggered real persecutions in the Middle Ages, we often call it "mythological," but in a sense judged metaphorical; we never ask ourselves if it might not be literally true. What prevents us from considering that possibility? Part of the answer obviously lies in the differences between myths and the persecution records I mentioned. These differences are fewer than the resemblances, but spectacular, too. They belong primarily to that part of the myths I have not yet mentioned, namely, the conclusions.

The conclusions of myths resemble each other: they are "happy endings." The collective murder or expulsion achieves more than the intended result, the termination of the trouble through the curbing of the troublemaker—so much more, indeed, that we cannot see anything real in those conclusions; we see them as a triumph for the irrational and the imaginary. In the Yahuna myth, a hitherto unknown edible palm grows out of the victim's body and becomes available for the first time. Once expelled from Thebes, Oedipus's body becomes a piece of religious property that is somewhat dangerous, to be sure, but so valuable that its possession is hotly contested among the protagonists of a later tragedy.

The benefits are so out of proportion with their only assignable cause that we do not really dare ascribe them to the shabby story that precedes. The latter cannot be the cause of the former. And yet it must be; it cannot be otherwise, from the standpoint of these myths: nothing else ever happens; the same sequence reappears in all the myths. Founding ancestors and tutelary divinities never do anything creative or positive. The only action they perform (or their very presence, if they do nothing at all) is so detrimental that it triggers collective violence against them, and that is all. From the collective violence, and from nothing else, a new cult is born, a totemic system is established, a new culture is founded. This sequence very much resembles a scapegoat process that would produce the kind of positive effects sought by the persecutors—the positive effects we always deny that scapegoating should and can produce.

In our world, and even in the medieval world, scapegoating never produces effects so radical as these. We see it as a contemptible process to which honorable men remain impervious. We cannot imagine that it could be responsible for the cultural mystery we call mythology. Even less can we imagine that concrete aspects of culture could be positively affected by it. But we do know that even in our world, scapegoating is not totally without effects. Even if the scapegoat is really an insider, the threat transforms him into an outsider, and the remaining insiders feel united as they never did before. They form a new and tighter inside. The alien threat displaces everything else; internal quarrels are forgotten. A new unity and comradeship prevails among those who, feeling attacked as a group, also feel they must defend themselves as a group.

These results are meager in comparison with the ones claimed by mythical conclusions, but they are not necessarily of a different order. Scapegoating cannot directly produce edible palms or miraculous relics, it cannot cure the plague, but nothing is more important to all aspects of the social enterprise than the social unity to which collective scapegoating still contributes, however faintly, in our contemporary world.

To reconcile our view of the mythical conclusions with our previous observations regarding the first part of the myths, we have only to assume that the generative scapegoating behind these myths is incomparably "stronger" or more intense than anything we can observe around us or even interpret in our historical records. Beyond a certain threshold of intensity—all other circumstances being favorable—the hostile polarization against a victim must empty the group of internal hostility, unifying it so tightly that a cultural rejuvenation can really occur.

You will object that a scapegoat, however intensely rejected, then embraced, cannot cure the plague. He certainly cannot, but he does not have to. To be productive of mythology, a scapegoat phenomenon must coincide with enough objective improvement in the situation, whenever there is an objectively bad situation, to promote the favorable psychosocial effect of intense scapegoating.

The only reality a scapegoat phenomenon can affect is the social climate, and we may assume that mythology is always due to a disturbance of that climate, followed by a scapegoat-induced return to serenity. It does not matter, of course, whether or not the real cause of that disturbance is exterior to the society, whether it is a real epidemic of plague or some bout of internal discord. If the disturbance has an exterior cause, however, we must assume that this cause has already ceased to act by the time the unanimous scapegoating intervened that truly reestablished the social peace and therefore resulted in some mythical and religious foundation.

What did I really mean above by a "stronger" or "more intense" scapegoat belief? One, obviously, that generates a more complete and stable belief. What kind of belief? Belief in the scapegoat means exclusively at first belief in his responsibility as a troublemaker. At the instant the scapegoat is selected, through a nonconscious process of mimetic suggestion, he obviously appears as the all-powerful cause of all trouble in a community that is itself nothing but trouble. The roles are reversed. The victimizers see themselves as the passive victims of their own victim, and they see their victim as supremely active, eminently capable of destroying them. The scapegoat always appears to be a more powerful agent, a more powerful cause than he really is.

The agitation and fear that preceded the selection of the scapegoat and the violence against him are followed, after his death, by a new mood of harmony and peace. To what or, rather, to whom will the change be attributed? Obviously, to the all-powerful cause that dominates the entire community: the scapegoat himself. Thus the scapegoat is credited with the reconciliation and the peace, after being credited with the earlier disruption. The absorption of all causality by the victim is so complete that he becomes a dynamic symbol of supreme benevolence as well as supreme malevolence, of social order as well as disorder.

This is the mysterious paradox of mythology—so mysterious, indeed, that mythology itself marvels at it and invariably comes up with supernatural intervention as an explanation. The change in the mood of the community, the change from panic to serenity, must be so swift and radical that it does not appear "natural." It must therefore be "supernatural," manipulated from outside; and since the scapegoat has subsumed all active causality unto himself, he cannot fail to be the grand manipulator, must be the sole and all-powerful agent in this affair.

Belief in the scapegoat is so strong that it supersedes even the power of death. The myth-makers sometimes assume that the victim they killed never dies; perhaps he was only wounded or ill, and was cured. In South America, there are myths in which the scapegoat hero only pretends to be dead and then springs back to his feet at the decisive moment. There are also myths that resurrect the scapegoat after his death. In all instances, however, the scapegoat is regarded as the one who planned and manipulated the entire crisis, so as to dispense the gift of a new beginning and be worshiped as the god or founding ancestor of his community.

I think the nature of primitive religions and institutions the world over can help us indirectly verify the universality and efficacy of this process. The three major pillars of human culture are myths, prohibitions, and rituals. We already understand what myths really are from the present perspective of genetic scapegoating. They are the recollection—typically distorted, yet reliable on some crucially specific points—of a scapegoat process so powerful that it turns its victim, in the eyes of the persecutors, who are also the myth-makers, into a transcendental symbol not only of violence and disorder, but of peace and order as well.

Assuming as we must, from the very nature of mythology, that this scapegoating process makes a formidable impression on the community, we can understand why primitive communities would refrain from certain actions in the name of the founding ancestor or god, and why they would perform certain actions (some of them the same, some different) also in the name of that ancestor or that god. Impressed as they are with their own scapegoating, these communities must inevitably feel that the god or ancestor does not want them to do what he did when he half destroyed them and was correctly punished for it, but that he wants them to do again what he did when they were saved. He is a teacher who must be imitated in the good things he did but not in the bad. The things you must not do are called *prohibitions* and the things you must do are called *rituals*.

The scapegoat genesis makes it possible to understand why divinities are always the guardians, even the founders of the laws they first transgressed; why there is a mysterious overlap between prohibition and ritual; and why the ritual action par excellence is the killing or expulsion of a victim, performed collectively as a rule, in the rites rightly regarded as "most primitive" by early anthropologists. It also makes it possible to understand why so many of these rituals follow a course that seems deliberately planned to provoke a scapegoat transference against the victim, similar to the scapegoating that occurs spontaneously in disturbed communities. The so-called scapegoat rituals of Frazer and others are those patterned so exactly after the spontaneous scapegoating in which the cult originates that modern observers cannot fail to notice the resemblance.

If my paper were not too long already, I would like to perform on rituals and prohibitions the type of analysis I have outlined for a few myths. In the past, such analysis has always led me to conclude that all aspects of primitive religion become intelligible in the light of a scapegoat effect analogous to what we find in medieval and modern scapegoating, but so much more powerful that we have not yet been able to detect it. This detection would become easier if we compared the scapegoat phenomena we are already able to analyze in the modern world with those of the medieval world. As we shift from the modern back to the medieval, we can observe certain modifications in the scapegoating process; for example, there is a greater acceptance of it in medieval times because it generates a more intense and widespread belief amid the populace. As a result, it looks more like an integral part of society and seems to sink into its substructure. This more intense scapegoating becomes more and more invisible, less and less intelligible to those who do, and even to those who do not, practice it.

Thus the phenomena of scapegoating can be arranged on two parallel scales that go in opposite directions. As we shift from modern to medieval times, we move down on the scale of knowledge and up on another scale that measures the coefficient of scapegoating intensity and efficiency. In other words, scapegoating becomes more and more effective as there is less and less knowledge, less awareness of it as a collective delusion.

If we extend these two scales beyond the point where scapegoating is intelligible, either to us or to the societies that practice it, we move back, I believe, into the domain of mythology and ritual. This is the world in which witchcraft is the norm because causality is primarily magical, at least in times of trouble and uncertainty. At such times, the search for a magical cause becomes identical with scapegoating.

The more socially "efficient" scapegoating is, the more capable it is of generating a positive transfiguration of the scapegoat, as well as the negative transfiguration of fear and hostility. The positive transfiguration is still present in the feudal and even the national traditions of military warfare. The enemy is respected as well as intensely disliked. This positive aspect weakens more and more in the modern world, as civil and ideological conflicts tend to predominate. The class enemy of the modern revolutionary never becomes ritualized as a good, even sacred enemy.

As we move back into the past, or to more primitive cultural conditions, we can certainly observe the reverse effect. Even though in the Middle Ages women in general and, more particularly, women accused of witchcraft had a low social status, there was another side to the phenomenon that throws a good deal of light on the primitive *sacer* (Sacred). The same medieval people who burned a woman on a pyre, thinking she was a witch, might almost simultaneously come close to worshiping her, begging her to perform some great miracle for them, still thinking she was a witch, always attributing to her a "power" she could use to help as well as to harm.

The Yahuna myth reflects exactly the same dual belief, and the same dual consequences. So does the Oedipus myth. Do we respect

mythology too much to recognize in it the effects of a familiar phenomenon? Are these effects rendered illegible by the intensification
and exaggeration required to produce authentic myths rather than
their weakened residue? Both factors, I feel, must contribute to our
inability to solve the enigma of mythical genesis.

V

I move to a third example, a myth from the Ojibway Indians, who
live on the northern shore of the Great Lakes. The following summary was written by Lévi-Strauss:

The five "original" clans are descended from six anthropomorphic supernatural beings who emerged from the ocean to mingle with human beings.
One of them had his eyes covered and dared not look at the Indians, though
he showed the greatest anxiety to do so. At last he could no longer restrain
his curiosity, and on one occasion he partially lifted his veil, and his eyes
fell on the form of a human being, who instantly fell dead "as if struck by
one of the thunderers." Though the intentions of this dread being were
friendly to men, yet the glance of his eye was too strong, and it inflicted
certain death. His fellows therefore caused him to return to the bosom of
the great water. The five others remained among the Indians, and "became
a great blessing to them." From them originate the five great clans or to-
tems: catfish, crane, loon, bear, and marten (Lévi-Strauss 1963: 19).

In this myth, we have not one but six supernatural visitors from
some never-never land. One of them kills an Indian merely by looking at him. This unintended murder plays the same role as the
plague in the Oedipus myth or the fish poisoning in the Milomaki
myth. This time, there is only one victim, but that makes no difference from the standpoint of the community. The threat is the same
as in our two previous myths.

If the "dread being" were allowed to stay in the community, more
people might be killed. It is imperative, therefore, that he himself be
either killed, like Milomaki, or banished, like Oedipus. He is sent
back to the bottom of the ocean, we are told. This ocean (or, rather,
this lake) is the place where this creature came from in the first
place; banishment there, we may feel, is not much of a punishment,
but had the creature happened to be a mere human being before he
evolved into a supernatural creature, it would have meant some-

thing worse: death by drowning. Whatever the case may be, there is little benevolence, we all know, in the classic invitation to visiting strangers: "Why don't you go back where you came from?"

One more feature in this third myth makes it similar to the first two. The "dread being" committed murder, all right, but out of innocent curiosity. His intentions were friendly. All he did was partially lift the veil that protected the natives from his excessively "strong glance." He hoped he could satisfy his desire to see his hosts without depriving them of the necessary protection. This little story gives the myth its distinctive flavor, its touch of the "uncanny," as Freud would say, but the net result is very much the same as in the other two myths. The personal guilt of the victim is lessened, but his responsibility for the catastrophe remains entire.

In the Oedipus myth, too, we have a hero whose actions were disastrous even though his intentions were good. Oedipus meant no harm to Thebes. He did not commit parricide and incest knowingly. Milomaki's case is a little less clear but seems quite similar. This hero, too, apparently harbored nothing but good intentions toward the community ravaged by his presence. How could the young boy have been aware of his deadly influence on those who ate fish after hearing his beautiful music? Milomaki could not warn the audience at his concerts about something he was unaware of. Oedipus could do nothing about something he did not suspect. Both heroes are personally forgivable therefore, but their very ignorance made the need to curb them even more urgent. Something had to be done, by whatever means.

All three myths have heroes with little or no subjective guilt and a lot of objective responsibility. We cannot blame them for acting the way they did, any more than we can blame those in the community who joined forces against them. No one is really guilty. The victims cannot be condemned for exerting their evil influence: they meant no harm; it was just part of their awesome nature. But the violence that directly or indirectly emanated from the community cannot be condemned, either: there was no other course.

All these stories recall the origin of some cult or of the society itself. I believe that this claim is legitimate, at least in part. Primitive mana, the numinous, *le sacré*, initially reflect very directly their origin in scapegoating. The transcendental power of the divinized scapegoat is very harmful as well as beneficial. The central figure of the myth is both a criminal and a savior. As time elapses, however, a very natural tendency seems to be at work among the people whose myths these stories became: they want to attribute as little reprehensible behavior to the actors in those myths as seems compatible with a faithful retransmission of the original message.

All these actors end up as sacred ancestors or divinities. Ideally, we may think, they should be blameless. I call this ideal "natural" because it is still operative in us. Despite abundant proof to the contrary, many anthropologists today remain unconvinced that the primitive Sacred, in its original form, is simultaneously "good" and "bad." They find many arguments in primitive religion itself, because as soon as primitive religion becomes a little less primitive than it was originally (originally being understood diachronically rather than historically), it is affected and modified by an attitude that recalls our own.

When this attitude is present, the thought of the hero's abominable crimes causes some shock and disbelief. We feel that all participants in the account of a society's sacred beginning should inspire a minimum of respect, especially the central victim, who generally plays the role not of one supernatural figure among others, but of the sacred ancestor par excellence. Very often, as in the case of Milomaki, he is the only character with a proper name. It is not very nice to discover that the first time our sacred ancestor showed up in the community, it was only to become a vicious killer of his own people.

No one wants that sort of thing. And yet, this is what we have in the Yahuna myth, in the Oedipus myth, in countless other myths. A tendency is at work, therefore, to rehabilitate the hero-victim. There is something, however, that prevents this tendency from fulfilling itself completely, at least at first. The visiting stranger certainly does not receive from the people who turn out to be his people (Oedipus, remember, turns out to be a Theban) the type of hospitality we would expect a sacred ancestor to receive. If the rehabilitation of the victim were too complete, if he turned out to be entirely innocent, then his persecutors would become the guilty ones. We would get rid of one vicious killer, but we would have a whole collection of vicious killers in his stead. And no one wants that, either.

It would be possible, of course, to eliminate the collective murder entirely. But it is the very heart of the story, its dramatic climax. And this story, after all, is the principal, even the sole reason that all these ancestors and mythical beings are remembered. It should be preserved as accurately as possible.

A time finally comes, no doubt, when the cult has completely lost its original vitality and its myths become indifferent stories that can be manipulated at will. Then the collective murder is likely to turn into an individual murder or even disappear entirely, as in the case of much Greek and Roman mythology. I will limit my observations here to an earlier stage of the mythical evolution. It can throw a good deal of light, I believe, on the true nature of mythology.

Let us restate the problem the community has to solve. The main founding ancestor should not be a total scoundrel. If he were totally innocent, however, the truth of the myth would become explicit, revealing the very origin I am trying to uncover, which is far from pretty. The truth is that there never was a righteous community justly mobilized against a dangerous enemy; rather, there was an outbreak of food poisoning, perhaps, or some epidemic, or a panic caused by something else, or by nothing at all, which dissolved the community into a crazy mob. Then, like all mobs, this one turned to violence: the people picked the first available victim, the likeliest scapegoat, the visiting stranger, but they never found out what really caused their violence; they believed in their own story too much.

As sacred ancestors go, the lynchers may be second best to the victim, but they are not insignificant. Even though individually less prominent, they too are sacred ancestors, and a pretty formidable lot. They have proved it. Besides, they are the most direct ancestors of those who regard these myths as *their myths*. They must not be discredited.

This is the problem, and there cannot be a clear-cut solution; there must be a compromise. Each side will have to give a little in order to get a little. The victim must be vindicated, but only to the extent compatible with the good reputation of his victimizers. Thus the myth can neither fully adopt nor fully reject the simplistic vision that mobilizes persecutors against their scapegoats in times of intolerable stress. It cannot face up to the naked truth of the event in which, for some unfathomable reason, the holy is rooted. And yet, being the account of that event, the myth wants to remember it as truthfully as possible, not as it should have been, but as it really was.

The formula of the involuntary murderer is the only solution to the problem at hand, as long as the basic structure of the drama is not seriously distorted. One can still sympathize with the victims, one can view them as heroes, and one can sympathize with their lynchers as well. One must excuse the violence inflicted on the visiting ancestor, and one must excuse the violence he supposedly inflicted on others. This solution lies midway between the nonconscious lie of the persecutors and the truth that no myth has ever uncovered.

All the themes in our three myths and the system they form recur too often to be the result of chance. Everything becomes intelligible if we assume that the scene has evolved from an earlier and rougher version of generative scapegoating. The version we have seeks to blunt the impact of the violence without revealing it for what it is. Our myths become intelligible in every detail if we only assume that latecomers tidied them up somewhat in order to improve their logic and, above all, make everybody in them look good, the victimizers as well as their victim.

We must not conclude from the modifications and attenuations of the original event that the myth-prettifiers see with any clarity what they are doing, repressing deeper down than the myth-makers themselves the truth of the scapegoat phenomenon. On this continued repression, which can assume the most diverse forms in later culture, the survival of the myth and everything that goes with it depends—the religious cult, the culture itself, and even, I believe, the values of nonreligious humanism.

Like the original lynchers, their successors know not what they do. They run away from this knowledge. They would not have to run, however, they would not need excuses for everybody, if they really suspected nothing at all. To modify their myths the way they do, they must feel a sense of malaise. If they had a complete knowledge of what really happened, they would give up their mythology;

if they knew nothing, they would not modify their myths. What makes them uncomfortable, therefore, is the sheer proximity of knowledge.

I see another clue to this malaise in something else that at least two and perhaps all three myths have in common. The violence we have been talking about is not merely "collective": it is spontaneously unanimous. This unanimity is the source of its power to unify the community. The ancient specialists of ritual, in India, for instance, often mention this unanimity as indispensable to the correct performance of sacrifice.

In order to harmonize the entire community, the unanimous violence would have to be the violence of all, without exception. Everybody should be involved, yet none of our three myths shows this universal involvement. Even the two that make the physical violence explicit—the Yahuna myth and, somewhat ambiguously, the Ojibway myth—attribute it not to the entire community but to a smaller group, carefully defined as, we might say, a special-interest group.

In the Yahuna myth, the lynch party includes only the relatives of those who were killed by the combined action of the bad fish and Milomaki. In the Ojibway myth, the posse is limited to the supernatural companions of the troublemaker. If they had not immediately restrained their thoughtless colleague, the other genies of the lake would have become as much of a terror as he was in the eyes of the Indians. Their corporate reputation was at stake, you might say, and they had a special interest in being the first to take punitive action.

We vaguely feel, however, that there may be another reason for the alleged passivity of mere mortals in the Ojibway myth. Overpowering a "dread being" is a delicate task at best, and rather than handle it on their own, if they had the choice, most human beings would prefer to delegate it to other dread beings. The myth describes the safer course, the most reassuring course from the standpoint of the community at large. But let us suppose that a real lynching took place, and that the only being anyone really dreaded was the victim. If no gods were around at the time to substitute for men, it is probable, nevertheless, that a lynching party was formed—most informally, if I may say, with membership unlimited, under the pressure of fear.

The idea of a lynching party limited to other dread beings must be a later development, and it is not completely illogical in view of the action performed, an action made more dreadful still by the dread nature of the victim. The whole affair is raised to the transcendental level. This was a welcome development, no doubt, because it freed the descendants of the lynchers from the fear they must have felt, retrospectively, at the thought of their own direct ancestors, all by themselves, unaided by any supernatural power, summarily dispatching the most sacred of all dread beings to the bottom of the great lake.

In many myths that deal with threats by a single person, similar to the ones described in our three myths, the lynching party extends to the entire community. In the Yahuna and the Ojibway myths, the threat is very much the same, but the lynchers are a smaller group. Thus we have a subgroup of lynchers who are as unanimous as the entire community would be; yet that community remains uninvolved, even though its reasons for being involved are the same as those of the subgroup. The wider community conspicuously abstains from the violence it might feel imperiled enough to commit.

This collective violence restricted to a smaller group is too frequent, all over the world, not to call for some general raison d'être. It can only suggest, I believe, a reluctance on the part of many communities to assume as their own a violence that must have been precisely that—the community's own, the responsibility of the whole community. This is strongly suggested, of course, by those more naïve, perhaps, and more primitive myths that do not restrict the collective violence to a subgroup and must be closer to the original event.

This interpretation is made more likely, I feel, by those religious or literary works that not only do not suppress, minimize, restrict, or otherwise marginalize the central lynching of the mythology from which they are derived, but emphasize it in the extreme. This return to the original emphasis gives them immense evocative power and yet does not unduly scandalize the morally sophisticated audiences of a later age, because the violence is restricted to a small group and can therefore be presented as the unenviable monopoly of a band of reprobates.

I am thinking now primarily of the interpretation Euripides gives of the Dionysus myth in *The Bacchae*. The subgroup, this time, is limited to women, all the women who have supposedly left their homes and turned *bacchae* to wander in the mountains. They are severely condemned, and the unanimous violence against Pentheus is condemned. They are presented as rebellious against the god even though they are perfectly obedient, and they are opposed to the "good Maenads" from whom nothing concrete distinguishes them.

The genius of Euripides powerfully suggests the dependence of the cult on the lynching scene, revealed as the model of an orgiastic ritual that culminates and concludes with the *diasparagmos*, the tearing apart of a live victim by a veritable mob of worshipers. The presence of that lynching scene in all episodes of the dionysiac mythology confirms its role as the common denominator of the entire cult.

The fact that the collective violence is limited to a subgroup enables Euripides to elude the disturbing consequences of the truth made dramatically manifest in his own play. He maintains the fiction of the lynching scene as a deviation from the true cult, even though it is ordained by the god, and the victim is still treated as guilty in part, rebellious against the god, and in part as a devout worshiper of that god. Left unexploited by the literary critics and the anthropologists alike, these contradictions are enormously suggestive. In this essay, I have tried to show that the lynching scene is really central, and that the interpreters should keep it at the center even in those myths that suggest otherwise—but a little too insistently to be taken at face value. The myth protesteth too much.

There are myths in which collective violence plays its role explicitly and is represented as the violence of the entire community. There are myths in which collective violence plays a marginal role and is represented as the violence of a subgroup. There are myths in which violence becomes the violence of a single villain, but traces of its former collective nature may remain (Girard 1982: 85-145). Finally, there are myths in which violence is not represented at all and seems to play no role. I am convinced that the second, third, and fourth types are not really independent configurations but have evolved from the first type through a process that can be retraced from beginning to end: a process of marginalization, then elimination of the unanimous murder scene.

Many nineteenth- and early-twentieth-century anthropologists had a tendency to classify as "more primitive" those myths—and rituals—in which the collective violence is relatively central and uninhibited. This tendency has been criticized, and most researchers today studiously avoid yielding to what they regard as an "ethnocentric" temptation. But this temptation seems inescapable at times. Why is it inescapable? Because it is a part of the same broad, uneducated, but powerful insight that causes us to designate a certain type of collective violence by the name of a ritual, the "scapegoat ritual."

A community that actively seeks and finds scapegoats is usually a community troubled by dissension or by some real or imaginary disaster. Such a community will establish a false causal link between its chosen scapegoat and the real or imaginary cause of its trouble, whatever that may be. The presence in all these myths of some disaster for which the victim is regarded as at least objectively, if not also personally, responsible could certainly result from the community's state of panic and from the systematic projections of all scapegoaters onto their scapegoats.

VI

We have observed some deviations from our pattern, such as the attenuation of the victim's guilt and the reduction of the lynching community to a specialized subgroup. We might observe more deviations. If we analyzed them, they would always lead to the same conclusion: they all result from nonconscious efforts to repress, distort, marginalize, or efface the original pattern itself, the telltale signs of collective scapegoating.

Is this a circular reasoning? Myths that contain exactly what is needed to reflect a pattern of nonconscious persecution I take at face value and regard as suggestive of the true nature of mythology, and myths that contain something else and therefore do not clearly support my case I regard as having been tampered with.

The test of the hypothesis lies in the explanatory value of the analyses required to bridge the gap between any given myth and the pattern of collective violence in its most transparent and pristine mythical form. The Yahuna myth comes close to this transparency,

I would think. That is why I analyzed it first. Is the generative principle that this transparency lets us glimpse something suggestive for one myth only, or at most for a limited number of myths—the dionysiac myths, perhaps—or is it useful for mythology in general? Will it throw light, for instance, on the most striking theme of the Ojibway myth, the theme of the veils? I think it will. In my opinion, this theme is a variation on the loss of one or both eyes. Either loss produces a sense of malaise in the onlookers, especially at the first contact—in other words, when the one-eyed or the blind are strangers.

Mythological heroes are often described as individuals with some infirmity, comparable to some mark or sign that turns them, quite literally, into marked men. They seem to attract the blows of destiny and the anger of the gods. Such, at least, is the language of myth and literary criticism. The truth, I am afraid, is more prosaic: persecutors everywhere are especially attracted to them.

Oedipus not only limps but, at the end of his myth, he is blind. Many heroes are also one-eyed, like the Greek Cyclops. The Roman hero Horatius Cocles is not really one-eyed, but when he frowns and his eyes narrow, he seems to be, and as a result, he can sometimes defeat his enemies just by looking at them. His name signifies "cyclops." The many blind and one-eyed mythical heroes accused of having the "evil eye" remind us, inevitably, of the veils in the Ojibway myth. These cover both eyes of five supernatural beings and one eye of the sixth. All six beings are supposedly endowed with the same excessively "strong glance," which kills at first sight.

In strange surroundings, the situation of the one-eyed man may be worse in some respects than that of the blind. Being completely helpless, the blind are ultimately less frightening. Alone in the midst of many, the one-eyed man cannot defend himself if attacked; he sees those who see him, but he draws no real advantage from this ability and much disadvantage. His one good eye seems more uncanny than the two bad ones of the blind. He returns the distrust of the glances that converge on him, thus inspiring even greater distrust and giving rise to the standard accusation of the evil eye.

Different as it seems from the arrival of a famous blind hero in a strange city, such as the arrival of Oedipus at Colonus, the arrival of the six genies among the Ojibway must be very much like it after all. In the American myth, the collective fear is not objectively described by a poet; it is subjectively and indirectly suggested by the supposed effectiveness of the evil eye. And as usual, the subject of the myth must be a panicked crowd.

Physical infirmities would not appear so frequently in mythology, either directly and explicitly, as in the Oedipus myth, or indirectly and implicitly, as in the Ojibway myth, if they did not obsess mythmakers everywhere. This obsession fits in with the hypothesis of generative scapegoating. The physically handicapped, we all know, are frequent victims of discrimination and persecution, especially but not exclusively among backward people. The physical and moral abnormalities of mythical victims suggest an obsession that is unlikely to content itself with pure contemplation. Like the other clues, this one would have little value if it were isolated, but it becomes highly significant in the context of all the others.

When we think of this mythical obsession, we must also remember the terrible disasters and strange crimes with which the mythical victims are always charged. We must remember the guilt of the victims, which is always taken for granted without the slightest element of rational evidence. We must remember the collective nature of the punishment normally inflicted on the so-called guilty. Finally, we must remember the curious manner in which so many myths marginalize, attenuate, camouflage, and finally suppress all the telltale signs of scapegoating I have listed, thus betraying an embarrassment that points toward the truth quite indirectly, though no less significantly than more positive clues.

Discussion

RENÉ GIRARD: First, let me say that my research always leads me to emphasize scapegoating as the generative principle of mythology, ritual, primitive religion, even culture as a whole. My paper was an attempt to show how the concrete analysis of religious material can lead back to scapegoating.

The notion of scapegoat ritual in past anthropology, or the role of collective violence in Freud's *Totem and Taboo*, makes it very easy to misunderstand what I am trying to do. These notions can only be rigid molds into which it is impossible to fit the diversity of religious forms without distortion. I am not trying to revive this type of enterprise. If I were doing this, my research would be a caricature of the older anthropology, with all its defects rather than its virtues increased. The conception of nonconscious scapegoating to which I resort is not a reductive notion. It is a dynamic principle of genesis and development that can operate as a hermeneutic tool.

This principle can certainly account for those religious institutions that present visible signs of scapegoat transference in the explicit and traditional sense, but that is not the only task for which it is suited. It can also account for those religious and cultural forms that present only the most indirect signs; it can reveal that many mythical themes and many ritual actions left uninterpreted in the past are, in fact, indirect signs of scapegoating.

Many people believe that the adoption of any universal principle in the study of primitive religion is necessarily reductionist. For the sake of hasty generalization, they fear, such a principle will ultimately "reduce" and impoverish the diversity of religious phenomena. I do not think this is the case with "scapegoating" in the sense in which I have used the term. The vocabulary of scapegoating cannot fail to be misleading at first, but I do not see how that can be avoided. Even though many more examples are needed and the preceding remarks are fragmentary, as well as deficient in other respects, I hope they will help prevent possible misunderstandings and make a positive contribution to our debate.

Secondly, I would like to point out that I am not a specialist of ritual. I was not trained as an anthropologist but as a historian, and my first book was one of literary criticism. My interest in Greek tragedy led me to the question of sacrifice. The more I studied sacrifice, the more convinced I became that its enigma can hardly be distinguished from the enigma of religion.

I believe that the immolation of victims is the fundamental ritual action and therefore the most characteristic form of religious behavior. In all this, I feel very close to Walter Burkert. And I feel very close to Walter as well in the belief that our investigation of these problems cannot fail to be interdisciplinary. I do not feel we have to justify this attitude methodologically. The reverse attitude is the one that needs justifying. I must admit, however, that my work has been interdisciplinary to a degree that may be regarded as excessive because it can become unmanageable.

I believe that most cultural data are pertinent to the study of sacrifice, even data in a society such as ours, which does not practice sacrificial immolation. The first example that comes to my mind is our own questioning of sacrifice at this very moment. There must be a relationship between this questioning and the fact that blood sacrifice is abhorrent not merely to a small elite but to our entire society, which is rapidly becoming worldwide.

In spite of this abhorrence, many of our customs and practices and much of our thinking may still be related to sacrifice in a manner we do not suspect. I believe that many phenomena in our history are too obviously pertinent to be excluded from an investigation of the subject. This is the case, for instance, with our attitude vis-à-vis certain forms of collective persecution, with our understanding and condemnation of collective prejudice, and of all forms of exclusionary practices. I also believe in the pertinence of many literary documents, such as Greek tragedy or the theater of Shakespeare. I also believe that the Jewish Bible and, above all, the New Testament are instrumental in all the progress that we have already made, and will make in the future, toward an understanding of sacrifice.

I have been led more and more to develop a global theory of religion centered on sacrifice or, rather, on a hypothesis concerning the origin of sacrifice. When I first turned to the subject, I had no such intention. I am fully aware that global theories are viewed with great suspicion at the present time, and I would still share that suspicion myself if my own research had not taken an irresistible turn toward the sort of enterprise I was taught to distrust. I have reacted strongly against many aspects of structuralism, but in some respects I remain influenced by it. I think it is possible to recover the genetic dimension without losing the positive aspect of structuralism.

Many anthropologists now regard the elaboration of a global theory of religion as a meaningless activity. The search for origins is condemned as mythical, regardless of the form it takes. Most influential anthropologists of the recent past and the present share that attitude, as far as I am aware. Evans-Pritchard, for instance, wrote a book on theories of religion in order to demonstrate that not one of them in the past has ever made any sense, and that none in the future will ever make any sense. It is true, indeed, that all past theories are more or less forgotten nowadays, and deservedly so if you evaluate them from the standpoint of their highest ambitions. I believe, however, that quite a few of them contain extremely valuable insights, and that they deserve to be studied carefully.

In the face of repeated failure, over a long period of time, researchers can adopt two attitudes. They can remain hopeful. They can continue to believe that the right answer must exist and has eluded earlier efforts, perhaps because the right approach has not been devised. Research should go on. This is the attitude of Walter Burkert, I feel, and it is mine as well. I think it is a minority attitude.

The second attitude does not believe there can be a right answer because it does not believe in the question itself. Words are slippery and no one can say for sure that the word religion means anything definite. The search for a global understanding is a waste of time. Research should shift to other subjects. This is an attitude most popular at this time, especially among researchers influenced by the latest trends in critical theory and philosophy, the most important of which are "poststructuralism" and analytical philosophy.

In all instances, it is argued that our usage of such words as ritual, sacrifice, and scapegoat is so influenced by our Western way of thinking that they have little or no value from the standpoint of the cultures we are studying. In this view, the renunciation of globalism is not a defeat for the discipline of anthropology but a positive move, a progress in the awareness of the ethnocentrism that determines not only the answers we give, but the questions we ask. The radical view of ethnocentrism is leading more and more anthropologists and other social scientists to limit enormously the type of questions they ask. All questions about human cultures that have broad philosophical and spiritual implications have fallen under some kind of *a priori* suspicion.

I certainly agree that sacrifice, in a society that practices it, is not questioned at all or is questioned in a sense different from our own questioning. As I suggested before, our questioning is unique, and its uniqueness reflects our society's uniqueness in regard to sacrifice. In my opinion, it is not merely probable but certain that this uniqueness determines both the kind of questions we can ask and the kind of answers we can give.

I am not reluctant to acknowledge that the modern sense of scapegoat (the psychosocial scapegoat of my introduction) is a post-medieval understanding of victimage that originates in the Christian West. On the contrary, I strongly emphasize this "ethnocentrism." It may cause distortions in our outlook that we do not perceive or that we perceive only belatedly, but in respect to the detection of unperceived victimage, it must be regarded as a unique strength. We are the only society, I feel, in which it becomes possible to perceive a relationship between the question of sacrifice and the question of arbitrary victimage.

Our standpoint is probably the only one, culturally and historically, from which sacrifice can become the problem that it is for us. I see nothing in this that necessarily condemns our research or that should deflect us from the task that lies ahead. Why did practically all societies before ours regard some form of sacrificial immolation as a normal part of culture? Why is sacrifice so abhorrent to us? Where does it come from? What is the origin and the raison d'être of sacrifice?

The concern with ethnocentrism was not invented by the coun-

terculture of the sixties. It is an essential feature of the Western intellectual tradition, and it remained exclusively Western until the
entire world became Westernized. It was already voiced in the Renaissance in almost exactly the same terms as today, not only by
exceptional thinkers such as Montaigne, but in a routine way by
many travelers to foreign lands, by the early anthropologists. This
concern for ethnocentrism is typical of Western culture in the last
four or five centuries, and it is not found anywhere else.

Should we conclude that our enduring obsession with our own
ethnocentric fallacies is only our own specific modality of the ethnocentric fallacy and should be rejected as such? I do not think so.
The struggle against ethnocentrism is at the heart of the culture that
invented the discipline of anthropology. It should not become a leit-
motif of self-disparagement; it must not be a logical trap and an
excuse for nihilistic inertia.

The effort to rid oneself of ethnocentric prejudices is essential to
the scientific spirit, and it should be ardently pursued. We should
always be on the lookout for our ethnocentric fallacies, including
those that consist in one-sided and excessive reactions to previous
fallacies. Moving away from a perceived error offers no guarantee
that the opposite stance is more truthful, and can be made still more
truthful by being pushed to the extreme.

The self-questioning mood of many social scientists today is potentially more positive than the self-satisfaction of the past, unless
it degenerates into a kind of allergy to all broadly based speculation.
To a discipline that has never achieved any consensus regarding any
theoretical framework, this type of speculation is necessary, especially now that fieldwork is practically at an end in the field of religion, and the need for it cannot be invoked as an excuse for reject-
ing "armchair anthropology." In regard to extinct cultures, either
we will have "armchair anthropology" or we will have no anthropology at all.

In the present situation, we may feel that the less ambitious we
are, the greater our chances to achieve solid results. This may be an
illusion. Whatever we do, we cannot avoid taking risks, and, at bottom, minimalism may be no safer than the most ambitious theorizing. We should never lose sight of the limitations inherent in our
position as researchers, but we should also be proud of the intellec-

tual ideals and practices we have inherited. Outside of a certain philosophical and even spiritual context, which was certainly "ethnocentric," at least in the sense that it was specifically Western, the enterprise of the modern natural sciences would never have been launched. The great initiators in that respect knew little or nothing of Eastern mysticism, or Polynesian ritual, or countless other cultural forms. If they had been influenced by these cultural forms rather than by their own Renaissance humanism, it is probable that their scientific enterprise would never have gotten off the ground. If the theoretical views that made many scientific discoveries possible contained "ethnocentric" aspects, the discoveries themselves did not, and for better or for worse, they must be responsible for the worldwide unification of human culture that is the foremost reality of the present world.

This is the greatness of our scientific tradition: that it never ceases to question its own premises in an effort to achieve greater objectivity. Even if this effort never proves entirely successful, it cannot be declared a failure, even in the social sciences. I think that anthropology should enjoy the same freedom to follow potentially productive intuitions as the natural sciences have always enjoyed. Anthropologists should disregard the puritanical nihilism of our time and feel uninhibited about global interpretations, even if they are framed, as they cannot fail to be, in a context that reflects our own intellectual and spiritual tradition.

I just said a word about the *a priori* arguments against a hypothesis such as mine. Now I will say something about the type of misunderstanding that keeps cropping up again and again because of the peculiar nature of this hypothesis. Too often, unanimous victimage is understood as a theme, ritual, or pararitual, rather than as a structuring device. This tendency manifests itself most spectacularly in the objection that is heard most often: the hypothesis is accused of being "reductionist."

The implication is that I am trying to force the extreme diversity of rituals and myths into a single mold, which would be the "scapegoat" theme or motif effectively present only in some myths and some rituals. The misunderstanding is difficult to disentangle because, out of the whole ritual corpus, Frazer and others have carved a special category, a dubious one at best, that they called "scapegoat rituals." Many people feel I must be talking about "something like that." I have tried to dispel the confusion, but I have had little success so far, and that is the reason I started my paper with a discussion of the various meanings of the word scapegoat. My fundamental meaning is the modern and vulgar usage, which should enable us to perceive the nonconscious dimension of the operation that interests me.

A text structured by some kind of collective victimage will reflect the view of the victimizers and therefore will not advertise itself for what it is. This text will present the victim as guilty, in the sense of Milomaki being guilty for the poison fish, even though no evidence whatever is provided. The only evidence we have is that the people who died ate fish, and to us, at least, this evidence suggests something different from what both the people who burn Milomaki and the myth itself obviously believe. If the people who died had eaten some bad fish, that could go a long way toward explaining their death. We modern men, with our uniquely ethnocentric view of food poisoning as a medical problem, feel no need to assume the additional explanation of some evil magical power that might emanate from the presence of some stranger in the community. Food poisoning sounds more objective to us as an explanation.

Is the Oedipus myth really more sophisticated in its choice of evidence against the hero than the story of Milomaki? It only seems so, probably because of the enormous cultural fuss around Oedipus in the twentieth century. The victimage that lies behind the myth can be deduced from lots of indirect clues, including the lameness of Oedipus or his position as a self-made man, which resembles the great popularity of Milomaki. Some modern critics vaguely present Oedipus as some kind of pharmakos, but they cannot point to an explicit pharmakos or scapegoat motif anywhere in the Oedipus myth. This goes for Milomaki as well. The only interpretation that makes sense is the one that postulates the real process of scapegoating as the generative and organizing force behind all themes. Would you expect a prosecutor to present as a "scapegoat" the man whose guilt he endeavors to demonstrate? A text is either generated by a real scapegoating process and contains no scapegoat theme, or it contains a scapegoat theme and is not generated by a scapegoating process. You cannot have it both ways.

In *Le Bouc émissaire*, to illustrate the crucial distinction between the scapegoating process, on the one hand, and the theme or motif of the scapegoat on the other, I resorted to medieval texts that can be regarded as near-myths, and that, to us at least, in the modern era, are quite obviously rooted in victimage. In one of his works, the fourteenth-century French poet and musician Guillaume de Machaut speaks about the Jews being responsible for many deaths in the preceding year. These Jews were justly punished. The author does not say where and when all this happened, but all historians agree he must be referring to the persecution of Jews during the Black Death. Since the injustice of the deed escapes him, no historian expects him to write that the Jews were being used as "scapegoats." And yet, all historians agree that they were. We do not have to be trained historians spontaneously to perform on Machaut's text the type of "scapegoat analysis" that I recommend for mythology proper.

If you compare this medieval text with Milomaki or Oedipus, you will see that there is no essential difference in the themes of their organization. Of course, we have a lot of information on the middle of the fourteenth century in France and almost nothing on the world that created the myth of Milomaki. We can see, however, that this historical information plays no essential role in our interpretation of the Machaut text as a reflection of scapegoating. The main cause is a conjunction of themes that we recognize as characteristic of this type of persecution, and this is the same conjunction we have in the myth of Milomaki and the myth of Oedipus.

Every theme of Machaut is determined by the reality of a "scapegoating" in which the author of the text participates as he reproduces uncritically the viewpoint of the actual persecutors. The text resembles the two myths we are discussing precisely because it projects the responsibility for an epidemic of plague upon an obviously innocent victim or victims. And in their desire to convince themselves that their substitute victim or victims are guilty, the medieval persecutors, like the authors of the Oedipus myth, tend to make up additional accusations that relate to family relations and sexuality, such as parricide, incest, infanticide, and bestiality. But the modern historian explicitly views the Jews as scapegoats, using this very word or words to the same effect. He makes the truth manifest and denounces the cruel illusion of Machaut. He writes a text with a scapegoat *theme* in it, and as a result, that text is no longer structured by a real process of scapegoating.

The text of Machaut is the very reverse. Being structured by a scapegoat process, it says nothing about it, and even though it relates *real events*, it systematically distorts them, but it distorts them in a manner so characteristic of this type of persecution everywhere that we find it relatively easy to see through the distortions and grasp the truth of what really happened, at least in a general way. Being fully visible to the historian and made visible in his text in the form of a theme or motif, the collective victimage has no more power to structure the vision that is communicated to us. The scapegoat structure cannot survive under the sharp scrutiny of unprejudiced observation. It cannot stand visibility.

Historical "texts of persecution," such as Machaut, or stories of the lynching of blacks in the American South, or the arguments of terrorists in the French Revolution, are often called "mythical" by those who refuse to be fooled, and they are so close, indeed, to mythology that we should find it natural to bring all these texts together and ask ourselves if bona fide myths are not simply more texts of persecution that have not yet revealed their secret and continue to fool us all for a number of reasons, but primarily because it has never entered our minds that we could deal with them in the same manner as I have just dealt with the text of Machaut.

Sensational and bizarre as it seems at first, the "theory" of mythology and ritual that I propose is not really a theory at all. It is a correction of persecutory distortions—a correction we have been practicing for three or four centuries on another category of texts— and it has become so acceptable and banal to us that we resort to it almost automatically, but only in the case of texts originating in our own historical world. My personal contribution consists only in saying that the time has come to extend that type of interpretation to the hard core of primitive religion.

It is true, of course, that deluded and mythical as they are, the historical "texts of persecution" never come up to the level of transfiguration that characterizes mythology proper. Even the most mystified persecutors of Jews or lepers in the Middle Ages did not metamorphose their victims (scapegoats) into divinities and sacred ancestors. But they did often endow them with a quasi-supernatural power to cure the diseases they simultaneously accused them of spreading.

We are discovering only analogies, but analogies so striking, perfect, and complete that they cannot be fortuitous. The power that transfigures a persecuted victim into a mythological being is still active in our world, but always greatly weakened, even when at its strongest, during the Middle Ages for instance.

During the past centuries, the growing capacity of the West, and then of the entire world, to decipher the enigma of scapegoat transfiguration that lies behind the arguments of deluded communities must correspond to more and more advanced phases in that weakening process. The present effort to extend this critique to mythology proper must represent one further advance in that gradual enlightenment, and we can see the day when the persecutory significance of mythology in the entire world will be just as obvious as it is in Machaut and all similar texts.

Mythology proper is more difficult to penetrate, because the coefficient of distortion and transfiguration is higher. The weakening of the force that generates mythology is one and the same as the strengthening of our power of elucidation in regard to that same mythology. Can we identify the antimythological force at work in the modern world? I am convinced that we can, and this is the most controversial aspect of my views even though, in many respects, it is the most obvious.

When we do our "scapegoat analysis" of Machaut and rectify much of the information he provides, without doubting the reality of the victims behind his text, we do something very similar to what the Bible does in the psalms, in Job, in the writings of the prophets, and in all of its best-loved stories. These stories superficially resemble myths because many themes are the same, but more important, they rehabilitate the victims and overturn the scapegoating on which mythology is founded.

You can see this immediately if you compare the Joseph story to the Oedipus myth. Oedipus is expelled from Thebes twice, and each time for a reason that the myth regards as valid. From the beginning, he constitutes a real danger to his family and to the entire city. The second time, he has really killed his father, he has slept with his mother, and he is responsible for the epidemic of plague. Joseph, too, is expelled twice, first as a child by his own family, and then as an adult by the entire Egyptian community, which regards him as guilty of sleeping with the wife of his protector. The crime is equivalent to the incest of Oedipus, but unlike the Egyptians and the Greeks, who believe that sort of accusation without proof, the Bible regards it as a lie.

Each time, Joseph is wrongly accused and unjustly punished. Unlike the Oedipus myth or the Milomaki myth, which regard their respective heroes as responsible for some dreadful social disaster, the Bible says that, far from being responsible for the destructive drought that occurred during his administration of the Egyptian economy, Joseph took wise measures and saved not only his own starving family, but the whole country. Instead of practicing vengeance, he saved his own persecutors.

The Joseph story, and the other biblical texts, systematically take a stand radically opposed to the standard mythological view. Even when biblical inspiration operates within a narrative framework similar to that of the Oedipus myth, it runs systematically contrary to mythology, since it overturns the illusion of some previous victimage. It keeps reinterpreting mythical themes from the standpoint of the rehabilitated victim.

The similarities and differences between mythology and these biblical stories are the same as those between the Machaut text and the modern historian's account of what happened to the Jews during the Black Death. The main difference is that instead of speaking in his own name, the biblical author chooses as his hero the principal victim, whose viewpoint prevails in an account that does not suppress the persecutors' version but regards it as deceptive. After they get rid of Joseph, for instance, the twelve brothers give their father a false account of his disappearance that may be tentatively identified as an allusion to some primitive myth demystified by the biblical story.

In the nineteenth century, students of comparative religion greatly emphasized the dramatic similarities between the Bible and the myths of the entire world. They hastily concluded that the Bible was a collection of myths similar to any other. Being Positivists, and seeing the more or less similar data everywhere, they perceived no real difference between the one and the other. Only one thinker perceived the crucial difference and his name is Friedrich Nietzsche.

In Nietzsche's later thought, the dichotomy between the masters and the slaves should be understood primarily as the opposition between the mythical religions on the one hand, which express the standpoint of the victimizers and regard all victims as expendable, and the Bible and, above all, the Gospels on the other, which "slander" and undermine the religions in the first group—all the other religions really, because the Gospels always denounce the injustice of sacrificing some innocent victim. I think Nietzsche was driven to madness by the folly of deliberately siding with the violence and deceptiveness of mythology against the nonviolence and truthfulness of the biblical attitude.

The Judeo-Christian scriptures should be regarded as the first complete revelation of the structuring power of victimage in pagan religions, and the question of their anthropological value can and should be examined as a purely scientific question, in the light of whether or not myths become intelligible when interpreted as more or less distant traces of misunderstood episodes of victimage. I believe that they do.

I conclude that the force of demythification in our world comes from the Bible. This answer is unacceptable to those who feel that anything that would place the Bible in a favorable light cannot be seriously envisioned by scholars because it must be a *religious*—and therefore an irrational—view, with no value whatsoever from the standpoint of anthropology.

This attitude is itself irrational, motivated by religious prejudice. Mythologists and classicists would not hesitate for one second to interpret the Machaut text as modern historians do, and yet it never enters their minds that the same type of interpretation could be appropriate for such myths as Milomaki's or Oedipus's. They are never tempted, it seems, even out of sheer curiosity, to try out in their own field a tool of demystification that has proved immensely successful with texts extremely similar to the ones they have been studying with much less success for a very long time. When I suggest they might go the same route as historians, the suggestion is often regarded, I can tell you, as an almost indecent suggestion, some kind of blasphemous extravagance.

And yet, what should be more natural to scholars than handling similar texts in a similar fashion, just to see what happens? There is an unperceived taboo against this kind of comparative analysis. The most powerful taboos are always invisible.

Like all powerful taboos, this particular one is antireligious, which is the same as religious. At the time of the Renaissance and later, modern intellectuals substituted ancient culture for the Judeo-Christian scriptures. The later humanism of Rousseau and his successors has excessively glorified primitive cultures, and it is also against the Bible.

If the reading I suggest is accepted, our long-standing system of academic values that exalts all nonbiblical cultures at the expense of the Bible will become untenable. It will become clear that genuine "demythification" works with mythology but not with the Bible, because the Bible already does it itself. The Bible really invented it. The Bible was the first to replace the scapegoat structure of mythology with a scapegoat theme that reveals the lie of mythology.

WALTER BURKERT: There are a lot of questions that can be put to this all-embracing thesis. I shall begin with a question of detail that concerns the interpretation of mythology. I venture to take this touching example of Milomaki you deal with in your paper. I must apologize for using a myth from outside my field (my source is Joseph Campbell). We have a story about the boy who sang beautifully and was killed, because whoever ate fish died. Now your interpretation is that this was a real incident of persecution. I have looked up in Campbell the continuation of that story, just a few sentences: after Milomaki died, a kind of palm tree grew out of his ashes, and "the people fashioned huge flutes of the wood of this palm and these gave forth the same wonderfully beautiful tones that formerly had been sung by Milomaki himself. Further, the men blow on such flutes to this day when the fruits are ripe, and they dance while doing so, in memory of Milomaki, who is the creator and giver of all fruits; but the women and children must not see these flutes, for if they did they would die."[1]

What I see in such a myth would be, first, a complex of myth and ritual; there's a clear reference to a festival of fruit gathering, and

[1]Campbell 1959: 221.—ED.

this festival is accompanied by music; and there is a special division between the men and the women and children. This is a wonderful festival with a dark background. I think I somehow understand this pattern because there are Greek myths that are very similar. For example, Orpheus, who sang so wonderfully, was tragically killed by the Thracian women; but still he kept on singing, and his head floated to Lesbos, and now all good poetry comes from Lesbos. (Sappho is from Lesbos.) Or Ikarios, the inventor of wine: people thought he had drugged and poisoned those who first drank wine, so he was killed; but still, as the giver of wine, one remembers him when drinking wine. Ikaria is a village that stands out in the Dionysus cult, and wine is something wonderful. So here again we have a wonderful festival with a dark background. I would try somehow to derive this "joy with a dark background" from the general sacrificial pattern, where joy presupposes something dreadful: a beautiful, "blameless" animal must be killed, or else there would be no feast. So there are disclaimers, attempts at restoration, honors paid the victim, and the festival takes place.

What I find interesting and important is precisely the structure, this kind of peripeteia between tragic background and a joyous festival, that is provided by this kind of myth. If ever somebody were killed in a regrettable way, such an accident would not be what gives life to the complex of myth and ritual. It is not a contingent event but this kind of living cultural pattern at work in society that gives life to the pattern.

GIRARD: Most contemporary anthropologists minimize what you call the "dark event," or they entirely deny its significance. You do not, and I greatly appreciate this aspect of your work. My own emphasis on this "dark event" constitutes the most distinctive aspect of my work, and I had time for nothing else in my paper but, like you, I see a "bright" and positive side to mythology and I want to understand how the "dark" and the "bright" relate to each other. My interpretation of the "dark event" as a trace of unanimous victimage cannot be significant if it does not account for the beneficial aspects of Milomaki's death—the flute playing and the discovery of the edible palm. Your question gives me an opportunity to say something about this.

First, I observe that in your two examples, as well as in the myth of Milomaki, the "dark event" is a collective murder. The collectively murdered victim is the one who teaches a new art or technique to the community, or is somehow responsible for this innovation. There is something similar in myths that relate to cultural prohibitions. They are said to originate with victims who were killed, not for upholding the prohibitions against trespassers, but, paradoxically, for being trespassers themselves. The collective murder is interpreted as a punishment for the trespassing.

Since these myths say that the law came into existence as a result of all this, and therefore did not yet exist when it happened, they seem to acknowledge, at least indirectly, the arbitrariness of the collective murder. In all these instances, some great good befalls the culture as a result of some unanimous violence against someone viewed as the benefactor as well as the original malefactor. In many instances, it is clear that the victim appears as a malefactor first and is punished as such. He turns into a benefactor as a result of the unanimous victimage. I think this sequence strongly suggests the positive consequences of a killing that cannot fail to be arbitrary but is never perceived as such.

You speak of "joy with a dark background." I see the "dark event" as much more than a background. In all our examples, the "dark event" is at the center, and all positive effects flow from it. In sacrificial rites, the immolation of the victim corresponds to the "dark event" of the myth, and it is really central to primitive religion. The collective murder functions like a triggering mechanism for the various benefits that accrue to the culture.

You want to derive the "dark event" from the killing of innocent animals during the hunt. If the "dark event" must be derived from anything, I agree that it can only derive from the hunt and your hypothesis should be adopted. But I cannot picture the mythical drama as derivative in any such sense. The dark event constitutes the one common denominator of all myths, and not merely of the myths about hunting. In order to respect the general economy of rituals and myths all over the world, the collective murder should not be derived, I feel, from any of the useful activities that it teaches the community. The whole direction of the analysis should be reversed: all useful activities must derive from the murder. But is it really possible? Can it be done without surrendering to some kind of mystique of collective violence?

BURKERT: I agree that there is a basic event. The only difference is that this basic, "dark event," for which I propose the *homo necans* concept, was not somehow a fortuitous accident, which happened once, but a necessary practice that developed in hunting.

GIRARD: I do not conceive my generative victimage as a kind of accident that cannot be repeated. This is a misunderstanding. It may result from a confusion between my hypothesis and the original murder in Freud's *Totem and Taboo*. I certainly take a more positive view of *Totem and Taboo* than most people do. I see one priceless insight in that book. Freud surveyed a great many data of primitive religion, and tremendous observer that he was, he detected a single common denominator to all of it: some form of collective murder. The time will come, I hope, when the truth of this insight will be acknowledged. I believe in this insight, but I disagree with Freud on how to interpret it.

The collective murder I am talking about must be regarded as a "normal" occurrence in prehuman and human groups during the whole prehistory of our species and some of its history as well. My idea is that violent forms of so-called scapegoating must put an end to a kind of intraspecific fighting that is normal, too, during the same stages of human development, but so intense and deadly that it would make human culture impossible if there were nothing to interrupt it.

I believe that intraspecific fighting among human beings is held in check by the "scapegoat" murder. I regard unanimous victimage as a self-regulatory device that can stabilize human communities because it provides a model for the whole elaboration of human culture, beginning with ritual sacrifice. To explain this unusual view, I must talk about something called *mimetic desire*, which is the basis for my conception of human conflict and of the unanimous murder itself. My thesis makes little sense unless all aspects are embraced simultaneously. I must summarize a great deal of material and omit all the supporting evidence, which can be found in my books.

The very diversity of cultural patterns suggests that people in groups influence and control one another's desires, negatively, of course, through the prohibitions and taboos that forbid men to desire this or that, but positively as well: many objects and types of behavior seem intrinsically desirable in one particular culture and completely indifferent or even highly repugnant in another. Such differences of "taste" can only be rooted in reciprocal influence, that is, imitation. I reserve the word desire for what happens to appetites and needs when they become contaminated with imitation or even entirely displaced by it. To me, therefore, desire proper has no specific biological basis and can be studied "phenomenologically."

For modern students of desire, the main question has been: what is the true object of human desire? To Freud, for instance, our "true" object is always our mother. From the mimetic standpoint, this makes no sense. Desire can be defined neither by its object nor by some disposition of the subject. Man is the creature who does not know what to desire, and he turns to others in order to make up his mind. We desire what others desire because we imitate their desires.

What are the consequences of imitation when, instead of patterning our desires according to the suggestions of some cultural model, we imitate one another in our choice of desirable objects? The model is anyone who suggests an object of desire to anyone else by desiring that object himself. The model and his imitator desire the *same* object, and they necessarily interfere with one another.

Rivalry is too much the rule, especially among the males of our species, to be always ascribable to scarcity or to the fortuitous convergence on the same object of two or more desires that arise independently of one another. The constant crisscrossing of desires must result from the type of imitation that great writers describe, especially in comedies and tragedies.

Take the four mixed-up adolescents in *A Midsummer Night's Dream*. They are inconstant; the two boys fall in love with different girls at different times, but at any given time they are always in love with the same girl, and therefore they are always rivals. They incriminate destiny, their parents, the fairies. They make up myths, but in reality they copy each other's desires. Shakespeare has a definition for this erotic mimicry: "To choose love by another's eye." This is the tragic and comic predicament par excellence, and I find it more helpful for an understanding of human behavior and the human psyche than all modern theories of desire put together.

As I imitate the desire of my neighbor, I reach for the object he is already reaching for, and we prevent each other from appropriating this object. His relation to my desire parallels my relation to his, and the more we cross each other, the more stubbornly we imitate each other. My interference intensifies his desire, just as his interference intensifies mine. This process of positive feedback can only lead to physical and other forms of violence. Violence is the continuation of mimetic desire by violent means. Violence does not play a primordial role in my perspective; only mimesis does. This point is often misunderstood. The word violence in the title *Violence and the Sacred* must be partly responsible for the misunderstanding.

Violence is a symmetrical, reciprocal process because it is mimetic. I am convinced that the association between violence and biological twins in many mythologies and rituals stems from a frequent but far from universal confusion between the physical similarity of identical twins and the mirrorlike reciprocity of mimetic conflict. In respect to this and many other themes, anthropologists have a lot to learn from the classical tradition of comedy and tragedy.

Mimetic rivalry is already observable in animal life. Even when food or females are not scarce, when many identical bananas, for instance, are available to a group of monkeys, fighting may erupt. We say that the purpose of these conflicts is dominance, prestige, etcetera. But the postulate of such a complex, purposeful activity is unbelievable. The cause of the fighting is simply that two or more monkeys have set their sight on the same banana, and no one wants to yield to someone else. There is nothing special about the disputed banana, except that the first to choose selected it, and this initial selection, however casual, triggered a chain reaction of mimetic desire that made that one banana seem preferable to all others.

Among animals, these rivalries normally do not result in death, which is why they can play the key role in the establishment of "dominance patterns." The dominant individual is the one who never has to yield because the others always yield first, with or without fighting. The dominance pattern is the consequence rather than the purpose of mimetic rivalry.

In human culture, similar phenomena do occur, especially in marginal areas, but symbolic patterns are the norm. These patterns are possibly but not necessarily hierarchical, and they exist independently of the individuals who temporarily occupy the various positions. As a result, they can persist unchanged from generation to generation. They are an essential part of the religious and cultural memory of human communities. The various positions are allocated not through actual fighting, as a rule, but according to modalities of inheritance, election, co-optation, etcetera. Why this enormous difference between human and animal societies?

Fixed symbolic patterns tend to prevent mimetic rivalries in the same way that dominance patterns do. Mimetic rivalries can nevertheless occur among men, and when they do, they are more ferocious than among animals and can easily become lethal. Even if one of the antagonists kills the other, a mimetic rivalry is not necessarily over. Some next of kin may take up the cause of the dead man and imitate the killer, doing to him, mimetically, what he had done to his victim: kill him. This diffusion of mimetic violence beyond the boundaries of the initial conflict is called vengeance. And the mimetic process being what it is, there is no reason for vengeance to be limited to a single act. It can transcend all limitations of time and space and turn into the interminable vendetta or blood feud.

We must envision the possibility of generalized "mimetic crises" that dissolve cultural differentiations into the dreadful reciprocity of chaotic violence. Even though this possibility is unthinkable to the civilized modern observer, at least until recently, it is greatly feared by primitive and traditional societies.

The mimetic conception of desire and violence makes it unnecessary to postulate a specifically human aggressive instinct to account for the murderous intensity of conflicts among human beings. Having a bigger brain, and being the most mimetic animal, as Aristotle was first to point out, man is also the animal with the fiercest mimetic rivalries. The natural tendency for weaker individuals to yield to the stronger does not suffice to counter the mimetic frenzy. The establishment of a society on the animal model becomes impossible.

This whole mimetic view is quite different from the "aggression" of the ethologists. The problem with aggression, I feel, is the implicit one-sidedness of the concept. The whole problematic seems influenced by the situation in modern urban cultures, where one-sided aggression is undoubtedly frequent, but resembles predation rather than an intraspecific conflict. Inside a primitive human community, unprovoked aggression—or, rather, violence with no antecedent rivalry—is most unlikely. With mimetic desire, the dynamic reciprocity of these conflicts, their tendency to escalate, becomes immediately intelligible. The problem with this type of escalation among men is that is can become infinitely destructive.

Human societies are very different from animal dominance patterns, yet reminiscent of them in some respects, because their rituals, their prohibitions, and their symbolic systems of segmentation replace animal dominance patterns as a means of preventing or moderating—most of the time—the mimetic rivalries that must be held in check.

Since men are unyielding in their rivalries, their symbolic cultures certainly did not originate in the gentlemanly "social contract" cooked up by eighteenth-century theorists. Lévi-Strauss has revived once again this absurd idea, blithely suggesting that one fine day prehuman groupings decided (after some kind of constitutional referendum, no doubt) that cultural differentiations, language, and other cultural institutions would be nice things to have.

The real solution to the problem must lie in the very unyielding intensity of mimetic rivalry. It must lie in the murderous violence itself. To be intellectually satisfying, this solution should involve no factors extraneous to the mimetic crisis as it was defined earlier: it should not depend on dragging some deus ex machina upon our scene of mimetic escalation. It must be purely mimetic, therefore. The "scapegoat" or unanimous-victimage hypothesis satisfies this requirement. When mimetic violence permeates an entire group and reaches a climactic intensity, it generates a form of collective victimage that tends toward unanimity precisely because of the participants' heightened mimetic susceptibility.

We are all vaguely aware of spontaneous and nonconscious scapegoating as a possibility. We know that an enraged mob can almost instantaneously solidify against some individual unanimously perceived as a "culprit," even though no reasonable evidence of guilt is available and the victim was obviously chosen at random. The members of the mob visibly influence, or *imitate*, one another in their selection of the victim. The atomistic dissemination of hostilities during the mimetic free-for-all gives way to a massive polarization on a single target. A lot of mimetic refocusing occurs on that particular target because it is the nature of the mimetic urge to polarize in this manner.

The entire process must be governed by the same mimetic urge from beginning to end, but it produces different results according to the successive phases of the cycle. First comes mimetic desire, which is divisive and conflictual. Next comes the mimetic rivalry. As it intensifies, it focuses less and less on the disputed object and more and more on the rivals themselves, who become obsessed with one another.

Paradoxically but logically, this intensely conflictual phase, at its most divisive, can become reunitive all of a sudden if it leads not two, not three, not even many, but all the participants without exception to adopt the same enemy through a snowballing of imitation, which the circumstances cannot fail to produce. The more intense the appetite for violence is, the less discriminating it becomes, and the more willing to substitute a widely acceptable target for its original one.

All the participants can satisfy their appetite for violence at the expense of the victim against whom their mimesis has polarized. Thus, in spite of its random and unpredictable aspects, the unanimous expulsion or death of the selected victim can bring an end to this type of disorder on a most regular and normal basis. In the *Eumenides*, Aeschylus observes that "unanimous hatred is the greatest medicine for a human community."

How could such a process lead to a stable religious and cultural system? The examination of the most violent rituals can solve that mystery, I believe. They often begin with reciprocal taunting and quarreling, then so-called simulated fighting breaks out. As the chaos spreads and intensifies, a remarkable shift of attention occurs. Instead of picking on one another, the participants start refocusing on only the one creature—generally an animal, but it can also be a man—that is destined for sacrifice and that is actually or symbolically mobbed by the entire group. Then, peace returns.

The disorderly phase of rituals makes little sense, it seems to me, from the standpoint of the hunting hypothesis. But it makes a good deal of sense if interpreted as the deliberate reenactment of a mimetic crisis climaxing in unanimous victimage. The rationale for the reenactment is the pacifying effect of the climactic conclusion, which corresponds, of course, to the sacrificial immolation.

If you examine the rules regarding the performance of sacrifice, you will see that, in the most diverse cultures, many of those rules do correspond to actual features of the collective phenomenon they want to reproduce. Many rituals, for instance, emphasize unanimous participation, or at least unanimous attendance; many others seek to introduce an element of randomness in the selection of the victim or of the place and time of the sacrifice. Only an origin in random victimage, shrewdly observed but naïvely misinterpreted as a supernatural intervention, can account for these features.

The purpose of the most brutal and apparently archaic rituals is not merely to relax taboos and have a nice "recreation" in the limited modern sense, but literally to re-create the community by reenacting a process of community disintegration and regeneration, through a unanimous victimage that was obviously experienced as a real starting point for all positive collaboration among the members of the community.

In my opinion, there is no reason to doubt what the participants themselves say about these rituals. They scrupulously reproduce the process from which the ritual originates. They provide us with a good mimetic image of what happens when a religious cult is born, and Durkheim had some inkling of this. This image of religious beginnings can also be regarded as a more confused image of the hominization process itself, when the threshold was first crossed between the dominance patterns of animals and ritualized victimage around which human culture began to crystallize.

Ritual is just as mimetic as its disorderly and violent model, but the mood is entirely different as a result of the sufferings and terror caused by the crisis. It is motivated by the desire to avoid further fighting and renew the benefits of unanimous victimage. To the entire community, the crisis and its resolution become a positive model of imitation and counterimitation.

The mimetic urge has now turned peaceful and culturally productive, because it consists in doing again and again what the victim did or suffered that resulted in a great good for the community (ritual sacrifice). It also consists in negative imitation, in never doing again whatever the victim did that greatly harmed the community (prohibition). Finally, it consists in remembering the whole process from the viewpoint of the befuddled and grateful victimizers, who project the whole responsibility for what happened onto that mysterious victim. We can now understand why they regard him as a benefactor as well as malefactor (myth). The entire mimetic cycle is projected onto him and interpreted as a supernatural visitation destined to teach the community what to do and not to do in the future.

The paradox of the mimetic cycle is that men can almost never share peacefully an object they all desire, but they can always share an enemy they all hate because they can join together in destroying him, and then no lingering hostilities remain, at least for a while.

Too much mimetic desire will cause an intraspecific free-for-all intense enough to generate the common enemy that is needed for the reconciliation. This collective victimage will trigger not only the cult of the victimized reconciler, but all useful communal enterprises and institutions, from kinship laws to food gathering and rites de passage, because each one of these demands the social harmony that can only be achieved through this process. That is the reason, I believe, why primitive religion associates all useful activities with some form of victimage that brought communal harmony because it was unanimously believed, unanimously *misunderstood*.

Many aspects of collective victimage are somewhat contingent, but the phenomenon can be made continuous with the entire process of human desire and intragroup conflict in such a way that the primitive confidence in the cultural and economic fecundity of what Walter calls "the dark event" begins to make sense. In my last three books, I tried to show, among other things, that the implicit contradictions between the "dos" and the "don'ts" that must emerge from the successfully misunderstood victimage, the inevitable tension between the ritual imperative and the prohibition imperative, can be regarded as the true source of cultural innovation in the nonhistorical phases of human culture.

The strength of the mimetic theory lies, I believe, in its ability to go along with sacrificial religions and reveal the reason behind their unreason to a degree that has never been possible before. Mimetic theory reveals the pertinence of many primitive ideas without surrendering to some kind of neoprimitive mystique. Unanimous victimage and sacrificial substitutions turn the disease of mimetic rivalry into its own medicine. The cure is really the same thing as the disease, and the problem of keeping the "good " sacrificial violence separate from the "bad" is a major religious problem. The mimetic reading enables us to understand better not only primitive ritual, but also the more elaborate reflections that remain dependent on it, such as pre-Socratic philosophy, Greek tragedy, and the *Brahmanas* of India. All these works are enormously useful as confirmations of the relationship between mimetic desire and sacrifice.

In *Des Choses cachées depuis la fondation du monde*, I tried to show that unanimous victimage must play, in the laboratory of human culture (which is this side of the threshold of hominization, represented in the Bible by the murder of Abel), the role formerly played by the surrender of the weaker animal in the establishment of dominance patterns. The victim must be the first object of non-instinctual attention, and he or she provides a good starting point for the creation of sign systems because the ritual imperative consists in a demand for substitute victims, thus introducing the practice of substitution that is the basis of all symbolization.

It seems to me that the mimetic victimage theory avoids the twin pitfalls that threaten the quest for human origins. On the one hand, the ethologists see so much continuity and similarity between animal and human culture that they minimize the difference. On the other hand, the symbolic anthropologists see so much difference and discontinuity that they deny the similarities and end up with no conception whatever of hominization and cultural genesis. The powerful insights of recent ethology are an embarrassment to them. That is the reason for the many efforts to discredit these insights through cheap political accusations.

JONATHAN SMITH: Can I return to the Milomaki myth, because it's an old friend? Walter's quite right; it's a ritual myth. It relates to the only pan-Amazonian religious ceremony there is. People say it's first fruits, but that is being too biblical. It is a spring fruit festival; it consists of blowing on these large wooden flutes. There are literally hundreds of myths that explain where the big wooden flutes come from. These myths are ritual etiologies, if you like. In fact, about fifteen or sixteen of Lévi-Strauss's South American myths are from this group, sometimes a name quite similar, sometimes a name quite different; but of two to three hundred myths that I know, only five have the motif of killing. What we've got is a very simple problem; it's a problem that deals with transformation. How did something that wasn't come to be?

At times the flute is given birth to, at times the flute is changed: it was once something else, and then it is transformed into being a flute. At times they stole the flute, either from a neighboring tribe or, more frequently, from the women, because they love to tell stories about stealing ritual objects from women. At other times they found it, somebody tripped over it and it made a noise spontaneously, and they got the idea, "Well, if we go on that will make the same noise again." At other times it really is—I hate to use the word—a kind of miracle. They walk by this tree and it starts tooting at them, and they take it and they toot with it.

In other words, there's a vast repertoire of what, I guess, a folklorist would want to call motifs. They're all attempting, it seems to me, in one way or another, to explain how we come to have this object, this cultural, this man-made object in the midst of the fruit ceremony. My question is how one knows to italicize one version as distinct from all the others. Does one understand in some way that the others are really dealing with the same thing but transforming or concealing the motifs? In other words, how do we assign priority?

GIRARD: We do not. I am not selecting one particular motif in the vast repertoire of the folklorists. My thinking is of an entirely different sort. I am talking about a generative process, and if I am right, this process cannot appear directly as a motif in the myth it generates.

I find no scapegoat motif in the myth of Milomaki. In other words, the people who burn Milomaki are not regarded as unjust, as arbitrary persecutors. The myth takes it for granted that Milomaki must be responsible for the death of these people's relatives. The attitude of the myth parallels that of Machaut, who believes the Jews are really responsible for at least some of the casualties in the epidemic of plague.

There is no more a scapegoat motif in Milomaki that in Machaut. The victim or victims are perceived as guilty. But the interpreter should understand in both instances that the entire myth, or quasi-myth, is determined and organized by the unspoken reality of scapegoating. My entire point is that the Milomaki myth can only result from a generative process similar to the one we never have any trouble detecting in the case of Machaut.

It is essential to my reading that there be no scapegoat motif in any myth. Obviously, you feel that there can be. The reason you do, in the case of Milomaki, is that the process of victimage is more visible behind the motifs of this particular myth than behind most myths. That is the reason I chose it, of course. Even the most skeptical observers find it difficult to deny that in the case of this myth, I have a point.

This makes my demonstration easier, but it can turn into a disadvantage, as I now see. Many observers will think, as you do, that the validity of the victimage reading is limited to the myths that are most transparent in regard to victimage. They will confuse this relative transparency with what we call a motif, or a theme. As a result, they will go on believing that a myth must talk explicitly about victimage in order to have something to do with it. They would never make that confusion in the case of Machaut. To understand my point, you must keep in mind at all times the incompatibility between a text that reflects the victimage it does not mention and a text that mentions the victimage it no longer reflects.

The myth is no more able to detect the scapegoat phenomenon behind the burning of Milomaki than Machaut can behind the burning of the Jews. If we acknowledge a relationship between this myth and scapegoating, the reason lies in our ability to decode the deceptiveness of the Machaut text. We must realize, however, that this same deceptiveness is present in the Milomaki myth, and that whatever scapegoat we find is not provided directly by the myth, but by our own insight, by our own decoding of the myth, which is just as legitimate as in the case of Machaut.

This is precisely what I want us to do, but I want us to be aware that we are doing it ourselves, and that the myth is not doing it for us. We must never confuse these two things: unanimous victimage or scapegoating as the generative force hidden behind a text, and the so-called scapegoat motif that undermines the hidden generative force.

The reading I suggest is contrary to the spirit of the myth, but we

should not worry about it any more than we do in the case of Machaut. This reading alone can provide us with our first real understanding of what the myth is about, just as a realization that the
Jews are scapegoats provides us with a real understanding of what
the Machaut text is about. If we read the myth as I propose, we
realize that Milomaki must have been selected as a culprit for no
other reason than his being a stranger in the community. Just as
medieval people killed the Jews during the Black Death because
they were enraged and panicked by the death of their friends and
relatives, the people who killed Milomaki must have been enraged
and panicked by the death of relatives who had eaten some bad fish.
They picked the visiting stranger for the same (un)reason that
moved medieval crowds to pick the Jews.

I do not believe that such a conjunction of themes, in or out of
our history, can occur for purely fortuitous or "poetical" reasons,
independent of victimage. In all probability, there was a real victim
behind the myth of Milomaki, but we cannot say anything about
him. This conclusion is prompted by purely textual reasons and has
nothing to do with an excessive faith in the historical value of
mythology.

The same must be true of countless other myths less transparent
than Milomaki's, but transparent enough if you examine them in a
comparative light. We are understandably reluctant to consider the
possibility that victimage could hide not merely behind a few particularly transparent myths, but behind myths that suggest it less
clearly or not at all, at least superficially understood.

To detect the process of victimage behind the Ojibway myth, you
must examine it much more carefully than the myth of Milomaki.
This is why I included it in my analysis. I wanted to show what can
be done with themes that at first seem alien to victimage, like the
lifting of the veil. You perceive the relationship to victimage only if
you identify it as a form of the "evil eye" that justifies the drowning
of a single "culprit." I am aware, of course, that much more is
needed to demonstrate the analytical power of the victimage process
in regard to mythical texts, but I said enough to show you that the
method has nothing to do with a reduction of all motifs to a "scapegoat motif" that really does not exist.

I am aware that many myths—a majority, no doubt—do not lend

themselves to an isolated demonstration of their genesis in unanimous victimage. To become intelligible as products of such a genesis, the analytical process must be broadened; if we want to analyze one particular myth, we must insert it as a link in a chain of related myths. We must begin with the interpretation of those myths that are most transparent in regard to victimage; then go on to less transparent myths, like the Ojibway myth; and finally move to myths that, at first glance, seem to contain no clue whatever in favor of my hypothesis. As we gradually become familiar with the telltale signs of victimage, your "scapegoat analysis" will become more and more skillful and will encompass myths that contain no visible clues to their own scapegoat genesis.

In *Le Bouc émissaire*, I tried to give examples of such analyses linked to one another in the manner of a chain. I was trying to trace the persistence of some less and less obvious telltale clues behind the successive metamorphoses they undergo. I feel there is an enormous potential in this method, but it should be practiced on a much vaster scale.

I am not completely satisfied with the results so far, not because I have doubts about the validity of the method, but because of the difficulties involved in its application. It demands a large amount of minute detail, and the final product is rather lengthy and intricate. It may well try the patience of readers beyond what can be safely expected at the present time. Let me give you an example of a myth that not only has nothing to do with unanimous victimage, but denies so deliberately and pointedly any involvement in it that, for this very reason, we can confidently assert that it, too, has a lot to do with unanimous victimage.

I seem to be joking, but you all know the myth about what happened to Zeus immediately after he was born. The infant god is threatened by his father Cronos, who wants to devour him. What does his mother do? She calls on the Curetes, who are a band of fierce-looking warriors. They form a circle around Zeus and place him at the center. Understandably, the baby is scared, and to prevent Cronos from discovering his hiding place, the Curetes brandish their weapons around the baby and drown his cries in their own ferocious vociferations.

Does not this myth remind you of an even better known mythical scene, about the infancy of another Greek god, Dionysus? The Titans brandish some kinds of toys to attract into their circle the little Dionysus, whom they immediately proceed to kill and devour.

In both scenes, we have a ferocious band of potential murderers who agitate certain objects and form a threatening circle around an impotent infant. The Curete scene looks very much like the collective murder of Dionysus, but this time there is no murder. There is a potential murderer in the story, but it is the infant's father, Cronos, not the Curetes, who are supposed to play a protective role.

It is a fact, however, that in light of Dionysus and the Titans, as well as in the light of other occurrences of child murder and cannibalism in Greek mythology, the spectacle of the Curetes howling and brandishing their weapons around a tiny baby is simply too suggestive of this dreadful pattern to be regarded as completely independent of it. In *Le Bouc émissaire*, I concluded that this curious scene must be based on an earlier one, quite similar to the episode of the Titans in the life of Dionysus, and that it must constitute a reinterpretation of the whole affair that aims at proving that Zeus was never killed and devoured by anybody, even though a well-remembered scene of his birth story may give the mistaken impression that he was.

The idea of a murderous Cronos must be a part of that reinterpretation. Far from being truly archaic, as the Freudians would have it, the murderous father must be a late invention, required by the metamorphosis of the real murderers, the Curetes, into protectors. The conjunction of the two new themes is destined to dissimulate the more truly archaic and fundamental pattern, which is the collective murder, of course.

I analyzed this scene in order to show how a myth with no collective murder in it, no actual scene of violence, can testify in favor of my thesis no less and even more eloquently than some additional collective murder that might have remained intact somewhere in the corpus of Greek mythology. We have enough of these scenes, and except for Freud, who was ridiculed for it, they have never aroused the curiosity of people interested in mythology.

It does not befit the dignity of Zeus that he would suffer the fate of so many less august deities. The myth of Zeus and the Curetes has obviously undergone a transformation that points negatively to the importance of unanimous victimage, especially if you place it in the context of other, not necessarily Greek myths. There are other myths no less awkward than the myth of the Curetes, but they do differ from it in their naïve insistence that they have nothing to do with the phenomenon we are talking about.

This is the case, I believe, with the Scandinavian myth of Baldur's death. In that myth, Baldur is bombarded with all sorts of weapons by the assembled gods, and he should not die from this bombardment because he is supposed to be invulnerable to all projectiles. His brothers, the gods, mean no harm; it is all supposed to be good, clean fun on their part, except that in the end, Baldur dies. The gods are innocent except for the villainous Loki, who took advantage of some minor flaw in Baldur's protective system.

It seems to me that in order to have such a scene, you need an earlier one in which Baldur was really killed by the united gods. You also need a community that feels ashamed of this scandalous murder and tries to do away with it, while retaining as many features of a revered text as it possibly can. We are dealing with a mythological revisionism that already resembles Plato's desire, or our own current desire, not to face up to the violence of mythology.

The people who tampered with such myths obviously shared some of our own attitudes, but they certainly did not treat the traces of collective victimage with the same indifference that we do. They did not regard the collective murder as an inconsequential scene, and mythologists might ask themselves, once in a while, if they did not suspect something to which we have become totally insensitive (in spite of Guillaume de Machaut and our obsession with the historical forms of persecution).

The details of my interpretation can certainly be questioned. But the possibility of myths, in systems rather distant from one another, that try to camouflage rather than eliminate the collective murder scene, should help direct the attention of the specialists toward the scene already identified by Freud as fundamental, if anything can. Could we have here something like a mythical analogon of the ritualistic "comedy of innocence" that Walter has emphasized?

SMITH: That there are myths that bear a distant relationship to one another, I have no doubt. What I have a problem with is that of the two or three hundred stories I know about the Milomaki-type figure, only fifteen or so are "dark"—to use your more neutral term. There are these other things going on here, and they seem also to represent a lot of other things. How do we account for something we once did not have, and we now have (which is a big issue in regard to ritual and ritual implements)? I guess what I want to know is, what can't you account for?

I have no problem with the fact that there are an enormous number of myths that have what you're calling a scapegoating pattern, but there are a great many myths, at least to my eyes, that bear no resemblance to them; and they are often found simultaneously in the same cultures, told about exactly the same object, in exactly the same situation. So what I really want to know is, is this a partial theory? If it is, I can understand it at one level. As you look ahead, will there be five or six other such complexes that will account for other sorts of things, or is there a way of reducing all of these mythic strategies to one? Are there myths and rituals that are non-scapegoating?

GIRARD: I do not know. There are many myths that I feel unable, at this time, to "generate" through the victimage process, but someone else may be able to do it. At some future date, I may or may not see some clue that I do not see now. I do not think that the power of the hypothesis depends on its ability to solve all problems through some kind of theoretical fiat. I believe, though, that the ultimate test for any global theory of mythology lies in the quality and quantity of intelligible relationships it can establish among the most diverse myths and mythical traditions. I feel that victimage, represented or disguised, unrevealed and revealed, in nonbiblical and in biblical religions, is so crucial to the mystery of religion that I am inclined to focus exclusively on the ramifications of this problem, which become more and more extensive, I feel, as I keep exploring more myths.

SMITH: Isn't there a more complex vocabulary? In other words, I would like to find a kind of verb underneath all of it. I propose the verb "to get." For example, this is the story of how we "get" a flute. We kill; that's one way. We give birth to it; that's another way. Find it; that's another way. Steal it; somebody gives it to us; we fall over it. These are all pretty basic translations of the phrase "to get," and

I want to know why you choose group murder as *the* way to "get." Walter has a way of telling me, with a kind of historical argument, why getting it by killing it might be earlier or more primordial or more originary than all these other ways. I have some problem with that; but the problem with you is that you don't present any kind of historical argument, and I don't quite understand what you're saying. You don't have singular origins, and that's a very important point. How then do you know that, of that whole panoply of modes of getting, we should focus on mob, victim, killings, etcetera, when the Amazonians don't do that?

GIRARD: A more complex vocabulary would help us make more refined distinctions between the innumerable motifs and themes in the sense of the folklorist, or the structuralist. To improve the kind of thematic descriptions we already have is certainly a worthy enterprise, but my own interest lies in another direction. It may be an impossible goal, but I would like to know how rituals and myths came about, and why. That is the reason I focus on the genetic possibilities of what I call mimetic violence and "scapegoating." It is another type of complexity that does not necessarily require a large vocabulary.

BURKERT: I shall try to answer Jonathan's question about forms of "to get." I would not try to reduce all forms to one, such as sacrifice. I would rather insist that "to get" is an absolutely basic function of life. The situation is similar to purifying: I see no problem in purifying with water, no problem in purifying with incense, because it makes a sweet smell and seems to make the air cleaner than before. But I see a problem in purifying with blood, because it really makes a stain, it does not make things clean, it makes them dirty. So we have to ask why this paradox is there: is there something beneath the surface, some kind of transposition going on? Similarly, as to "getting," I see no problem in just finding something, or taking it, or stumbling on it, and perhaps not even in giving birth to it. (Why shouldn't some woman give birth to something strange?) But I do see a problem when you must kill somebody to get food, kill "the creator and giver of all fruits." Here again, I find a difference between what is told on the surface and some deeper motif, and there the sacrificial pattern comes in. But I do not say that it is privileged by percentage, just that it is a phenomenon that I find difficult to understand. Perhaps this is subjective, but it is still some criterion.

GIRARD: I agree with Walter. I am intrigued, too, when I see that to get some food you must kill the creator and giver of all fruits. No, it is not a question of percentages. But it is important that this phenomenon we do not comprehend should be extremely widespread, not only in primitive mythologies, but in mythologies that have made an effort to get rid of it, and that somehow cannot really succeed, like the Greek Olympian mythology. When we feel we understand a large number of connected phenomena, except for one that keeps recurring again and again and does not quite fit the general picture, the chances are that our whole system of interpretation has already failed. In order to discover a better one, we should not shove under the rug the phenomenon that stubbornly resists our efforts—this is what the myths themselves already do. We should actively focus our attention on it. To my mind, the crucial part of a myth is Walter's "dark event." The crucial part of a ritual is the sacrificial equivalent of that same event, the immolation of the victim. I think the real future of our studies lies in the investigation of the "dark event," not in the side issues that may be raised in order to avoid the central issue.

JOHN LAWRENCE: The real purpose of René's theory and the purpose of this conference is to explore some important connections between religious rituals and violence. I think that René is very straightforward in saying he has a maximal theory, which is exposed to a maximum kind of risk, and its power should be explored in relationship to this distance from the data. I'd like to refer to what seems to me to be an important kind of historical data, connecting religion and violence, which seem to me to be alien to his model. I guess we might call them "rituals of Manicheism." It seems to me that many cultures, including our own and extending back into the ancient world, have developed rituals with a highly ideological character, through which they differentiate between themselves as the righteous ones and some other group that is utterly unrighteous and unworthy of existing, and so should be destroyed. There is a typical scenario of innocence, wherein the group that wants to

exterminate the other group proclaims itself as being utterly innocent and utterly righteous, and that is the prelude to some kind of
exterminating action, the premise of which is Manichean. It seems
to me that as a model of the kind of violence with religious motivation that exists in the world today, this one is much more preva-
lent than a model related to the scapegoating. So I would join in
with Jonathan to a certain extent, on the principle of selectivity, and
ask: if our concern is the present shape of the world, why is this
model chosen in preference to some other model, which is certainly
also prominent in history? I want to let Bob Jewett get in on the tail
of my comment because he knows more about this history than I
do.

ROBERT JEWETT: Well, just very briefly, the contention that the
Bible is always on the opposite side of the knowledge, that it refuses
victimage, does not seem to match the evidence in our particular
cultural tradition, which has been shaped so decisively by biblical
models. My own work on zealous nationalism has led me to a more
dialectical approach to biblical materials, because when you look at
the Indian massacre rationale from the beginning, and at major figures of zealous nationalism such as John Brown, you'll see that major actors in these patterns of violence model their behavior on the
great conquest narratives of the Old Testament, on the pattern of
Phineas in Numbers 25, Elijah, and Elisha. Now I concur with you,
René, that there are biblical counterweights to that zealous pattern;
but in our tradition, that holy war ideology, which has been secu-
larized in popular media, reaches its apotheosis, I think, in the Rea-
gan administration, which carries out exactly the same Manichean
policies that we can trace right back to biblical paradigms. I guess
the point here is that there is one side of the biblical heritage, which
I think we should in all frankness admit, that takes sides in a Manichean direction with the heroes of zealous violence. As was said in
the Numbers account of Phineas, when he broke into the marriage
tent and speared the Israelite man and the Midianite woman to
avert the plague, "His zeal was the zeal of Yahweh" (Num. 25:6-
13); he had a short circuit of zeal in which human rage was flatly
identified with divine rage, thus relieving him of responsibility, and
his action relieved the plague and redeemed the community. The

pattern of redemptive violence that we can trace throughout many of the strands of biblically oriented communities is directly connected with that kind of a paradigm.

GIRARD: It seems to me that everything John Lawrence said militates in favor of the scapegoat genesis. In my view, what you call "rituals of Manicheism" are not entirely specific to cultures influenced by the Bible, but they may be more widespread there, because of a conflict between the growing awareness of scapegoating, as a result of the Judeo-Christian influence, and the difficulty of giving up the practice. You have to make your scapegoating more convincing to yourself by displacing it and also by accusing your victims of being the chief victimizers, in order to justify your own victimization of them. This is what political propaganda is mostly about, I am afraid.

If you look around, you will see how widespread this devious injection of the Christian problematic into our conflicts really is. Even the most banal political discussions illustrate this modern phenomenon—"How do you dare reproach me for the Gulag when all you do is justify and defend the Pinochets of this world?"—etcetera, etcetera. However nauseating this type of argumentation always is, it should be studied carefully because of its unique religious significance. Never before in history have people spent so much time throwing victims at one another's heads as a substitute for other weapons. This can only happen in a world that though far from Christian, to be sure, is totally permeated by the values of the gospel. Nietzsche was correct in saying this. Nietzsche tried to convince himself that this process of mutual recrimination and *ressentiment* expresses the genuine essence of the Gospels, but this view cannot stand a serious examination. The greater a truth, the more perverted it will be in the hands of sinful men. *Corruptio optimi pessima*. This process of corruption is now reaching a level of intensity that would amaze even Nietzsche himself.

The question of the type of world we live in as a result of the Judeo-Christian influence on us is an important one. It is inseparable, of course, from the question of whether or not the Judeo-Christian scriptures reveal the "scapegoat" or victimage infrastructure of all religions. But the question of that revelation must also be considered separately. This is the only question I have discussed so far. I certainly do not believe that the Bible gives us a political recipe for escaping violence and turning the world into a utopia. Rather, the Bible discloses certain truths about violence, which the readers are free to use as they see fit. So it is possible that the Bible can make many people more violent and, indirectly, help generate the Manichean ideologies you are talking about. Religious truth and social usefulness do not necessarily go hand in hand. This is Dostoyevski's point in the legend of the Grand Inquisitor.

In the Hebrew Bible, there is clearly a dynamic that moves in the direction of the rehabilitation of the victims, but it is not a cut-and-dried thing. Rather, it is a process under way, a text in travail; it is not a chronologically progressive process, but a struggle that advances and retreats. I see the Gospels as the climactic achievement of that trend, and therefore as the essential text in the cultural upheaval of the modern world.

The question I wish to put to modern anthropology concerning the Bible is why the privilege granted the Bible by Western people is to be considered only the result of ethnocentrism. Could there not be good substantive reason for that privilege—reason arising out of the Bible's power to disclose the truth about human society? For instance, Frazer says that a proof of the nonspecial nature of the Bible is that the centrality of the death of Jesus Christ makes the New Testament just like the many other religious sources that have a dying savior at their core. Thus the same anthropologists who do not want to consider murder an important element in the creation of mythology, when they start talking about the Bible, curiously agree that the proof that the Gospels are the same thing as mythology is the Passion. Thus, rather curiously, they express precisely what I contend: that at the center of all myth, at the center of culture, stands the same great event, the event of the scapegoat. This the New Testament discloses.

The Crucifixion is the same event as in the myths, looked at from a point of view other than that of the persecutors. What this point of view is, is difficult to specify. One can get some idea of it by looking at how the persecutors are portrayed. They are all the "powers of the world," as the psalm quoted by Peter at the beginning of Acts says: "All the kings and powers of this world are united against the Lord and against his anointed" (Acts 4:26). You have the ecclesiastical authority, you have Pilate (even if he doesn't want it), you have Herod, and finally you have the most important thing of all, to which all powers of this world return: the mob.

Not only those powers but also the disciples are against Jesus. Peter's denial is reported to make this point. In other words, the Gospels tell us there are moments in which there is absolutely no truth in culture; and I do not think any other source tells us that with quite the same conviction. There are some anticipations in Greek culture, in particular the death of Socrates, but in the accounts of the death of Socrates, philosophy always knows the truth, whereas in Christianity, the Christians themselves say "Peter, our leader, was ignorant." In other words, the New Testament says that truth is not a human truth, that truth is outside of culture and has to be introduced into the world against the grain of culture itself; and it's not going to get there without doing a lot of damage, it's not going to get there by suddenly transforming the world into a utopia. It might even give some a new opportunity for evil, a reverse mode.

We go on persecuting, but in our world everybody persecutes in the name of being against persecution; that's what we call propaganda. We have our own scapegoats, but they are always the people who make scapegoats, and we never persecute directly any more. The honesty of the primitive culture is that you do what you do and do not pretend. So the gospel tells us there will be many victims, but they will always be helped by the Paraclete. I long pondered what that could mean, and suddenly I realized it's so simple. Satan means "the accuser," the word of accusation made true. Paraclete means "the lawyer for the defense," the defender of victims—nothing else. The Holy Spirit is the defender of victims.

So history makes sense in that way. Even if the gospel tells the truth, man is free and is going to do anything he wants with it. Therefore the gospel is going to be disguised and is going to create an extremely complex world. But certainly not one in which the people—especially the people who pretend to speak in the name of the gospel—would infallibly have the truth, as the example of Peter shows. The Gospels warn you, "Look what happens." It would be a mistake, therefore, to read them as justifying a Manichean attitude.

JEWETT: The point is, the violent history of the Western world is to a substantial degree oriented to the other side of the biblical heritage, climaxing in the Book of Revelation. It lacks that kind of openness toward the victim, or sympathy toward the victim, that you get in the Gospels.

GIRARD: I agree that there are differences, but we should not judge too hastily. We all feel highly sympathetic to "real" victims, but our "real" victims are not always the same as our neighbor's "real" victims. Do we really know what total sympathy toward all victims would entail? Certain aspects of the Gospels sound very harsh in the light of modern sentimentalism. This does not necessarily mean that our sympathy toward real victims is greater. I personally believe this sympathy can only be an emanation from the Gospels, and very often a caricatural emanation.

BURTON MACK: I want to see if I can rephrase what I think is going on with several questions, in my own way. When I read *Le Bouc émissaire*, I thought, René, that you had moved away a little bit from the type of argument that you used when you went from "mimetic desire" to "violence and the sacred," in the direction of what I thought was a datum of social history. As I understand you now, that might not be true. Nevertheless, you were quite concerned to talk about the reality of these things, and based your point of departure heavily on the actuality of the plague and the persecutions there.

GIRARD: Well, I can clear up that point very quickly. The first part of *Le Bouc émissaire* is a comparative analysis of medieval persecution and a number of myths. I wanted to show that mythology can be read as a reflection of the scapegoaters' viewpoint, independently from the theory of mimetic desire. This does not mean that mimetic desire has lost its importance in my eyes. I see no contradiction. In the present discussion, I have outlined both approaches.

MACK: What is the status of the historical social data for you, that is, what is the status of the realia of the social dynamics as you explain them in other ways?

GIRARD: I don't take a position on these problems.

MACK: Okay, I can handle that, let's leave it at the level of text, and say that there is a reality reference and we're not going to touch that in terms of methodology, in terms of social history, but you are concerned about mythology having an effect.

GIRARD: Mythology primarily. If you can have a genetic theory of mythology simply by seeing the reality of the victim, I don't say I'm reconstituting any historical scheme. I don't say I know anything about the Milomaki text, except for the fact that if it were a historical text I would smell the real victim.

MACK: Okay, the way I want to phrase my question then, is this. The scapegoat mechanism is for you, at least primarily, a matter of nonconsciousness, as you have phrased it. And even though you have worked out a schema to show various ways of adjudicating that and finally talking about a disclosure, the disclosure comes from another text, the Gospels, which then, because of the way you've answered the questions here, especially from John Lawrence and Bob Jewett, also really works at a concealment level. That is, you were quite easily drawn into using this kind of social-historical data as an inverse argument, or seeing it as an inversion of the scapegoat mechanism vis-à-vis the Gospels. You could use that to argue for the scapegoat mechanism, but you didn't say anything about how you could use the same kind of data that are put before us here to talk about the status of the Gospels. In other words, it's almost as if you have reified the gospel text over against the mythological text in the same way. They both work at the level of concealment; nevertheless, the gospel text also somehow discloses.

GIRARD: No, no, I wouldn't say that the text of the gospel conceals. It's all revelation, but we are not able to take it in.

MACK: But what does it mean if it's a revelation that we can't take?

GIRARD: Ah, but we can take it gradually. It's seeping in through history, and it has more and more effect, even though we don't recognize it. I refer you to the words of John's gospel, "I have yet many things to say to you but you cannot bear them now" (John 16:12).

MACK: Unrecognized revelation?

GIRARD: Unrecognized revelation, which is all the gospel is about—which is, "You don't understand these things now, but someday you will." We understand more and more.

MACK: Okay, I just wanted to hear you say that.

GIRARD: I wouldn't say that we have the right revelation now. I would say our history, in contact with the text of the Gospels, teaches us a certain significance of that text and a certain action of that text. Therefore there are invisible aspects of that text that have become more perceptible today. That text is alive.

TERRELL BUTLER: What is important to me about this conversation is the distinction that you made in *Le Bouc émissaire* between a text of persecution or a myth on the one hand, and the Bible on the other. In the former, the scapegoat mechanism is left out, while in the latter, it is put in.

GIRARD: The important distinction I make is between the case where the victim appears and his status as victim is justified—"it is right to hate the enemy" and so forth, where that justification is the result of the nonconscious operation of the scapegoat mechanism—and the case where we are told explicitly that the victim is a scapegoat, "the Lamb of God who takes away the sins of the world." The former is a text that conceals, whereas the latter is a text that reveals.

MACK: But it is double damnation if that revelatory text is used in the way that Bob Jewett and John Lawrence say it is by some contemporaries.

GIRARD: Why? That's what's predicted. The fact is the Christians have never been able precisely to see or to state the point made in the text, "Caiaphas, who was high priest that year, said to them, 'You know nothing at all; you do not understand that it is expedient for you that one man should die for the people, and that the whole nation should not perish'" (John 11:49-50).

MACK: The Christians have never been able to see that?

GIRARD: Well, it would be wrong to say they've never been able to see it; rather, let me say that they have never been able to formulate it in the language of modern theory, as I do. They have been able to conceive of all sorts of in-between statements, but nothing clear-cut. And that corresponds to the situation: nothing is clear-cut. We are in a place between the full revelation of the scapegoat and the totally mythical. In history, we are always between the gospel and myth.

Two

WALTER BURKERT

The Problem of Ritual Killing

THE PRESENT "RITUAL CONVERSATIONS" are to concentrate on theory and method. This is necessary, since we wish to confront and possibly reconcile different views and theses that have arisen independently, but that seem largely to overlap when dealing with the same issues. We shall, for the most part, not deal with what is the lifeblood of research—namely, the immediate contact with detailed evidence, the thrill of unexpected findings and new perspectives. If the beginning of philosophy is to wonder, to be "struck" by the phenomena, the discussion of method is, in a manner of speaking, "to strike back"; this may make ill-founded constructions crumble and cause clear outlines to disappear in the dust.

We can hardly expect a definite theory to emerge. If scientific theory means a limited number of propositions from which further statements can be deduced to be controlled by the data and thus falsified or corroborated, we must remember that in the humanities we are usually dealing with chance selections of data, especially in all fields of history, and even more, that our data are already interpretations, acquiring their meaning in a preconceived system of meaning. This is why theories ad libitum may be possible, forming the data, by choice and interpretation, into strange and striking configurations. Yet an absolutely objective scientific theory would not be gratifying as long as we endeavor to "understand" the phenomena, to assimilate them into our own outlook on life. There remains a framework to the hermeneutical process that is ineradicably subjective. We cannot but deal with simplified pictures of the world in relation to our own environmental and mental situation. The best we can do is be prepared to widen and deepen our understanding in a common effort of question and response.

I

In the history of religions, the concept of ritual, based on the use of *ritus/rituale* in the Christian church, was first discovered from the viewpoint of "survivals"; subsequently it became a major concern of functionalist theories with Emile Durkheim and J. E. Harrison; and recently it has been further developed by structuralist semiology. (Cf. Burkert 1979: 35-39; 1983: 22-29. For a semiotic approach, see Calame 1973; Staal 1979.) It should be clear at once that the functional and the semiotic aspects need not be in conflict with each other: signs do have functions in a given system, even if they are not reducible to them.

I hope we agree about the framework for a definition of ritual: rituals, *dromena* in Greek ("things done," besides "things said" and "things shown," especially in mysteries), are action patterns used as signs, in other words, stereotyped demonstrative action; the demonstrative element might as well be called "rhetorical" (Mack) or even "symbolic," though this depends on the definition of the controversial concept of symbol. (Cf. Rappaport 1971: esp. 67. The communicative element is denied by Staal 1979.) Ritual is thus a form of nonverbal communication, analogous to language at least to some extent. Ritual is a pattern, a sequence of actions that can be perceived, identified, and described as such, and that can be repeated in consequence. We know that action goes together with motives, emotions,[1] projective "ideas," but we need not refer to these for the identification and description of ritual; even the fact of communication is observable from its effects, from behavioral responses. Interaction in any society may be both pragmatic and communicative; we speak of ritual if the communicative function is dominant (i.e., independent to some extent of the pragmatic situation), which in turn makes possible stereotyped patterns, and is manifest from them.[2]

We should still distinguish "ritual" in a strict sense, a stereotype

[1]Scheff (1977) makes ritual "distanced reenactment" of "emotional distress," taking funeral rites as his model; this would hardly apply to preparative ritual or to a sacrificial feast.

[2]The detachment from the "accidents of ordinary life " is correlated to what Jonathan Smith sees as the essence of ritual, "performing the way things ought to be," "the creation of a controlled environment" (Smith 1980: 124f).

prescribed and predictable in detail, from a looser sense in which we may speak of a ritual hunt, a ritual war, a ritual theft: such actions may be expected and prescribed in certain societies, and surrounded by ritual in the strict sense, but their course and outcome are unpredictably pragmatic.

This concept of ritual is equally applicable to animal behavior; it has been adopted by Sir Julian Huxley and especially by Konrad Lorenz, the most forceful promoter of modern ethology. "A behavioral pattern," to use Lorenz's words,[3] that "acquires an entirely new function, that of communication," is observable in many species of animals as action redirected for demonstration, and the very variety of species allows for the systematic study of its evolution through all its steps.

This view is not popular with the many representatives of human studies who insist on the basic distinction between "human" and "animal." It should be clear, however, that the term "animal" contains a terrible simplification: a chimpanzee is closer to man than to a snail on practically all counts. The most revealing studies on animal rituals come, nevertheless, from less-related species, such as crested grebes or greylags, where the stereotypy is more marked. Of course, human behavior is largely learned, whereas much of animal behavior is innate, but this distinction becomes blurred with mammals, especially primates. There are innate rituals (i.e., significant behavior patterns that are proper to man and culture-independent), such as smiling, laughing, and weeping, whereas gestures of greeting, sympathy, or threat are found in very similar forms in chimpanzees. Other gestures are culturally transmitted and differ accordingly—for example, how to say no. Yet the "arbitrariness of the sign" (*l'arbitraire du signe*) noted by Ferdinand de Saussure in linguistics does not generally apply in ritual communication: you cannot show pride by hanging your head, or peaceful intentions by raising a fist.

A basic fact established by ethology is the priority of ritual communication over language. The priority of phylogeny is indeed repeated in ontogeny: every baby has to respond to behavior long

[3]Lorenz 1966: 72, accepted by Burkert 1983: 22-29; see also Rappaport 1971; d'Aquili et al. 1979; and esp. W. Smith 1979; not accepted by E. Wilson (1978: 179), who stresses the complexity of human as against animal "ritual."

before it acquires the ability to speak. This should warn us not to base a theory of ritual on verbalized concepts.

In this context, a discussion opened by Philip Lieberman is of great interest (see Lieberman 1972; Lieberman et al. 1972; Lieberman 1975; Kruntz 1980). His thesis is that "Neanderthal man" of the Lower Paleolithic still lacked the physiological equipment to produce articulate speech, as do the chimpanzees. This would make the language of *homo sapiens* only about forty thousand years old. It seems to account best for the disappearance of Neanderthal man and the comparatively rapid spread of *homo sapiens*, introducing new forms of symbolizations such as paintings and plastic art. Yet Neanderthal man already had elaborate rituals that are currently qualified as "religious": even if the deposits of bear skulls on which Karl Meuli relied as the first testimonies for sacrifice are controversial (cf. Burkert 1983: 14; Leroi-Gourhan 1971: 30-36), there remain clear cases of burial, including the use of red paint, ochre, and some uncanny collections and treatments of human skulls.[4] This means symbolic activity in an interplay of life and death. Lieberman's findings have been criticized and modified by some and defended by others; I am not able to pass an expert's judgment in the matter. The problem is further complicated by the fact that famous experiments have revealed a capacity for language in chimpanzees (in the form of sign language) that exceeds all expectations (see R. W. Brown in Young 1982: 197-204). In a sense, there must have been language before language. It remains to state that ritual communication must have accompanied all stages in this complicated evolution, and to speculate about its importance in the process.

At any rate, ritual behavior must have been a major factor in evolution (Burkert 1983: 26f; cf. Rappaport 1971; Wilson 1978: 177f). Every person has to learn language or risk being treated as an idiot; the disappearance of Neanderthal man has just been mentioned. Similar risks and consequences will apply to ritual communication in a close-knit society: there are no chances of survival for a "ritual idiot," whereas the genes of those who effectively use the rituals to increase their personal prestige will multiply. Rituals are prominent

---

[4]Müller-Karpe 1966: 229-42 (burial); P. V. Tobias in Young 1982: 48 (ochre); Wreschner 1980; Edwards 1978. For a special treatment of skulls, the most intriguing find is from Monte Circé (Leroi-Gourhan 1971: 44f).

in courting ceremonies, and thus clearly become factors in natural selection; other rituals may have indirect effects of the same kind. Ritual is, after all, communication of a special sort: it is action rooted in pragmatic interaction, and thus not only transports information, but often directly affects the addressee and possibly the "sender" as well. This has been called the operative or influential function of communication. Biology has drawn attention to the phenomenon of "imprinting," an irreversible modification by experience, distinct from normal learning by trial and error; it is most notable in the early stages of life. In fact, religious attitudes seem to be largely shaped by childhood experience and can hardly be changed by arguments; this points to the imprinting effects of ritual tradition. But there are also more direct pragmatic effects of ritual activity, such as the transfer of food or wealth to certain groups. After all, ritual killing is real killing, and the ritual expulsion of a pharmakos is directly effective on the societal level. The ethological perspective suggests that this has been working for thousands of generations. It is all the more remarkable that the result has not yet been an antlike, perfectly functional, finite, and stable system of human society.

The problem of religious ritual has already been touched on. The importance of ritual for religion has been observed and discussed ever since Robertson Smith. This is not to say that religion is to be reduced to ritual, only that ritual seems to provide a substructure that is essential and that is not to be derived from "higher" aspects such as myth or theology. A purely "cognitive theory of religion" must be a failure. There seems to be no religion without ritual.

This leaves the question of the *differentia specifica*: what is it that makes ritual religious ritual? The simplest answer seems to be that it is the intervention of language[5] and verbalized concepts, including names, to denote "superior beings." This creates another problem for the "religion" of Neanderthal man, who was possibly not endowed with speech, but we need not solve this now. The normal observer will take the testimony of language about demons, ghosts,

[5]Cf. Rappaport (1971: 66-72) on the "semantic content" added to ritual by language, which is not coextensive with the "social message" conveyed by it; he finds the essence of "sanctity" in "the quality of unquestionable truthfulness" (p. 69). This creates problems in the myth-and-ritual complex: myth is not "unquestionable."

or gods as the criterium that we are dealing with religion. The more central problem is whether the advent of language should be thought to imply a reversal of structures, so that ritual communication, though older and originally independent, has been transformed under the domination of speech and verbalized concepts and has thus lost all connections with what was there before, especially "animal" ritual.

In spite of the spell the concepts of innovation and creativity may exert in modern discussions, it can be held that it is easier to find the germs of religion in ritual than to derive the necessity of ritual from conceptual religion. Indeed, some form of displacement, of reorientation, of turning away from the pragmatic context, is the very essence of ritual. Hence an element of "as if" is inherent in ritual from the start, creating some void to be filled out by mythical designations (see Burkert 1979: 50-52). This seems to prepare the way for imaginary partners.

On another but not unrelated line, the concepts of synergetics may be brought in. Synergetics is a comparatively recent branch of physics that studies the emergence of states of order out of chaos, and vice versa; an example is laser light. Most remarkable is the sudden appearance of an "order parameter" that "enslaves" the performance of the single constituents, atoms and their electrons in this case, and makes one regular pattern emerge (see Haken 1978, 1981). The emergence of a pattern in communicative interaction (e.g., rhythmical chanting in a crowd of people) could be described in this way. Thus Greek gods such as Paian, Iakkhos, and Dithyrambos, who have been recognized to be "personifications" of the respective songs, are, rather, the "order parameters," suddenly appearing and disappearing again, of synergetic phenomena in ritual behavior.

There is no doubt that the transmission of religion heavily relies on the experience of ritual. No less a witness than Plato emphasizes how children both see their parents dealing in supreme seriousness with invisible powers and live through the joyous views of the festivals themselves: this is why they should be immune to the danger of atheism (Leg. 887de). The orator Dion (or. 12, 33) describes a mystery initiation, with abrupt changes of light and darkness, puzzling views and sounds, dancers whirling around and around: all this will make the initiate, Dion says, surmise some deeper sense and wisdom behind the confusing appearances. These texts point to characteristics of religious ritual that are manifest even from a behavioral point of view: an intricate yet somehow integrated complexity that leads to a postulation of "sense," and supreme, almost compulsive seriousness, at least with certain participants or at certain phases of the proceedings. This corresponds to what is often described as "awe" in the phenomenology of religion. It is no doubt a major factor in imprinting.

There is no denying that ritual, including religious ritual, has so far been approached in terms of functionalism. Functional interpretations of religious ritual have been developed by Durkheim, Harrison, and Radcliffe-Brown. In this perspective, religious ceremonies are seen to be a form of communication that creates, commemorates, and preserves solidarity among the members of the group (cf. Burkert 1983: 24-28). Social roles are played out by dramatizing both antithesis and thesis; they are thus determined, confirmed, and brought to attention. Society thereby ensures its own stability, both in the synchronic and the diachronic dimension; this brings in what has been said on the educational and imprinting effects of ritual. Thus ritual, especially religious ritual, is self-perpetuating.

Functionalism has been out of favor for some decades,[6] and no doubt the automatism of tradition that would result from its premises is neither attractive nor verifiable. Yet before dropping the functional approach, we should not lose sight of the remarkable advance it made in interpreting ritual. I wish to make three points:

1. Functionalism makes clear that ritual is interpersonal. It is not one person's invention, not an individual's quest for sense, but a system taken over, experienced, nay suffered, by every single being. This is especially true of religious ritual. The boy suffers circumcision before he has any possibility of deciding for himself. To use the analogy of language once more: nobody in the last forty thousand years has invented language; we learn it, we use it, sometimes improving or changing details, but we have already been shaped by it and experience the world through its framework. In a similar way,

---

[6]Stone (1981: 9-11) even speaks of the "disease of functionalism." On the other hand, the approach of Rappaport has been termed "neo-functionalist"; see also Goldschmidt 1966.

nobody in millennia has invented religious ritual; every *homo religiosus* has been shaped by it. Some struggle with it, some succeed in working effective change, some may free themselves totally if society allows for "religious idiots." But there still remains the power of religious tradition, shaping generation after generation in the accepted way.

2. Functionalism coincides with the self-interpretation of traditional religions. Bronislaw Malinowski wrote on the function of initiation ceremonies (1948: 40): "They are a ritual and dramatic expression of the supreme power and value of tradition in primitive societies; they also serve to impress this power and value upon the minds of each generation." "This much I know," a pagan Greek proclaimed as his faith, "that one must maintain the ancestral customs, and that it would be improper to excuse oneself for this before others" (Ath. 297d). To worship the gods and to honor the ancestors were parallel obligations; in the *patrios nomos*, as in the *mos maiorum* (ancestral customs), was found the main or even the only legitimation of religion. With Judaism, Christianity, and Islam, a sacred scripture has come in to provide a new foundation, which, however, is all the more the basis for purportedly immutable authoritative tradition.

3. The consequence is what I once ventured to call a "Copernican Revolution" (Burkert 1972a: 37): ritual is not to be understood as incorporating an "antecedent idea," not as the secondary manifestation of spiritual belief, but as communicative activity prescribed by tradition; ideas and beliefs are produced by ritual, rather than vice versa. In other words, we should not presuppose that people perform religious acts because they believe, but rather that they believe because they have learned to perform religious acts, or even more plausibly, that they act in the accepted way, whether they believe or not. This may seem to correspond just too well to contemporary practice; but for earlier periods, too, close inspection will show that it is the interplay of traditions and interests that determines the individual's choice, not "pure" religion in isolation.

Functionalism has been close to Darwinism, which is a functional theory in itself. There have been attempts at "social Darwinism," applying the principle of "survival of the fittest" to competing groups. In about 1900, it could have been said that religious communities were more coherent and hence more successful in the struggle for existence, and that this explained the tenacious success of religion in the evolution of mankind (e.g., Gruppe 1921: 243); some historical evidence could have been brought in for illustration. But the modern approach of sociobiology, using game theory and the computer, has exploded the concept of "group selection": it is only and always the individual's "selfish genes" that survive, which seems to favor the egoist, the hypocrite, the trickster (Dawkins 1976; cf. also E. Wilson 1978: 169-93). Computers have run hot recently in attempts to explain how altruism could come about all the same (Hofstadter 1983b). Yet I am afraid that altruism may be neither the core of morality nor the core of religion, and we should not even look for the religious gene. It is a commonplace that, in human evolution, genetic tradition has been supplemented and largely supplanted by cultural, learned tradition. It may nevertheless be useful to see this tradition, or rather the multiplicity of traditions, in sociobiological terms, as "strategies" in a game continuing through many generations. Sociobiology is looking for "evolutionarily stable strategies"; these would be the most successful and stable traditions. It is important to note that forms of "grudge" and retribution necessarily seem to enter successful strategies: "Tit for tat."[7] Has this something to do with the concepts of reciprocity, retribution, and justice, which loom so large in religious traditions—and which seem to be totally foreign to chimpanzees? Is ritual a means developed to inculcate and to rehearse fundamental rules, successful "strategies" in the continuing social game?

Some sociobiologists have gone on to speculate about the evolution of human tradition as a "selection of memes" analogous to the Darwinian "selection of genes." (See Dawkins 1976: 203-15; Colman 1982: 288f; and cf. J. L. Machic in Colman 1982: 271-84; Hofstadter 1983a.) The word meme, though, remains painful to a Hellenist. What is more important: it is of no avail, I think, to look for the logical structure of memes (e.g., some sort of self-reference) to explain their power of "success" and "replication." There is, rather, some psychological mechanism that shields the individual from the superabundant influx of sensory data and singles out what

---

[7]Dawkins 1976: 79f (retaliation) and 199f (grudge); Hofstadter 1983b (tit for tat).

is "memorable," which draws the person's attention by alerting him. This, however, once again introduces the quality of "seriousness," which was seen to characterize religious ritual, and recalls the phenomenon of "imprinting."

It is probably too early to expect definitive results in a field that has just recently been opened for discussion, but there does seem to be the possibility of rephrasing the concepts of functionalism in terms of the new perspectives and thus of reinterpreting even religious ritual. A tentative conclusion could be: rituals are communicative forms of behavior combining innate elements with imprinting and learning; they are transmitted through the generations in the context of successful strategies of interaction. Religious rituals are highly integrated and complex forms that, with the character of absolute seriousness, shape and replicate societal groups and thus perpetuate themselves.

A basic concept that has emerged, be it from the viewpoint of functionalism or of sociobiology, is that of tradition, of persisting supra-individual rules. It is hardly a popular one. The aboriginal age and continuity of religious traditions were more easily accepted by earlier generations, which had an interest in "origins" and "survivals." At present, the insistence is, rather, on the revolts against tradition and creative beginnings, on breaks, innovations, and discontinuities. A characteristic example is the critical analysis of the Hainuwele myth by Jonathan Z. Smith (1976).

Nobody will deny that religious traditions are extremely conservative, and that religious institutions are among the oldest institutions that survive to the present day. Judaism and Buddhism may by now claim to be about twenty-five hundred years old; if religions based on scripture should be judged a special case, one may point to Vedic ritual, older still, which continues to be practiced. Yet normally the proof of continuity becomes impossible for illiterate and prehistoric societies, whereas in certain cases interruptions, change, and innovation can be observed to occur notwithstanding the persistent appeal to ancestral customs, *mos maiorum*.

The emergence of new religions, on the other hand, the achievements of religious founders, never imply a radical break with tradition. There has never been a reinvention of religion as such. As to ritual in particular, older forms are often taken up: the essential features of the *hadj* are pre-Islamic, and baptism is pre-Christian. And even through its negation, the force of tradition can still be operative.

Even in the absence of direct evidence, the hypothesis of discontinuity is neither more cautious nor more logical than the hypothesis of continuity. Two parallel phenomena should give us pause. As to language, there can be no reasonable doubt that there has never been an independent invention for the last forty thousand years, but always continuous tradition, even if written testimonies do not lead back farther than about five thousand years, and linguistic reconstructions not too much beyond this term. Yet the idea that human language might have been creatively invented several times has nothing to recommend it: in this very special form of learned behavior, there has been evolution and diversification on the basis of unbroken continuity. Life itself, on the other hand, depends on the continuous replication of genes, of DNA. In spite of the general and ubiquitous chemical laws, it is not by multiple fresh formations that life has been on this planet for so many millions of years. The forms of behavioral communication could possibly be situated somewhere in between; there is no reason to assume that they were less continuous. As to the emotional equivalents that correspond to observable behavior, a striking example for continuity has been adduced by Konrad Lorenz (1966: 259-61; cf. Burkert 1979: 51): in anxiety as well as in enthusiasm, we feel "shivers of awe" running down our back—and remember the role of "awe" in religion. These shivers are, physiologically, the residual nerves and muscles once used to raise the hair at back and head for aggressive display, as gorillas impressively do. The emotional experience still complies with what had been demonstrative action, ritual at the subhuman level; and artificial signals such as Hector's crested helmet may be adopted to make good for the lost abilities. Thus the sign is restored to its meaning.

This does not mean that all traits of ritual should be traced back to prehuman levels; yet often their "etymology" is revealing beyond mere curiosity. Interpretation proper will always concentrate on definite social units at definite time levels; yet none of these is autonomous. The very instability of cultural systems, as abundantly proved by history, is the reason they cannot be seen as perfect, closed, and self-sufficient, but must be seen as shaped by and often struggling with tradition, conditioned by earlier states whose solutions may become problems in the course of time. The question "Where from?" remains a legitimate or even necessary complement to functional and structural interpretations. Ethology reopens and enlarges the perspective of history.

It remains to consider some alternative concepts of ritual, especially those that seem to question the interpersonal, communicative aspect of ritual. Are there not private rituals that are attributed to either neurotic trauma or magical intent? Jonathan Z. Smith has used the example of the farmer who every morning takes up a handful of earth to rub his hands with before starting to work (1978: 291f). This is an instance of private ritual. Even so, it is not without communicative character, marking distinctions to the farmer himself, as well as to others. Primarily, it seems to be self-communication, though probably not without relation to what had been communicated to the farmer by his elders about dirt and tidiness. But it is also pointed out to others; it would become religious ritual if and only if it were handed down and prescribed in a closed community.

Similar considerations apply to compulsive neurotic behavior that may be called ritualistic (Freud 1907; Reik 1931): these are patterns of behavior apparently used for self-communication, while normal communication with other people is disturbed; such patterns could become rituals of the kind that concern the history of religions only if and insofar as they were drawn into the interpersonal stream of communicative tradition. Private, neurotic "rituals" can sometimes be explained on the basis of traumatic experience, and similar origins "by accident" have been attributed to certain taboos and avoidances; the Pythagorean taboo on beans is said to have originated in a special allergy still found in Mediterranean countries.[8] This may or may not be "origin"; food taboos often seem to defy explanation. At any rate, a "real" experience, however shocking, cannot be transmitted unless it enters the system of communication, which means that it is shaped according to the preexisting framework. There may be elements in a ritual tradition that

[8]Burkert 1972b: 184. For discussions of food taboos and their explanation, see Ross 1978; Diener & Robbin 1978.

really go back to some "accident" of the kind, but it would be wrong to derive ritual tradition itself from this source.

Another attempt to explain ritual within the individual's perspective is the magical interpretation, as exemplified especially in the work of Sir George Frazer. Ritual action is seen as purposeful manipulation in order to obtain a desired result, such as rainmaking or curing the sick. Insofar as this seems to result in the symbolic imitation of pragmatic activities, "action re-done or pre-done" (Harrison 1921: xliii), the interpretation becomes largely parallel to the ethological perspective that looks for displaced action patterns. The difference is that instead of communicative functions, the "magical" hypothesis tended to assume some "primitive mentality" unable to make proper distinctions between reality and wishful thinking. This construct of a primitive mentality has been exploded by Malinowski (1948: esp. 25-36), among others, and will hardly find favor today. The tendency now is to understand magic in terms of communication, as a kind of "language." It may be noted that magicians used to have their special teachers (i.e., they relied heavily on tradition), and that the effect of magic art evidently depends on signals that reach the common people; a magician or witch whose powers nobody knew of would be reduced to nonexistence. Yet magic remains a special case, and its relation to religion has not at all been settled. Suffice it to say that magical ritual is more than just wishful thinking and imitation; it has its tradition, and it has a seriousness of its own as it proves effective in reality.

Let us not forget that the preceding outlines have necessarily been working with abstractions on the basis of reduced and simplified models. Nothing has been said about motivations and interpretations, the integrative power of myth, the conceptual and moral orientations that go along with religious rituals. A notable phenomenon is what I would call the "good conscience complex," the unscrupulous security of divine legitimation that, from a humane point of view, may become quite dangerous. Another qualification needs to be added: if, in the wake of functionalism, we speak of society communicating messages of solidarity through ritual, this is not to overlook the heterogeneous plurality of the persons concerned, the social differentiations, the interests of institutions and individuals. There are normally those for whom it is profitable to perform religious ceremonies, and they take the lead.[9] The profit may consist in prestige and authority—this seems to be the case with the families and officials of the ancient polis, but in a sense, every father and mother of a pious family take their share. In most societies, however, there are those who make a living out of religion, be it totally or in part—priests, monks, ascetics, charismatics of various caliber. Even if ritual is interpersonal, not invented by the individual but acquired or suffered through the force of tradition, it was used by an intelligent and cunning species in olden as in more recent days. The irrational and the rational, far from excluding each other, may enter strange coalitions.

II

Turning to the special problem of sacrifice, and thus limiting the scope of inquiry, let us concentrate on the area of study with which most of us are familiar—namely, animal sacrifice in Jewish, Greek, and Roman religion, including its sublimation in Christian theology. This does not forbid us to look for similarities and divergences in other cultures, though such evidence will not decisively corroborate or falsify the findings. Whether the sacrifice we choose is a typical or a very special case is another question. I do not wish to contradict Frits Staal's claim that the most promising field for ritual studies is the Indian and Chinese tradition.

I shall not dwell on the well-known data. They have been studied extensively in recent times by the Paris school of Vernant-Detienne and, in part, by myself (Detienne & Vernant 1979, with bibliography; Burkert 1983).[10] The basic paradox that continues to draw attention is best described by the title of René Girard's book *Violence and the Sacred*, which shows slaughter, blood, and killing as the central ritual of religion. This is the main form of communica-

---

[9]Julius Caesar had already made this observation with regard to the Druids and their disciples: *tantis excitati praemiis* . . . (*Bellum Gallicum* 6.14.2). See also Herrenschmidt 1978.

[10]In accordance with the ancient use of *sacrificare*, my approach starts from animal sacrifice and puts this in the context of ritual killing; in such a view, the resulting picture can only partly overlap the approach of van Baal (1976), who starts from "offering" and excludes ritual killing from the concept of "sacrifice."

tion with the gods, and it is at the same time the most effective "status dramatization," defining inclusion and exclusion, position and rank, in all forms of community, notably in oaths and alliances. There is an impressive continuity of the practice from the Pentateuch to the Jewish catastrophe, from Homer to Constantine, with some good evidence even from the Bronze Age, and striking survivals, especially among Greeks and Armenians, down to the present day. The ritual tradition is seen to date back at least four thousand years.

I shall not discuss sacrificial ideology, either, be it in tragedy, patriotic rhetoric, or theology proper. I take for granted the "anomaly" (Mack) inherent in this ritual, its puzzling, nay shocking, character. This is not just personal sentimentality; criticism seems to be as old as the Prometheus myth, and the resounding protest of Empedocles belongs to the classical age. It is the intriguing equivalence of animal and man, as expressed in mythology in the metaphors of tragedy, but also in rituals of substitution, that casts the shadow of human sacrifice over all those holy altars in front of the temples. Later, Christianity transformed the world, only to bring sacrificial ideology to a climax in the theology of redemption.

In an attempt to explain the "anomaly," both René Girard and I have had recourse to an "original scene" of necessary violence that became the foundation of human society and thus, even through the veils of religion, continued to exert its influence. This is to be taken not as a "just-so story" equivalent to legend, but as the projection of relations onto an image from which the original functions as well as the later displacements should become more clearly visible.

Let us be warned in advance that we are probably in danger of too easily assuming monogenetic developments. Trained by scientific logic, we are used to seeing just one line of cause and effect. In the complex process of human evolution through the vast spaces of prehistory, we should, rather, think in terms of a multidimensional network of interrelations. As for the problem of murder, no less than four varieties of intraspecific killing have been observed in ape societies within the last decade: a "war" between two troops (communication of J. Goodall, Dec. 18, 1981), and cannibalism within one group of chimpanzees (Goodall 1977); the killing of nonrelated babies among gorillas (Fossey 1981: 511f); and the drowning of a sibling out of jealousy among orangutans (Galdikas 1980: 830-32). Already at the prehuman level, the stock of destructive behavior is seen to be too rich and multifarious for only one line of cause and effect.

From Hunt to Sacrifice

Following Karl Meuli's pioneering essay on Greek sacrificial practices (1946), I have attempted to derive sacrificial ritual from Paleolithic hunting. This is the perspective of "where from?," explaining the later from the earlier stages, the ritualized communicative action from pragmatic activity, presupposing basic continuity in the evolution of behavior, psychic responses, and institutions. The central, practical, and necessary act would be to kill animals for food. Sacrifice is ritual slaughter (Meuli 1946: 224), followed by the communal meal, which in this perspective is not an infringement on "pure religion" but the very telos.

There are at least three facts that should be borne in mind in connection with this thesis: (1) the biological importance of a diet rich in proteins, together with the psychological adaptation of our species for such a diet; for the overwhelming majority of people, the taste of meat is still the very essence of a good meal; (2) the opposition of this development to primate tradition, which started with the ability to climb trees and to grasp for fruit and leaves; and (3) the universal combination of a meat diet with rules for the distribution of food. (See Goldschmidt 1966: 87-92; G. Isaac 1978a, b; Isaac in Young 1982: 177-81; Lancaster 1978; Baudy 1983.)

In a simplified, popular form, this means that man is the primate that turned carnivore, the "hunting ape." The implications of this adaptation are manifold and yet specific. It is possible to derive from it a kind of blueprint of human society in general.

This is the "hunting hypothesis" of hominization.[11] It includes cooperation for hunting and the distribution of meat; sexual differentiation, with men hunting and thus feeding the females, and fe-

---

[11] *The Hunting Hypothesis* is the title of Robert Ardrey's 1976 book; the more recent discussion started with Dart 1953; see Freeman 1964; Morris 1967; Washburn & Lancaster 1968.

males tending the fire for cooking and thus feeding the males;[12] the use of fire and weapons; and upright posture for running and transport. Basic human actions, represented by basic verbs in most languages, thus come into existence: to get, to bring, to give—and to kill. All this can be seen to be mirrored in sacrifice: to bring, to kill, to give. The span of time involved in the process, however, is staggering: about twenty million years. It also seems clear that hominization did not occur in one simple straight line; there were many blind alleys of evolution.

To be more precise, several steps must evidently be distinguished. I did not know, in 1972, that incipient hunting behavior, including cases of cannibalism, had been observed in chimpanzees. Normal chimpanzee hunting is done almost exclusively by males (Teleki 1973a, b, and restatement in Harding & Teleki 1981: 303-43; P. Wilson 1975). Following the hunt, there is some "distribution of meat." It is not a ceremonious dinner but a process of begging and granting; still, it is the only occasion when chimpanzees do share food, apart from the special and different mother-child relation (Silk 1978). We can notice the germ of what seem to be practically universals in human civilizations: the hunt as men's business, and men feeding the family (Galdikas & Teleki 1981; Wolpoff 1982). There is no analogy to this in other mammals. Sacrifice preserves the image, the founding of community by communal eating, with a previous kill and a prestigious "Lord of Sacrifice" at the center.

Far beyond the chimpanzee stage is what we figure to have been early Paleolithic hunting. It is characterized by the cooperation of hunting males using fire and weapons; the first effective hunting weapon was the wooden spear hardened by fire. This situation seems to be indicated, for example, by the findings at Chou Kou Tien (Wu & Lin 1983)—of a "Peking man" who used fire and was able to hunt large animals, especially cervids, with great success. The *Männerbund* (male hunting group), with the use of weapons and sacrificial banquets, has remained a powerful configuration in ritual and symbolism.

[12]Modern trends are against this differentiation, but the association of male prestige and hunting is practically universal; see Watenabe 1968: 74: "It is the individualistic hunting of larger mammals that is invariably the task of males." See also, on Bushmen, Marshall 1976: 180f.

Meuli's most original and permanent contribution was to draw attention to the Siberian hunters' ritual.[13] The hunt itself is a pragmatic activity; ritual stereotypes, rather, concern the framework, the beginning and the ending: there are forms of avoidances and purifications before the hunt; there are attempts at compensation or restoration afterward, with disclaimers of responsibility and expressions of guilt and mourning; Meuli coined the memorable term "comedy of innocence." Most of these rites will not leave tangible traces to be ascertained by prehistory; but there are the customs of depositing skulls and bones, especially thighbones, in certain places, and Bächler and others claimed to have discovered such deposits from the Lower Paleolithic period. Meuli relied on them, as did I, but more recent discussions by prehistorians seem to have seriously invalidated Bächler's findings. Yet some evidence from the Upper Paleolithic has remained, as far as I can see, to allow comparison with later sacrificial ritual: setting up the cranium of a reindeer on a pole, putting a bear's hide on a clay model in a cave. Naturally, the Paleolithic evidence is lacunar and difficult to interpret; one may claim that the first task is still to see even Paleolithic evidence in its own context, which leaves much room for controversies among specialists about hunting magic, shamanism, and the like.

The next crucial step was the creation of animal sacrifice proper amid Neolithic husbandry.[14] This meant bringing in domesticated animals instead of wild ones to be slaughtered in local "sanctuaries"; this would finally lead to the temples of urban high culture. That a basic continuity of ritual should be assumed in this process of the "Neolithic" and the "urban revolution" is a daring hypothesis. It is easy to point out the differences in structure and function of the respective societies. Sacrifice at the new level is a transfer of property, a "gift" instead of forceful appropriation. The domesti-

[13]Meuli 1946: 224-52; for Africa add Baumann 1950; for South America, Reichel-Dolmatoff 1971. The rituals of excuse and appeasement are always brought in in connection with the hunt; I see no reason to postulate that they have been taken over from pastoralists, as J. Z. Smith does. It is true that the account of Trilles (1933) on the elephant ceremony of the pygmies (used e.g. in Burkert 1983: 68 n.44) has been called into question by the findings of Piskaty (1957).

[14]The thesis of E. Isaac (1963), that animals were first domesticated for the purpose of sacrifice (cf. Burkert 1983: 43), does not imply that the origin of sacrifice is in the Neolithic, but, on the contrary, implies that there was a preexisting "purpose," there was ideology and ritual.

cated animal can be paraded as a consenting victim, which is impossible with a "wild" one. (The problem is overcome in the "bear festivals," for which they rear and tame a young bear; Kitagawa 1961: 141.) Yet there remain those striking similarities between hunting ritual and sacrificial ritual on which Meuli relied. Strong corroboration has come from the excavations at Çatal Hüyük (Mellaart 1967; Burkert 1983: 43). As the "sanctuaries" in this Neolithic town, from about 6000 B.C., impressively show, hunting wild bulls was at the center of religious activity and imagery, with deposits of actual bulls' horns beneath the plastic figure of a Great Goddess giving birth (Burkert 1979: 119); bones of the dead were interred in these places. These memorable documents of prehistoric religion point as much to Paleolithic hunting as to the ceremonies and images of classical urban civilization.

Further confirming evidence may be found in the elements of hunting still to be found in later sacrificial ritual, such as "setting free" the animal destined for sacrifice (Burkert 1983: 16). In relation to Çatal Hüyük, the Great Goddess of Anatolia is a most interesting case. She is a huntress, still honored with actual bull hunts. What has mistakenly been called the many "breasts" of Artemis of Ephesus are bulls' testicles fastened to the image (G. Seiterle, *Antike Welt*, 10.3 [1979]: 3-16). This is giving back the source of life to the goddess, comparable—with understandable physiological misapprehension—to the role of kidneys in Hebrew ritual, or the collection of seals' gallbladders by Eskimo hunters (see Meuli 1946: 247; Burkert 1979: 202f). Nothing seems to block the line from hunting to sacrifice.

There is no need to stress that there are hordes of problems in this reconstruction. To mention the two most important lines of criticism known to me: it is claimed that the importance of hunting for hominization has been exaggerated and should be reduced considerably, and that the complex of bad conscience, guilt, and compensation in killing animals, so impressively set out by Karl Meuli, has been given undue prominence, too.

Some critical reaction to popularizing books such as those by Robert Ardrey and Desmond Morris is natural, and symposia of specialists will usually pile up criticisms and qualifications of details. I am not a specialist on the Paleolithic period, and I detest hunting, but this much I venture to say: the importance of hunting is not to be measured by the percentage of calories provided for the diet.[15] The hunt has been, and still is, something special, entailing men's pride and preoccupation far beyond what is economically reasonable. Paleolithic men may have succeeded in getting 100 percent of the prestige for contributing 20 percent or less to their groups' subsistence. The preoccupation with animals, with animals for hunting, is abundantly clear from the cave paintings of the Upper Paleolithic, and it is still equally visible in the profusion of animal statuettes in Greek sanctuaries. For the Greeks, a painter is an "animal-drawer" (*zographos*). If there is exaggeration of the importance of hunting and of animals in general, this is not the modern scholar's idiosyncrasy but the predilection of a very early tradition, especially the tradition of religious sacrifice.

The "respect for life" that Meuli discovered in the hunters' behavior seems to be, alas, less universal. It is neither innate nor taught in all societies. The bushmen of South Africa, a model case of a primitive hunting society, are said to laugh at the convulsions of the dying animal; the joy of getting food is overwhelming. Yet once more the important question is not about statistics, the percentage of positive or negative responses to killing. What is required for the thesis of continuous evolution from hunt to sacrifice is not that all human beings necessarily act or react in a certain way, but only that (1) some groups of hunters installed rituals that made the killing of animals for food a striking and labyrinthine affair that drew attention, affecting the life and consciousness of all members, and (2) these customs did not constitute a "blind alley" in the evolution of civilization, but set the path for further development through the Near Eastern Neolithic to the Mediterranean high cultures. This line of tradition still seems viable.

Possibilities of Psychological Interpretation

For methodological reasons, I have so far avoided bringing in psychological considerations or, at any rate, using them as arguments. Psychology is obviously essential for understanding, for our

[15]Lee (in Lee & DeVore 1968: 30-48) gives an estimated average of 35 percent that hunters contribute to nutrition in "hunting cultures"; on male preponderance, see n. 12.

empathy with the phenomena described. Yet continuity of behavior—its communicative function for creating social solidarity, the hunt and the hunters' customs—can be described without recourse to psychic experience, to the internal motives and responses of the actors involved. This seems to be the prudent course. In fact, modern scientific psychology, which works with experiments, questionnaires, statistics, is not of much help in our conversations about man's problematic heritage, whereas haphazard "eclectic" psychology is not of probative value.

The psychological categories I used in *Homo Necans* concentrate on aggression, remorse, and compensation (*Wiedergutmachung*). I was much impressed by Konrad Lorenz's book *On Aggression* (1966), and especially by his model of how aggressive behavior, ritualized, is transformed into a bond of personal solidarity and friendship. I shall not again describe the behavior of Lorenz's greylags here. An effect of sudden solidarity in a situation of aggression has often been described as a function of wars. (Solidarization against an aggressor is also found in monkeys; see K. R. L. Hall in Carthy & Ebling 1964: 53.) I extended the principle to include sacrifice in both its violent and its society-founding aspects, and combined this with Meuli's derivation of sacrifice from hunting and the anthropological thesis of hominization through the hunt.

Lorenz's theory of aggression has met with vigorous attacks from anthropologists and sociologists, and it does not seem to stand up too well against all the objections. (A bibliography of the tortuous discussions is not possible here; see E. Wilson 1978: 96-115; Burkert 1983: 1.) No doubt some extrascientific motives have entered the debate: cultural anthropologists dislike the animal perspective; progressive ideologists dislike pronouncements on "human nature"; the trend of our media, and possibly the hope of our generation, is toward man being nice and sociable. But some points of Lorenz's theory seem to be seriously undermined, such as his assertions about spontaneous, instinctive aggression in humans. I have not found any extensive discussion of the phenomenon that concerns us here, "the bond," i.e. solidarity wrought by common aggression; it seems to have been shuffled into the background, which is possibly a sign of some uneasiness. It is intriguing to note in this respect that the most dangerous variety, the welding together of a population in time of war by an outburst of patriotic enthusiasm, was tremendously effective in 1914 but did not work at all in the United States during the Vietnam War. Evidently there is no simple, predictable mechanism. I suspect the change has something to do with the news media. Aggressive solidarity, on the other hand, is still found to work nicely at protest demonstrations: confronting the authorities and the police, youngsters still experience the sacred shivers of awe.

Critics of aggression theories have often remarked that aggression itself is not too well defined. Are there just different variants of aggression, or are totally separate phenomena involved in the concept? Already, Konrad Lorenz has made a clear distinction between a carnivore's behavior in catching its prey and intraspecific aggression, which is accompanied by bad temper, grim facial expression, menacing gestures. Others have made more subtle distinctions.[16] I held that the human hunter would be a special case: being trained to kill against his instincts and heritage, man would experience the man-animal equivalence and thus mix impulses of aggression with the craft of hunting (Burkert 1983: 19f). It is difficult to prove this empirically.

There might well be present, or develop in certain individuals, a special "killing instinct," a unique and thrilling experience, an experience of power, of breakthrough, of triumph.[17] Is this a psychic response in its own right, proper to humans, or is it, as the "sacred shiver of awe" may indicate, still another mask of general aggressive behavior?

Whatever the answer may be, the difference for a theory of hunt and sacrifice would not be decisive. We are still entitled to assume a "shock of killing," a mixture of triumph and anxiety, a catharsis of destructive impulses and the readiness to make amends. This is what the evidence from attested hunting rituals and sacrificial rituals indicates—the shrill cry (*ololyge*), the expressions of guilt, the "comedy of innocence," wailing, disclaimers of responsibility, chas-

---

[16]See Moyer 1968. Compare Johnson 1972: 21: "While aggression and predation should not be confused, it is not always possible to make simplistic distinctions between the two."

[17]Compare the explanation of human sacrifice proposed by Davies (1981: 282): "Reaching out for something higher than himself, man was driven to kill so as to placate his idols with the greatest prize of all, a human life." Washburn and Lancaster (1968: 299f) speak of the "pleasures of killing."

ing the sacrificer, attempts at restoration. In this context, it is essential to remember what has been said about ritual tradition in general: there is no need to postulate general human emotions to generate rituals; rather, it is a certain ritual tradition that has encouraged—nay, selected and taught—special responses, and that has proved to be a successful strategy in the competitive games of historical evolution. The ritualization of killing, the rules of guilt and amends, may be viewed as an age-long education to responsibility in a context of authority and solidarity; religious civilization has emerged as an "evolutionarily stable strategy."

Nothing of the like is found in chimpanzees: they apparently have no feelings of guilt, they exhibit just the faintest signs of grudge. They evidently fail to realize the time dimension, the consequences of the past, the demands of the future. Man, by contrast, is painfully aware of this dimension, the main characteristic of which is irreversibility. The most drastic experience of irreversibility, however, is death. This is both acknowledged and overcome by ceremonial killing. It is striking to see how much sacrifice in ancient religion is concerned with the time dimension: through prayers, vows, and thanksgiving with new vows, sacrifices form a continuous chain that must never be broken; any important enterprise starts with sacrifice as a first step that cannot be taken back. On the synchronic level, reciprocity is installed in a community through sacrifice, the sharing of guilt, and the sharing of food; on the diachronic level, fictional reciprocity is also seen to occur, from remuneration to resurrection. Thus the experience of sacrifice may be seen not only in its emotional, but also in its cognitive relevance. No wonder the two main forms of religious ritual in the large sense are concerned with death: burial rites and sacrificial rites.

Alternative Models

I still find it remarkable that *Violence and the Sacred* and *Homo Necans* were originally published in the same year (1972). Both books have much that is parallel in argument and elaboration, including the interest in Greek tragedy; some common background, of course, is provided by Freud's *Totem and Taboo* and Lorenz's *On Aggression*. The main difference consists in the reconstruction of the "original scene" (to avoid the Freudian term "primal scene").

Instead of deriving ceremonial killing and eating from the hunt, René Girard describes an outbreak of intrahuman violence as the hidden center of social dynamics: an accumulation of "mimetic desire" erupts into violence that concentrates on a victim chosen by chance; after the victim's annihilation, order is restored at the price of the secret crime.

There are clear advantages to this construct, as compared with the many controversial items of evolutionary history adduced in *Homo Necans*. There is no need to hypothesize about evolution or even animal behavior, and the equivalence of man and animal plays quite a secondary role. In fact, Girard is not primarily interested in ritual; works of literature turn out to be the more revealing sources. He insists on the real occurrence of persecution; however, it is not the bare facts, but the psychological mechanisms that produce, transform, and hide them that are the objects of inquiry.

What troubles me from the viewpoint of Mediterranean religious rituals is that Girard's "original scene" seems to combine what appear to be two distinct patterns: the scapegoat, or pharmakos, and the Dionysiac *sparagmos* (tearing to pieces). The elaborations in classical literature would be *Oedipus the King* on the one side, and Euripides's *Bacchae* on the other. The salient difference is that Oedipus, assuming the role of the pharmakos, is not killed violently but voluntarily led away (cf. Burkert 1979: 59-77; and on rituals of aversion, Burkert 1981). If there is annihilation in the scapegoat complex, it is characteristically left to "the others," to hostile forces, be they demons or real enemies. The basic action seems to be abandonment. It is different with normal sacrifice, which through killing leads to the communal meal. *Sparagmos* may be seen as an exaggerated, paranoiac variant of this, with the Bacchae regressively transformed into bestial predators: "Now share the meal" (Eur. Bacch. 1184; on abnormal forms of sacrifice as an expression of marginal or protest groups, see Detienne 1979: chap. 4). This is linked to another difficulty I have with Girard's model: the basic fact that man has always eaten animals in sacrifice comes in only as an additional, secondary trait, a form of deterioration. Similar preconceptions may be found in many an account of sacrifice in standard works on the history of religion. Scholars concentrate on what they consider to be the pure and religious side of the matter and leave in the dark the practical question of what finally happens to the "offerings"; only additional inquiry will show that these are normally brought back for human consumption.

Yet the scapegoat complex, raised to such prominence through the work of Girard, is an important phenomenon that is not accounted for in *Homo Necans*. The abandonment of the scapegoat and related forms of "purification" sacrifice, and even ritual killings termed purge and substitution, cannot be directly derived from the hunting-and-eating complex. Perhaps this is a case where monogenetic theories break down. Even Meuli did not claim to explain all forms of sacrifice with his model of hunting, but only the "Olympian" form of the Greek sacrificial feast. In my book *Structure and History* (1979: 71), I sketch quite another "original scene": the group surrounded by predators that will give up only if at least one member of the group falls victim to them.

The dominant force in this complex, as far as I see, is not aggression and violence, but anxiety. There may be seasonal cathartic "purges," but the main testimonies point to exceptional situations of danger—notably famine, war, and disease. The main message conveyed by the ritual is the separation of the victim bound for annihilation from all those others destined for salvation. There is often an insistence on the "free will" of the victim (which recalls the hunters' "comedy of innocence"); a strange and strong ambivalence is seen to arise: the victim is the outcast and the savior at the same time. It can be argued that with this we are closer to the essence of sacrifice than with the sacralized feast.

There need not be direct killing in the pharmakos complex, though it must be ensured that the scapegoat does not return: this would mean catastrophe. Hence instead of slaughter we often find other forms of annihilation, such as drowning or burning. The Aztec myth about the birth of sun and moon from victims "voluntarily" leaping into the fire, treated in Girard's recent book (1982: 85ff), is a memorable example. But there are also elaborate forms of slaughter and the manipulation of blood in rituals of aversion, and they are expressly said to mean the substitution of life for life. This is especially explicit in rituals from ancient Mesopotamia, where the demons are imagined as greedy carnivores and must accordingly be fed with surrogate victims, and in "Saturnus" inscriptions from Roman Africa.

Perhaps it is not by chance that scapegoat has become a part of our modern vocabulary, a metaphor for reactions and events that still happen in our society. It is possible that behavior of this kind results spontaneously under certain circumstances—presupposing, of course, the role of aggression in group organization and individual reactions. In this case, I do not claim a direct continuity of ritual from the "original scene" of threatening predators. Our reactions and images of anxiety may well go back to prehuman levels, but it is only with the specifically human realization of the time dimension that the prevenient expulsion of a victim can take place. Nothing of the kind has been observed in chimpanzees.

In the Mediterranean civilizations, nevertheless, scapegoating was an established ritual tradition, and comparable data are reported from elsewhere. If we try to interpret the signals contained in such action patterns, we may note the reversal from passive anxiety to aggressive activity as there emerge from the crowd both the active executioners—the priests, the Lord of Sacrifice—and the chosen victim. Catastrophe is going to happen, but it is determined and limited by the sacred officials. Anxiety is transformed into manipulation, and the fixed pattern seems to ensure the auspicious outcome. Comparable actions, well attested in ethnography, are self-wounding and finger sacrifice.

We may be content to state the coexistence of several forms of sacrifice. In ancient Greece, this would be *apotropaia thyein* versus *charisteria thyein*, or aversion-sacrifice versus feast-sacrifice; in Mesopotamia, blood offerings to demons versus divine worship. Yet it is precisely ceremonial killing that draws together the separate lines; clear distinction will be difficult in many cases. There must have been considerable overlapping in the course of time. If the reversal from passivity to activity can be more precisely termed a change of roles from the hunted to the hunter, overcoming the fear of death by the power of killing, we would be back to the model of the primate turned carnivore. What is more, we do find a sort of cooperation of the two roles in the institution of priesthood: the Lord of Sacrifice, owner of property but haunted by insecurity, gives up part of his possessions to the priests who, through butchering and the distribution of meat, act out the hunter's legacy (cf. Burkert 1979: 119 on *galloi*) and make their living. Such a synthesis might be the foundation of sacrifice proper. But more material would be needed to substantiate this idea.

Theophrastus, in his influential book *On Piety*, argued that Phoenician and Greek sacrifice had developed from cannibalism (see Bernays 1866; Pötscher 1964). This was how he explained both the labyrinthine preliminaries and disclaimers and the central role of eating in sacrificial ritual. Cannibalism has been observed among chimpanzees. Some findings of the Lower Paleolithic—indeed, nearly the first indications of symbolic activity by man—are uncannily suggestive of cannibalism.[18] This applies to the skulls of Monte Circé and possibly already to the Peking man of Chou Kou Tien. There is evidence from the Upper Paleolithic, the Neolithic, and even later periods that can hardly be denied. A startling discovery recently came from Minoan Knossos (Warren 1981). In classical Greece, the rumors about the Lykaia festival in Arcadia were the most notorious case, apart from what was told about secret terrorist organizations (Burkert 1983: 84-93; Heinrichs 1972: 31-37, 48-53). Myths abound with motives of anthropophagy. But cannibalistic ideology has even entered religious formulas. A well-known example occurs in the ancient Egyptian pyramid texts. The Gnostic "Gospel of Philip" writes: "God is a man-eater. For this reason men are [sacrificed] to him. Before men were sacrificed, animals were being sacrificed, since those to whom they were sacrificed were no gods" (C.G. II 62f.; Robinson 1977: 138). A strange form of progress indeed. I refrain from quoting the New Testament.

Anthropologists have noted that there are hardly any eyewitness accounts of cannibalism; the practice is usually attributed to "the others"; some have doubted whether it ever occurred as an institution in reality. I think we cannot be too optimistic. I am afraid one could, in the wake of Theophrastus, in fact construe an "original scene" in which horror and joy, breakthrough, triumph, and remorse were inherent in such a way as to elicit the experience of "the Sacred," and one could draft "evolutionarily stable strategies" with

[18]Skull rituals are even earlier attested than burial; see P. V. Tobias (in Young 1982: 48), and for a survey on cannibalism, Davies 1981.

moderate cannibalism as a successful device. The force of such a tradition might still be seen in the fact that on the secret market of video, as can be read in our newspapers, cannibalism is a very big hit just now.

Protest against such a hypothetical construction must finally rely on common sense, on the hopeful argument that the normal and sane should be prior to the abnormal, the necessary and functional prior to the bizarre. In my view, the "hunting hypothesis" still envisages the one situation in which killing is as legitimate and necessary as it can possibly be, namely, the quest for food in the competitive system of life. I tried to show the hermeneutical value of the hypothesis in interpreting myths and festivals in *Homo Necans*; from this, though, plausibility may arise, but no proof. The multiplicity of concurrent factors is not to be denied; every account can give only a reduced and simplified picture. Possibly some of the inadequacies can be relieved by a common effort in "conversations."

This has been an attempt at a theory of tradition. I am afraid it does not help much in dealing with the problems of our time, problems of a world profoundly changed through technology and totally new forms of communication. It would be absurd even to think of reintroducing sacrificial ritual. Yet we are apparently less able than before to control violence, which remains both real and fascinating. We largely agree about human rights and human values, but we are at a loss about the moral education of our children; we have lost the "good conscience complex." We may still hope to arrive, at least, through our studies, at a "condensed reflection of the human situation" (Mack); we still perceive some kind of wisdom in the ancient traditions, wisdom pertaining to compensation and balance in a limited world pervaded by the continuing process of death and life.

Discussion

WALTER BURKERT: The paper I wrote for this conference does not claim to solve every problem; it is an attempt to localize certain questions. It has two parts: one deals with ritual in general; the other, with animal sacrifice in particular. I shall not dwell too much on the first part, which is surely preliminary and one-sided. Its main purpose is to show that ritual is tradition, that those who practice it have not invented it: it is learned, on the lines prescribed by the biological blueprint we all share. It is often not understood initially by those who practice it, but it gradually becomes integrated into a cosmos of sense.

The second part takes as its basis two groups of what I think are hard facts. Animal sacrifice, at least the form most practiced in ancient Greece, Israel, and many other contexts, is a scandal, because it makes killing animals and eating them a sacred affair, a religious act, or even *the* religious act. (Sacrifice has usually been understood as an "offering," but this involves problems already indicated by Hesiod; after all, why must we *kill* the animals in order to turn them over to the gods, the lords of life?) On the other hand, sharing meat is a fundamental phenomenon in human society. The distribution of food is unique to man; it is one of the few universals of human civilization; and it is basically linked to the distribution of meat, not cucumbers or coconuts. Food sharing is not found among primates, except for a certain behavior among chimpanzees when they hunt and eat small animals. (Distribution in this case is rather a process of begging; nevertheless, this seems to be related to the human distribution of meat as a kind of foreshadowing.)

Thus the sequence "to kill–to distribute–to eat" is a very general and most important configuration in the construction of human society. It evidently evolved in Paleolithic hunting and provided the guidelines for animal sacrifice. Ritual killing and eating are religious acts because they are essentially the ritual representation of the distribution and consumption of meat. Insofar as sacrifice is termed an offering, the phenomenon of food sharing is presupposed.

There is another form of "sacrifice" that I have outlined in *Structure and History*:[1] the handing over of another person, or an animal, to persecutors in lieu of oneself. This is the scapegoat pattern, a sacrifice made out of anxiety, out of a feeling of being persecuted. A parallel form seems to be self-mutilation—for example, finger sacrifice, as known in many civilizations and even in Greek mythology. This may represent a special line of psychological response to anxiety that could be ritualized (i.e., become a repeatable pattern to be used when dealing with anxiety). I have not succeeded in linking together these two kinds of sacrifice, the latter sacrifice of aversion and the former feast-sacrifice. They may perhaps be linked by the fact that the experience or expertise of killing is involved in both, even in the scapegoat pattern.

RENÉ GIRARD: I have a question about the special line of sacrifice that derives from hunting. How can you isolate such a line, since there are no parts of primitive culture that are not connected with sacrifice? The enthronement of the king, justice, the processing of metal—all of these involve sacrifice. Voltaire said that religion is everywhere, having been carried there by greedy, selfish priests for their own purposes. But if he's wrong and the priests are not really to blame, then it must have gotten everywhere in another manner.

In your paper, you say that hunting is *the* activity in which killing is necessary. Now, I don't see a necessary conflict between my position and the hunting hypothesis, but could hunting not have come from sacrifice, rather than the other way around?

And, by the way, where you distinguish pharmakos and *sparagmos*, you confuse what I say. The big mistake people make about me is to think that I take one part of ritual behavior and annex everything else to it. Nevertheless, I must admit that I have not distinguished well enough between these two. For example, I would

[1]Burkert 1979: 71 ff.—ED.

say that the mob murder of Louis XIV's court favorite involved both a pharmakos and a *sparagmos*.

BURKERT: We may speak about human behavior at three levels: ritual, myth, and "reality" or "real history." There may be an underlying pattern common to all—in this case, something like an outbreak of mob violence. In *Violence and the Sacred*, you did speak about the level of ritual, not just about the third, the historical level.

GIRARD: Yes, I do mix up the level of ritual with that of the historical too much in that book.

BURKERT: Regarding the question of the sequence of hunting and sacrifice, it's possible to say, logically, that either hunting comes from sacrifice or sacrifice comes from hunting. But if one looks at the historical evidence, the second alternative seems more likely. As to the universality of sacrifice, I tried to show, using Lorenz, that the hunt is a special form of cooperation, which would make understandable why all forms of association are founded on sacrifice.

JONATHAN SMITH: Let me try to defend Burkert against Burkert. Though we share little, what I find impressive about his work is his ability to say a lot, and to make distinctions while saying a lot. I find this insistence on making distinctions critical because, if all is religion or all is scapegoat, then we've learned nothing.

GIRARD: I must protest!

SMITH: The second point I want to make concerns the way Burkert relates the phenomena he distinguishes. The question then becomes how one should understand those relationships—are they genetic, formal, or what? If we are to make distinctions, then we must also deal with definitions. I know of no ethnographic monograph published in the last twenty years in which the term sacrifice appears in the index. My conclusion is that there is no "sacrifice" until we invent it. We imagine it and then go out and find it.[2] My major question has to do with how you articulate this relationship between hunting and sacrifice. Sometimes it seems genetic, sometimes formal, sometimes even psychological. I hope you will not concede the

[2]See J. Smith 1982a.—ED.

universality of sacrifice, even though that would make my job easier.

GIRARD: Jonathan has said something very important here, namely, that all our notions of sacrifice are determined by our Judeo-Christian concepts. But would we have a better view of sacrifice if we were Polynesians? Not necessarily. This radical skepticism is right, but it is only half the truth. The first appearance of the term scapegoat in the common, vulgar sense was in the sixteenth century. I'm sure the Greeks and Romans couldn't have formed the concept in just that way, but that doesn't mean the process was absent in their societies.

BURKERT: I do think distinctions are very important. The question of the *genus proximum*, the phenomenon itself, within which we wish to make distinctions, is no less important. I cannot really agree with the thesis that there is no such thing as "sacrifice." For one thing, ethnography is no longer very interested in religion, so perhaps it is only natural that the term does not appear in monographs.

Marcel Detienne, too, wrote that sacrifice is a modern notion, arbitrarily constructed on a Judeo-Christian basis; but he would not doubt that *thysia* existed in the ancient Greek polis.[3] We may then, as Theophrastus did, discern similar rites among the Phoenicians, the Hebrews, and others. Amongst all of these there are differences, but there are also similarities. We are entitled to speak of a "family" of phenomena called "sacrifice" (here I am thinking of Wittgenstein's concept of "family" relations).

Regarding the universality of sacrifice, what I thought René meant was, for example, making a sacrifice when you build a house, when someone is sick, etcetera. These activities remain in the same "family" of phenomena. Finally, Jonathan says that if everything is scapegoat, we have learned nothing; but I don't quite agree. This structure is very complicated, paradoxical, and effective; one does gain something by elucidating and understanding it.

SMITH: Let me pick up on your word tradition. (I don't like sacrifice, but I do like tradition.) I need to understand better how you're charting the traditions you are investigating. In your work, there is

[3]See Detienne 1979: 34.—ED.

a relatively direct line between the quest for food and the language of sacrifice, but there is only a relatively indirect line of relationship between the different forms of sacrifice itself. So, the items animal/food quest/sacrifice are directly related. *Then* we get to the small span of the historical, and things get much more complicated. Why is it that, if the four thousand years are so complicated, the preceding four million years are so uncomplicated?

BURKERT: That is because of the kind of evidence we have. For the historical period, we have texts, and so things are seen to be quite complicated. It is like using a microscope that brings out all the details. For the rest, we don't have the microscope. One might say everything is then only guesswork; but there is some justification for a macroscopic view; there are some configurations that can be understood. One can reconstruct models that, though clumsy, may tentatively be correlated with examples we happen to know in some detail.

SMITH: That's true, of course; but imaginatively—do we not have to imagine the pre-writing era as being just as complex as the later period? Do we imagine a simplicity or that, as far back as we can go, all the ambiguities would be there?

BURTON MACK: Let me rephrase Jonathan's question. In your paper, Walter, you referred to Jonathan's concept of discontinuities; and he seems to be asking about that now. He sees in *Homo Necans* a pattern of linear continuity for that early period, but when you come to the Greek period, you have to deal with shifts, breaks, misunderstandings, etcetera. You might need to talk about a more human basis of religion, rather than an ethological one.

BURKERT: But it might be the case that the evolution of civilization did proceed at different paces in different periods. It could be that there was less change in prehistoric times, and that lines of continuity could have been maintained, without interruption, better than in historical times. We may also note that even through breaks and misunderstandings there is a chance of maintaining some understanding of sense, and hence some stability of tradition.

SMITH: Take the example of setting up the bones of slaughtered animals. It could be that many different understandings are represented by ostensibly identical actions. The question is whether or not, in theory, we must presume the same understanding for all lone setups. The bones could represent an insignia, a trophy, a resurrection—there are all sorts of possibilities. Secondly, we do know certain kinds of histories, especially from the ethnographic literature. It's obvious that pre-writing cultures are embroiled in many of the same kinds of disagreements as we are. So, don't we have to assume disagreement even from the first two guys who crawled out of Olduvai Gorge? And finally, there is the question of whether we have to assume cultural crosscurrents and syncretism from the very beginning.

BURKERT: You're right, there could be many different interpretations; but if we look at the situation from the viewpoint of ritual, that is, of what people do, then it looks much more stable and continuous.

GIRARD: In the relationship of the hunter to the animal, you attach much importance to the "comedy of innocence." Can that come originally from humans interacting just with animals?

BURKERT: That's a very good question. The "comedy" is not found among bushmen, for instance.

SMITH: It's not found where people aren't pastoralists.

BURKERT: As I say, it's not found among everyone, but one thing is clear: other primates don't behave that way.

GIRARD: One must note the fact that, in sacrifice, before the victim is sacrificed, he, she, or it is made to appear guilty. The maneuvers between victim and sacrificers are multiple and varied, and will not be the same in every culture.

BURKERT: In a way, we're talking about two sides of the same coin. Both show sacrificers dealing with the victim in an atmosphere of responsibility, that is, of guilt.

GIRARD: So we are brought back to some original duality of the victim, the latter being both very bad and very good. Isn't it necessary to have some original matrix, from which things could go either way?

BURKERT: I think this might be possible. The fact of guilt discloses two sides.

GIRARD: For me, the invention of guilt itself can't be psychological. It must be based on the scapegoat mechanism. I'm looking for a genetic scheme, where all the potentials are present at the beginning; some are exploited, others are not.

MACK: The two originary scenes are up against each other here. René is asking: if the invention of guilt is to be accounted for by the mechanism of the scapegoat, then how can the animal have been the first scapegoat? doesn't it have to have been a human at first?

BURKERT: It could have been the similarity between the animal and the human: in the hunt, you *must* treat an animal, which is so similar to a human, in just the way you must *not* treat a human.

GIRARD: But if we have a genetic scheme beginning from the scapegoat mechanism, that act will serve as a model. It can become the hunt, the sacrifice—whatever. We can trace all these forms back to the scapegoat without reducing them.

BURKERT: That is a fascinating possibility. The reason I started from the hunt is that it's simple and universal, and would have been practiced for a long time. In your hypothesis, there are problems similar to those of *Totem and Taboo*. You must presuppose a certain mechanism of human psychology that makes all this possible. The evolutionary question is, then, how did this mechanism come about? At one time? Gradually?

GIRARD: At a certain level, it doesn't matter who the scapegoat is. If it's an animal, then the situation must be tied up with a mimetic fascination for that animal. So many myths and novels tell of animals acting collectively to kill. Think, for example, of the scene in *The Jungle Book* where Mowgli is threatened by a pack of dogs. He escapes by stirring up a swarm of bees, which then turn on the dogs. It is as though there were a ring of concentric circles, with Mowgli at the center, surrounded by dogs, surrounded by bees.

FRITS STAAL: Jonathan's point about "sacrifice" falling out of use in ethnography is right, but this may be only a matter of terminology. If you were to look at India today, you would find much ritual but little sacrifice. I am reminded of the fact that, in most monasteries of Tibet, there is an ibex head on the wall. It doesn't figure in Buddhist rites, but it does in exorcisms. In the Vedic period, the simplest rituals were those using vegetables; more complex were animal rituals, and more complex still were the soma rituals. The distinction among the three types, from the point of view of the ritualists, was not great. You don't find anything like a "comedy of innocence" in Vedic ritual. You do find rituals of expiation, in case a mistake is made in the performance of the original ritual.

BURKERT: These ibex heads you mention are probably related to a form of apotropaic ritual. They are used in warding off evil of one sort or another. Your comment about the scarcity of sacrifice in modern India is well taken, but there has no doubt been a historical development there. Regarding the three types of sacrifice you listed, if you dispense with the soma innovation, you have animal sacrifice at the top of the hierarchy, just as in Mediterranean religions.

GIRARD: Simon Levi has written about Vedic ritual. He says that soma is a god and is not happy to be sacrificed. One is never to deal commercially with soma. When one is ready to sacrifice it, one gives the leaves to a vagabond and buys them back so that the god gets mad at him, not you. Also, when the sacrifice is made, one thinks of an enemy.

STAAL: Yes, these associations between sacrifice and violence are felt, but the soma-merchant reference can be taken simply to show that the trading of soma was illegal. Why, we do not know. After all, the priests buy all the other accoutrements of the sacrifice. Someone comes to the priests with soma, they haggle, then the priests simply grab it.

GIRARD: Here the similarity to the pharmakos is quite striking.

BURKERT: Buying the animal for sacrifice also plays some role in Greek religion.

GIRARD: And recently, there has been evidence that money may have originated in sacrificial ritual.

TERRELL BUTLER: I'd like to refer back to Jonathan's earlier comments on making distinctions. René is able to make distinctions, and with the use of a simple concept.

STAAL: But it should not be *too* simple.

GIRARD: No, there is no concept, because the concept is ritualized.

BURKERT: A model?

GIRARD: No, I want to show that the vulgar sense of scapegoat goes back to the time when Western society stopped punishing witches. The first use of psychological repression comes when one says that even though there is a collectivity of people in agreement, they can still all be wrong. We live in a world that can assume that there is no truth. No primitive culture could say that.

SMITH: You can't mean that. Every version of a myth represents a process of intellection.

GIRARD: But I am saying that there is a certain kind of myth represented by mob action, and that that was never questioned.

SMITH: It *was* questioned. One group would say, "This is *our* turf," and another group would say, "No, it's *ours*."

GIRARD: But no one would say, "It's all bunk."

SMITH: I think they would. The disintegration of culture began with culture itself.

GIRARD: Greek tragedy does try to question collective representation, very underhandedly. Also, look at Job. He says, "Thanks to me the good people feel better, and the bad people feel worse. I hold society together."

SMITH: When you have the unmasking of the actors after the ceremony, is that an act of criticism of collective representation, or has the unmasking been subsumed by that representation? Look at the Ndembu.[4] Their ceremony constitutes a serious questioning of the adequacy of representation.

GIRARD: I'd say ritual is alive when it's subsumed, but it's not subsumed to the extent that the sense of worship is dead. This ambiguity you're talking about is not the destruction of ritual.

SMITH: But criticism is not destruction. My question was whether the unmasking amounted to a criticism.

[4]Turner 1967, 1968.—ED.

GIRARD: But every myth or ritual includes criticism of the structure it sets up. That is its genius. The process of criticism is not static. It's one thing to burn someone at the stake, but quite another to engage in scholarly debate.

ROBERT HAMERTON-KELLY: Walter, in your paper, you talk about the originary scene proposed in *Structure and History*, pages 71ff. Does this scene represent an approximation of your views to René's scapegoat mechanism?

BURKERT: I think it is a form of René's scene, and it seems to be inherent in certain forms of sacrifice. The difference is that I am not talking about killing in this context, but about abandoning a selected substitute to the pursuer.

HAMERTON-KELLY: But are these two processes different? Whether you kill it or abandon it, it dies just the same.

GIRARD: Right. For instance, when you see the abandonment of malformed children, it seems different from the scapegoat mechanism because it appears to be more functional. The parents want to get rid of the child because it is ugly, because it will require more care, because they do not want it to reproduce—whatever. Therefore, it is regarded differently from seemingly senseless activities. Its claim to being any sort of "religious" behavior is discounted. The rule of thumb seems to be: if it's crazy, it must be "real" religion. Trampling grapes to produce wine isn't. Now, as to the contention in Jonathan Smith's paper that sacrifice occurs only among pastoralists, I feel that sacrifice comes before domestication. Look at the bear ceremony of the Ainu. They treat the victim like a child, but you cannot domesticate a bear. The societies that succeed with domestication are those that happen to pick animals that can be domesticated.

BURKERT: Jonathan, I agree that cultural disintegration began with culture, but isn't it true that certain institutions, such as religion, have been constructed to maintain continuity?

SMITH: Of course. But I'm asking whether one institutionalizes the institution and winks, or whether one institutionalizes the wink. What I question is whether there are institutions that don't wink at all. It's claimed that these institutions occur in some pristine unity among "primitive" peoples, but all you need is one wink and the whole thing starts to fall apart. I want to look for these institutional winks. Unless I assume these people are utterly "other," they must know about these winks. For example, the Ainu say that they actually nurse the bear. Now, surely they say yes, and surely they say no.

GIRARD: The nursing of the bear is a dramatization of taking the bear as one's own.

SMITH: But that presupposes that they know what they're doing.

BURKERT: Isn't the question, "What do the Ainu tell themselves?"

LANGDON ELSBREE: Isn't the question, "When does the wink become a sneer?" Parody and irony are quite distinct. Parody doesn't destroy what it parodies; irony does.

GIRARD: And often parodic behavior is the extreme of naïve and trusting faith. Take, for example, the medieval parodies of the mass.

STAAL: A typical element of ritual seems to be that people continue to do the same thing but change their interpretations of it.

GIRARD: So, you are a *ritual* man! It's been said that people sacrificed long before they had religion, but my question is, why did they sacrifice?

BURKERT: I think there are different levels of winking. For instance, there are foundational myths, which seem quite serious, but there are also trickster myths, which seem to question everything. Perhaps in any mythological system there is a kernel of seriousness that is not brought into question, and margins that are.

CESÁREO BANDERA: But even the question of believing or disbelieving is not of fundamental importance. The only important thing is to do the rituals in the prescribed manner. Until recently in rural Spain, it was customary to hire professional mourners for a funeral. Does the one paying actually believe they mourn? It doesn't matter; the practice was still taken very seriously.

SMITH: There's an enormous anachronism to the notion of the collective. Where we have good ethnography, it's always clear that myth and ritual are owned by certain subsets within the collective. But there are very few instances where the performance is restricted to the subset that owns it. The point is to question an assumption about collectivities that is undergirding much of this discussion. There is no myth or ritual that is not performed before people who are not a part of it, and who therefore would not argue about it. Pluralism is as old as humankind.

GIRARD: Are you questioning the social nature of ritual?

SMITH: I'm not questioning it in terms of fact, but in terms of scale. The diversity and pluralism of any so-called primitive society can be found to be as complicated as modern San Francisco.

BURKERT: But you could go on to say that actually you have individuals who, in ritual, may be united in certain groups that can then act collectively.

STAAL: In India, the Brahmans in effect "own" ritual, since only they can perform it, but myths can be told by anyone.

SMITH: Yes, there is a sense in which ritual is more stable than myth.

Three

JONATHAN Z. SMITH

The Domestication of Sacrifice

In their eagerness to plumb ritual's dark symbolic or functional
depths, to find in ritual more than meets the eye, anthropologists
have, perhaps increasingly, tended to overlook ritual's surface,
that which does meet the eye. Yet, it is on its surfaces, in its form,
that we may discern whatever may be peculiar to ritual.

R. A. Rappaport

I

One consensual element that appears to inform this "conversation on a theory of ritual" is a marked restlessness with the reduction of ritual to myth, and a concomitant concern with "action" as
a mode of human expression and experience that has a necessary
integrity of its own.[1] In the elaboration of such a point of view, little
will be gained by simply inverting past valences,[2] by adopting
Goethe's stratagem of substituting "in the beginning was the deed"
for "was the word." Although such an inversion could be questioned on logical grounds alone, there are other reasons more press-
ing to the concerns of this conversation. Chief among these is that,
in the case of man, speech and action are given together. Neither is
prior, in fact or in thought.[3] The connection is both so necessary

[1] Although from a theoretical perspective quite different from any adopted by the
major participants in this "conversation," see R. A. Rappaport's eloquent formulation (1979: 174): "It becomes apparent through a consideration of ritual's form that
ritual is not simply an alternative way to express certain things, but that certain
things can be expressed only in ritual." The epigraph is from the same page.

[2] I am speaking here at the level of theory. There is much to commend the detailed
investigations of a variety of scholars from Lévi-Strauss to Tambiah, which have
demonstrated that, in a wide variety of cultural situations, myth and rite often stand
in an inverse relationship to one another.

[3] Here, as elsewhere, I mean "social man."

and so intimate as to challenge all analogies where this duality is lacking (e.g., the animal on the one hand, the computer on the other). If action is not an "acting out" of speech, neither is speech a "secondary rationalization" of deed. In the history of this debate, much mischief has been done by the seemingly one-sided association of speech with thought and rationality, rather than perceiving action and speech, ritual and myth, as being coeval modes of human cognition.

Likewise, little will be gained by reinstating the old hierarchy by way of the back door. I have been struck by the desire of many who hold to the priority of action/ritual to find a story or a "primal scene" at the "origin" (itself, a narrative or mythological notion) of rite, be this expressed as tale or emotion, as articulate or inarticulate. In the one case, action has slid, all too easily, into "drama"; in the other, a consequence has been affirmed, all too readily, as a cause.

In thinking about a "theory of ritual," it would seem more fruitful to focus on the characteristics of those actions that, by one definition or another, *we* designate as "rituals," and to abstain from initial concern for content, which, among other problems, inevitably forces a premature return to myth. For me, in undertaking such an enterprise, the central theoretical works are two: Freud's brief essay "Zwangshandlungen und Religionsübungen" (1907) and the exasperating and controversial "Finale" to Lévi-Strauss's *L'Homme nu* (1971).

As is well known, Freud, in this first essay on religion, remarked on the resemblance between "what are called obsessive actions in sufferers from nervous afflictions and the observances by means of which believers give expression to their piety." The connection was to be found in the notion of "obsession," in the compulsion to do particular things and to abstain from others. The things done and the things not done are ordinary, "everyday" activities that are elaborated and made "rhythmic" by additions and repetitions. Obsessive acts in both individuals and rituals are described as the overwhelming concern for

little preoccupations, performances, restrictions and arrangements in certain activities of everyday life which have to be carried out always in the same or in a methodically varied way . . . elaborated by petty modifications [and] little details [accompanied by the] tendency to displacement [which] turns apparently trivial matters into those of great and urgent import.

In this early essay, the defining characteristic of ritual is "conscientiousness [toward] details": "Thus in slight cases the ceremonial seems to be no more than an exaggeration of an orderly procedure that is customary and justifiable; but the special conscientiousness with which it is carried out . . . stamps the ceremonial as a sacred act."[4]

In Freud's essay, although a set of five summarized cases are offered as examples of individual obsessive behavior, no specific examples of religious ceremonial are provided. In the chapter in Lévi-Strauss, the religious examples are specified as those instances where "a ritual ceremony has been recorded and transcribed in its entirety," which may "fill a whole volume, sometimes a very large one" and take "days" to perform.[5] Lévi-Strauss's characterizations of ritual are drawn from "thick" ethnographic texts, from transcripts of an entire ritual rather than from a brief ethnographic "snapshot." As such, they are to be given particular value.

Lévi-Strauss begins with the two questions that confront any theorist of ritual: how are we to define ritual? how are the actions in ritual to be distinguished from their close counterparts in everyday life? He answers both of these questions (like Freud) by way of a characterization: "In all cases, ritual makes constant use of two procedures: parcelling out [*morcellement*] and repetition." Parcelling out is defined as that activity where, "within classes of objects and types of gesture, ritual makes infinite distinctions and ascribes discriminatory values to the slightest shades of difference" (1981: 672 [1971: 601]). Parcelling out is what he elsewhere describes as the processes of "micro-adjustment" (*micro-péréquation*), which he holds to be the characteristic activity of ritual (1966: 10).

---

[4]Freud (1907: 26, 34). In presenting this aspect of Freud, I have deliberately abstained from his genetic account, which is here less important than his characterization, since it is only an analogy that is being proposed. A theory of ritual, in any case, could not be constructed on the basis of the 1907 essay alone. A far more interesting genetic proposal (although equally remote from my concerns) is his late notion of a "compulsion to repeat," as sketched out in *Beyond the Pleasure Principle* (1920). See Gay 1975; 1979: esp. Chap. 3.

[5]Lévi-Strauss's specific examples make clear that he is primarily thinking of the accounts in those thick, green *Reports* of the Bureau of American Ethnology. The documents he has in mind as parallel from Africa and Oceania are not specified.

Alongside this "infinite attention to detail" is the second characteristic, that of a "riot of repetition." Lévi-Strauss proposes a further reduction of these two characteristics: "At first glance, the two devices of parcelling out and repetition are in opposition to each other. . . . But, in fact, the first procedure is equivalent to the second, which represents, so to speak, its extreme development" (1981: 673). One does not have to be persuaded of the cogency of this reduction to accept the accuracy of the two characteristics.[6]

I have not cited these two theorists in order to urge acceptance of their theories (which are, in fact, thoroughly incompatible), but rather to insist on the accuracy of their complementary characterizations of the surface appearance of ritual. They have presented us with a prima facie case for what is distinctive in ritual. Freely paraphrasing, both insist that ritual activities are an exaggeration of everyday activities, but an exaggeration that reduces rather than enlarges, that clarifies by miniaturizing in order to achieve sharp focus. Collecting their terms, ritual is the realm of the "little," the "petty," the "trivial." It is the realm of "infinite distinctions" and "micro-adjustments." Ritual is primarily a matter not of nouns and verbs, but of qualifiers—of adjectives and adverbs. Ritual precises ambiguities.

While I would derive a host of implications from these characterizations for a "general theory of ritual,"[7] one is of particular impor-

[6]As in the case of Freud, so here I have abstained from accepting the implications that Lévi-Strauss perceives in this characterization of ritual (although they appear highly cogent to me, whereas his appeal to Dumézil does not). If myth (and language) are perceived as dichotomizing and contrastive, then "ritual, by fragmenting operations and repeating them unwearyingly in infinite detail, takes upon itself the laborious task of patching up holes and stopping gaps, and it thus encourages the illusion that it is possible to run counter to myth, and to move back from the discontinuous to the continuous" (Lévi-Strauss 1981: 674). Compare the formulation in Rappaport (1979: 206): "The distinctions of language cut the world into bits—into categories, classes, oppositions and contrasts. It is in the nature of language to search out all differences and turn them into distinctions. [It is] in the nature of liturgical orders to unite or reunite. . . . Liturgical orders are meta-orders. . . . They mend ever again worlds forever breaking apart under the blows of usage and the slashing distinctions of language." (See also pp. 127-28, 204, and passim.)

[7]These theoretical presuppositions underlie my attempt to develop a vocabulary for speaking of ritual. The notions of *focus* and *perfection* developed in "The Bare Facts of Ritual" (1980) have been more or less adequately described in Mack's Introduction; the notions of *experimentation* and, especially, *rectification*, developed in "A Pearl of Great Price" (1976), regrettably were not. (See note 10, below.)

tance for this conversation. To put it crudely, ritual is "no big deal."[8] The object of action that receives ritual attention is, more often than not, commonplace. The choice of this or that object for ritual attention often appears arbitrary.[9] But what is of prime importance is its infinite and infinitesimal elaboration in the manner that Freud and Lévi-Strauss have suggested.[10] One cannot single out a highly condensed or dramatic moment from the total ritual ensemble as if this, in some sense, was the "essence" of the ritual.

These considerations underscore the position that a theory of sacrifice (our specific topic for this conversation) cannot be found in a quest for origins, but can only be found through the detailed examination of elaborations. The idioms of sacrifice are diverse; the everyday acts it elaborates are manifold (e.g., butchering, eating, exchanging, gift-giving, greeting, displaying); the contexts in which sacrifice gets applied and rationalized are highly variegated. Until there is an adequate typology, accompanied by "thick descriptions" of exemplary ritual processes and ensembles, little progress will be made. To my knowledge, neither of these preconditions has been adequately fulfilled.

Let me make clear that this is not a request for more data, but a theoretical stance. I have tried to express this stance, in a quite different context, as a denial of

the privilege given to spontaneity as over against the fixed, to originality as over against the dependent, to the direct as over against the mediated. . . . This is expressed in the learned literature in a variety of dichotomies: religion/magic, individual/collective, charisma/routinization, communion/formalism, the text as direct speech over against the commentary and the gloss, the original or primordial over against the secondary or historical. In elegant form this privilege is expressed in the writings of a scholar such as

[8]As opposed to myth or to the mythology of a ritual, which may very well be a "big deal." (See note 6, above.)

[9]See the development of this in "The Bare Facts of Ritual" (1980). The object may, after all, as well be a cucumber as an ox. It is for this reason that I abstain from all questions about the etiology of the object of ritual attention (*pace* Mack's persistent questions to me on this point). I doubt, in most cases, whether the originating element is recoverable. If it is, it would be without theoretical interest.

[10]I have developed this, at some length, as the dynamic of *reduction* and *ingenuity* in "Sacred Persistence" (1982c: esp. 40-42), which is a statement explicitly intended to be read in conjunction with "Bare Facts"—and unfortunately ignored in Mack's summary.

Adolf Jensen for whom all truth, meaning, and value is located in what he describes as a primal moment of ontic "seizure," a "revelation," a "direct cognition." The first verbal "formulation" of this experience, its first "concretization" is an "intuitive, spontaneous experiencing" which he terms, "expression." All subsequent "formalizations" and "concretizations" are reinterpretations of this primal experience which Jensen terms "applications" (for him, a pejorative). All "applications" fall under the iron "law of degeneration" resulting in the original "spontaneity" becoming a "fixed but no longer understood routine." [In contradistinction, I would propose an enterprise that would insist on] the value of the prosaic, the expository, the articulate. It is to explore the creativity of what I have termed in another context, "exegetical ingenuity," as a basic constituent of human culture. It is to gain an appreciation of the complex dynamics of tradition and its necessary dialectics of self-limitation and freedom. To do these things . . . is to give expression to what I believe is the central contribution that religious studies might make, . . . the realization that, in culture, there is no text, it is all commentary; that there is no primordium, it is all history; that all is application. The realization that, regardless of whether we are dealing with "texts" from literate or non-literate cultures, we are dealing with historical processes of reinterpretation, with tradition. That, for a given group at a given time to choose this or that way of interpreting their tradition is to opt for a particular way of relating themselves to their historical past and their social present.[11]

Despite the above, although a quite different enterprise from my usual agendum, in accommodation to what appears to be one of the dominant concerns of the present conversation, I will venture a highly tentative suggestion on the possible activity that achieved prime elaboration in sacrifice.

II

From the immense variety of human ritual activities, a few have been lifted out by scholars as privileged examples on which to build theories of ritual—preeminently sacrifice, New Year's scenarios, and male initiatory rites. Each of these three seems to entail quite different consequences for scholarship. The choice of which one is to be

[11]J. Smith 1983: 223-24. This is a fundamental attitude underlying my recent work, as adumbrated in the Foreword to *Imagining Religion* (1982a), as well as in "Sacred Persistence," "Bare Facts," and "Pearl of Great Price," to mention those essays most directly relevant to our conversation.

taken as exemplary is one of great significance. Having said this much, let me note that, among this small group, animal sacrifice has often appeared to be primus inter pares, primarily because it has seemed (at least to the scholarly imagination) quintessentially "primitive." Perhaps the first question that ought to be asked is, Is this the case?[12]

The putative "evidence" for the primitivity of animal sacrifice is far from compelling. Though there are obvious questions of definition, of what counts, I know of no unambiguous instance of animal sacrifice that is not of a domesticated animal. The Paleolithic indications for sacrifice are dubious. I know of no unambiguous instance of animal sacrifice performed by hunters. *Animal sacrifice appears to be, universally, the ritual killing of a domesticated animal by agrarian or pastoralist societies.* Where it occurs in groups otherwise classified, it is still of a domesticated animal, usually in the context of a highly developed "exchange (or display)" ideology.[13] Furthermore, though I am unhappy with many of the interpretative implications developed from the familiar dual typology, where there are articulate native systems of animal sacrifice, they do appear to fall into the categories of gift-offering-display and/or pollution removal. Neither gives comfort to primitivity. The former seems to require a developed notion of property, the latter the complex ideological and social hierarchies of pure/impure. As best as I can judge, sacrifice is not a primitive element in culture. Sacrifice is a component of secondary and tertiary cultures. It is, primarily, a product of "civilization."

Why, then, the preoccupation with the primitivity of sacrifice? Beyond its obvious resonances with elements of our past, with Greco-Roman and Judeo-Christian religious systems and practices, I suspect that sacrifice allows some scholars the notion that here, in this

[12]I have abstained from the question of human sacrifice and other modes of the ritual killing of humans (headhunting, cannibalism, "sacral regicide," etc.), which are often too readily homologized with animal sacrifice. The evidence for these practices is frequently less certain than for animal sacrifice—often being more illustrative of intercultural polemics than cultural facts. Nevertheless, a rapid review would indicate that documented human sacrifice is present only in agricultural and pastoral cultures. The other modes of ritual killing, while requiring their own interpretations where their occurrence appears credible, are not to be classified as "sacrifice" (as Jensen, among others, has quite properly argued).

[13]See my "Note on the Primitivity of Animal Sacrifice" at the end of the paper.

religious phenomenon at least (or at last), is a dramatic encounter with an "other," the slaying of a beast. As I have suggested elsewhere, such a notion rests on an agrarian mythologization of the hunt and is not characteristic of what we can learn of the attitudes of hunting and gathering peoples toward the activities of hunting (1982a: 57-58). This agrarian reinterpretation (interesting and important as it is in itself) has allowed the scholarly fantasy that ritual is an affair of the *tremendum* rather than a quite ordinary mode of human social labor. It has allowed the notion that ritual—and therefore religion—is somehow grounded in "brute fact" rather than in the work and imagination and intellection of culture.

It may well be for these reasons that one of the other privileged modes of ritual, initiation, has not been so vigorously put forth as the exemplum of primitivity. This is surprising in light of the fact that many of those early reports that asserted that this or that primitive group had "no religion" (reports that led, ultimately, to the overdrawn theses of *Urmonotheismus*, particularly in the form of the "otiose High God"; see J. Smith 1982a: Chap. 5) specifically noted no sacrificial practices, but did report (often in lurid terms) the presence of initiatory practices and secret societies. It is my sense, after surveying a wide sample of literature, that sacrifice and initiation stand in an inverse ratio to each other: where there are elaborate initiatory rituals, sacrifice seems relatively undeveloped; where there are complex sacrificial cycles and ideologies, initiation seems relatively undeveloped. Indeed, I am tempted to suggest that initiation is for the hunter and gatherer and primitive agriculturalist what sacrifice is for the agrarian and pastoralist. But initiation is relentlessly an affair of "culture" rather than "nature," and one of making ordinary what appears to be an experience of the *tremendum*.[14] Furthermore, the temporal dimensions of initiation (at times an affair of twenty years, with highly ambiguous limits),[15] in contrast to the extreme binary compression and irreversibility of the sacrificial

[14]On imitation as an affair of culture, consider, for example, the lack of correlation between biological puberty and the so-called puberty initiations, already clearly perceived by A. van Gennep (1960: 65-71). On the making ordinary of the experience of the *tremendum*, consider, for example, the frequent phenomenon of the unmasking of the putative deities. (Cf. the survey in di Nola 1972 and the comments in J. Smith 1978a: 300-302.)

[15]For an extremely detailed description of an elegant example, see Tuzin 1980.

kill, make clear that initiation is an affair more of social labor than of drama.

Given these observations, I hazard the opinion that the starting point for a theory of sacrifice, that which looms largest in a redescription of sacrifice, ought no longer to be the verb "to kill," or the noun "animal," but the adjective "domesticated." Sacrifice is, in part, a meditation on domestication. A theory of sacrifice must begin with the domesticated animal and with the sociocultural process of domestication itself. In such an enterprise, we are aided by a recent rich literature on the historical processes of domestication, and on "domesticity" as a native, taxonomic category.[16]

Following current usage, domestication may be defined as the process of human interference in or alteration of the genetics of plants and animals (i.e., selective breeding). It is frequently, although not necessarily, associated with agriculture, which may be defined as the process of human interference in or alteration of the environment of plants and animals. Such processes of interference presuppose a variety of social developments and result in a variety of social consequences.

For an understanding of sacrifice (and other agrarian ritual activities), the most important consequence is an alteration of the sense of space and time. The most obvious spatial and temporal reorientation associated with domestication is signaled by the term "sedentary community." This marks a shift from the hunter-and-gatherer's social world of immediacy, skill, and chance to a social world of futurity and planning—of the capacity for continuity of time and place. This is apparent with respect to animals. Here the art of breeding is, as well, the art of selective killing. Some animals must be held separated out for several years until they reach sexual maturity. The bulk of the herd must be slaughtered while immature. In the domesticated situation (as the archaeological stratigraphy bears out), immature animals will be killed more frequently than mature ones, males more frequently than females, and so forth and so on. For the domesticator, killing is an act of precise discrimination with an eye to the future. It is dependent on the social acceptance of a

---

[16]For the historical processes, see, among others, Ucko & Dimbley 1969; E. Isaac 1970. For domestication as a taxonomic category, see, among others, Leach 1964; Tambiah 1969. See further J. Smith 1974.

"delayed payoff," as well as on the social acquisition of the intricate technology of sexuality and the concomitant pattern of settled dwelling.

If this everyday and continual activity of domestication is agrarian and pastoral man's prime mode of relating to the animal, then we can specify with precision the commonplace activity that is elaborated obsessively and intellectually in sacrifice, as well as its difference from the hunter's relationship to game: *sacrifice is an elaboration of the selective kill, in contradistinction to the fortuitous kill.*

Though I do not wish to strain the point, it does appear that the other elements characteristic of domestication have their concomitant elaborations in sacrifice. The notion of the "delayed payoff" is central to any but the most mechanical *do ut des* understanding of the gift structure of some sacrificial systems, but it is present in some pollution systems as well. (For example, in the Israelitic cult, washing with water works for immediate, advertent pollutions, whereas the *hatta'th* is for inadvertent impurities that one may or may not be aware of, or for pollutions that last more than a week.[17]) Furthermore, sacrifice is not fortuitous with respect to either time or place—it is highly determined and presumes a sedentary pattern.[18] Finally, in many sacrificial systems, the complex requirements for the physical and/or behavioral characteristics of a particular animal chosen (bred) for sacrifice, whether before or after the kill, represent to an extreme degree the same kinds of details that are sexually selected for by the breeder.[19]

All of these elements, governed in the majority of cases by elaborate, highly formalized rules, suggest that sacrifice is an exaggeration of domestication, a meditation on one cultural process by means of another. If domestication is a "focusing" on selected characteristics in the animal, a process of sexual "experimentation" that strives to achieve a "perfection" or "rectification" of the natural animal species (these terms, it will be recalled, are key elements in my

[17]This understanding of this element in the Israelitic system and its implications has been especially well worked out by Jacob Milgrom. See, among other works, Milgrom 1970; 1976: esp. 766-68.

[18]This characteristic was clearly perceived by Jensen (1963: 162), who used it as a point of marked contrast to headhunting.

[19]Each of these elements, presented here impressionistically, would have to be tested for frequency by means of detailed cross-cultural comparisons.

vocabulary for ritual; see Smith 1982a: 40-42), then sacrifice becomes a focus on this focus, an experimentation with this experimentation, a perfecting of this perfection, a rectification of this rectification. It can do this precisely because it is a ritual. *Sacrifice, in its agrarian or pastoral context, is the artificial (i.e., ritualized) killing of an artificial (i.e., domesticated) animal.*[20] Because sacrifice is inextricably related to alimentation and, therefore, to what I have elsewhere described as a basic cultural process of reduction and ingenuity, of food and cuisine (see Smith 1982a: 40-42), it is, perhaps, especially suited for this sort of meditation.

What has been proposed thus far could be further elaborated with respect to the taxonomies of domesticated animals in relation to humans, on the one hand, and to animals on the other.[21] Just as the role of the mask in initiation ceremonies, as interpreted by Victor Turner (1967: 105-8), where the artificial, radical mixture or juxtaposition of anatomical features from humans and animals serves as an occasion for cultural meditation on difference and relationship; so too in the case of a domesticated animal, which is, in some sense, a hybrid, a fabrication.[22] Furthermore, if the domesticated animal stands, in native taxonomies, between man and the wild animal, then, to invoke a more familiar scholarly idiom for sacrifice, the sacrificial animal stands in an analogous position between man and "the gods." The transactional character of both positions relativizes the apparent absolute difference. (Hence the frequently observed correspondence of kin taxonomies and rules for sexual relations to taxonomies for domesticated animals and rules for their eating or sacrifice.) Sacrifice accomplishes this not by sacramental-

[20]Perhaps this may account for the agrarian mythologization of the hunt, which exaggerates the "otherness" (i.e., the nonfabricated nature) of the wild beast. (See above; and J. Smith 1982a: 57-58.)

[21]See Leach 1964; Tambiah 1969. Here is an excellent example of the relation of ritual to myth (see note 6, above). The myths of domestication are relentlessly binary and contrastive. The etiquette and rituals concerning domesticated animals, in relation to both wild animals and humans, reduce this binary and contrastive characteristic by providing instances of almost infinite degrees of difference. Note that this is raised to the level of theory by Leach (1964: 62-63).

[22]This is in contradistinction to Lévi-Strauss's understanding of sacrifice as belonging to the "realms of continuity" (1966: Chap. 8, where this notion is developed in a contrast between sacrifice and totemism), which appears to be in contradistinction to his later theory of ritual as described above on the basis of *L'Homme nu.*

ism, but by an etiquette of infinite degrees and baroque complexities (for a good example, see Tambiah 1969: 142-43). But to develop such a thesis with any cogency and conviction demands particularities rather than generalities: the comparison of specific exemplary taxonomies of domesticates with specific exemplary sacrificial ensembles. The detail such a discussion would require goes well beyond the bounds of civil "conversation."

If Lévi-Strauss, through a discussion of wild animals in the "totemic" systems of hunters and gatherers, has taught us well that animals are "good to eat" and "good to think," then the domesticated animals in the sacrificial systems of agriculturalists and pastoralists may teach us, in analogous ways, that animals are "goods to eat" and "goods to think."

A NOTE ON THE PRIMITIVITY OF ANIMAL SACRIFICE

As is well known, the observations that "ritual killing is completely absent in the oldest known strata of culture," and that animal sacrifices are "almost exclusively of domestic animals, for they all occur in agricultural cultures" stand at the foundation of A. E. Jensen's theory of sacrifice and ritual killing (1963: esp. 162-90; quotes from pp. 162-63). Jensen uses these observations to reason to a different set of conclusions than those proposed here.

It would require a lengthy monograph to review critically all the putative evidence that has been adduced for the primitivity of animal sacrifice and to cite the evidence for the stark assertions made above. Since the issue of primitivity is without interest for me, someone else will have to provide such a work. (I would propose J. van Baal, the distinguished scholar of *dema*, who has more than once offered a similar assessment, although I share none of his presuppositions. See, among others, van Baal 1976: esp. 162; 1981: 67-73, 219-25, and passim.) However, some brief indications may be provided:

1. The Paleolithic evidence remains opaque to interpretation. Since the work of F. E. Koby (1951), the evidence for Paleolithic bear sacrifice has been rendered exceedingly doubtful (see Leroi-Gourhan 1971: 30-36; Burkert 1979: 167, n.3). This is extremely important because the only contemporary putative evidence for a wild animal being used in sacrifice is the circum-polar bear festival.

In fact, the bear festival does not fit, although it was used as the hermeneutic key to interpret the Paleolithic remains. (a) The peoples who practice the bear festivals are pastoralists, not hunters. While the figure of the "Master of the Animals" appears to be shared by them and some hunters (especially the Amerindians), among the latter there is no recorded sacrifice of wild game. The conception of the "Master" among the reindeer pastoralists is in the idiom of pastoralism (penning the animals and the like). It is possible that this is a notion independent from that of the "Master" among hunters. If not, it is a radical reinterpretation that forbids any easy synthesis. (b) In the circum-polar bear ritual, the animal is domesticated for a period of years before being slain. (c) In the case of the Ainu (for whom there is the best ethnographic documentation), both the most distinguished native Ainu anthropologist, K. Kindaichi (1949), and the bear festival's most distinguished recent interpreter, J. M. Kitagawa (1961), vigorously deny that the ritual should be classified as a sacrifice, seeing it instead as part of a complex structure of visit-and-return. (See further Smith 1982a: 59, and the literature cited on p. 144, n.24.) At the very least, the complex tissue of parallelism, invoked since the pioneering article by W. Koppers (1933), will have to be carefully reevaluated. Both terms of the proposed equation are in difficulty. The equation has been decisive in the literature on the primitivity of animal sacrifice.

2. On the issue of Paleolithic sacrifices, the evaluation of the evidence has been one of steady retreat from confidence to uncertainty. For example, J. Maringer, who confidently declared in 1952 that "the practice of sacrificing the head, skull and long bones of animals survived from earliest times right up to the Upper Paleolithic" (1960: 90), retreated by 1968 to declaring that sacrifice is not evident in Lower and Middle Paleolithic deposits, and that it is possible to speak "with relatively great certainty" ("*mit mehr oder minder grosser Sicherheit*") of animal sacrifices only in the Upper Paleolithic (1968: 271). Yet even here, strong alternative hypotheses that account for the "evidence" as nonsacrificial have been proposed (e.g., Pohlhausen 1953), as Maringer acknowledges (1968: 269-70).

3. The fact that sacrifices are invariably of domesticated animals in contrast to wild ones (and hence from a different "sphere" than

religious practices associated with hunters or Paleolithic man) was already quite properly insisted upon by L. Franz (1937). Several months of checking in a variety of ethnographic monographs have turned up no exceptions. Here, I distinguish between killing an animal in sacrifice and the postmortem offering of some portion of an animal routinely killed for food. The latter is certainly present among some hunters and gatherers.

There are occasions of the ritual killing and eating of wild animals in connection with initiatory rituals, most particularly initiations into secret societies. The Lele pangolin, made famous by M. Douglas (1957; and other works), would be an obvious example, although she gives no reliable description. I sharply distinguish this from sacrifice, and would classify the bulk of the instances known to me as modes of ordeal.

I would also note the interesting thesis—first developed by E. Hahn, C. O. Sauer, and others, and recently revived by E. Isaac (1963; 1970: 105-10; and elsewhere)—that animals were first domesticated for the purpose of sacrifice.

4. In the discussion of the primitivity of animal sacrifice, much depends on how one imagines hunters (Paleolithic or contemporary). I join in the consensus that there never was, and certainly is not now, a stage of pure hunting. Hunting is always in combination with gathering, with plant products making up the bulk of the diet (except in unusual cases, such as that of the Eskimos).

It is, of course, impossible to determine the diet of Paleolithic man. Only animal bones, mollusk shells, and the like can be preserved, not soft parts and vegetable substances. For contemporary hunters and gatherers, a figure that approximately 70 percent of their normal diet is vegetable occurs in a variety of cultural locales, from the Amazon to Australia (e.g., Reichel-Dolmatoff 1971: 11; Meggitt 1957: 143). Furthermore, if one examines a wide variety of ethnographic reports, it becomes clear that the meat portion of the diet, that which is the result of hunting, is composed largely of small mammals, birds, reptiles, eggs, insects, fish, and mollusks. *Mano a mano* combat with large carnivores is largely unreported. For example, among the Desana, although their mythology is largely concerned with jaguars, Reichel-Dolmatoff reports that "a man who goes to hunt for two or three days per week obtains approximately three catches, for example, a small rodent, an armadillo, and a few birds. In a month he can get three or four wild guinea pigs, two cavies and a monkey; a deer or a peccary every two months; and a tapir once a year" (1971: 13). If bored-through teeth (trophies?) are any indication of the results of a Paleolithic hunt, 56 percent of a wide sample of such teeth are those of fox and deer, and only 3 percent are of bear or wolf (Leroi-Gourhan 1971: 28).

Finally, as I insisted in "The Bare Facts of Ritual" (1980), we need to recognize the strong ideological component in hunting. Although men routinely gather, and women in some societies routinely hunt (e.g., Efe pygmies, Klamath Indians, Tasmanians, the Australian Tiwi), hunting is strongly marked as a prestigious male activity, even when the males rarely hunt. Though the native descriptions of killing strongly emphasize its *mano a mano* character, in some of those same societies, traps, stampedes, ambushes, and the like are widely employed.

5. I have not raised the issue, widely discussed in some German anthropological circles, that many of our present hunting-and-gathering societies may be derivative from earlier agricultural societies (e.g., Narr 1952: esp. 504). But this may need to be taken into account in evaluating a particular report, as does the more recent influence of agrarians on pastoralists and hunters and gatherers (especially in Africa and northern Eurasia).

Discussion

JONATHAN SMITH: My paper has two parts: the first is dead serious; the second is a bit of *jeu d'esprit*. To write the second part, I had to say to myself: "I don't ever talk like this, but how would I sound if I did?" We have here a discussion among assumptions about things that we can't know for sure. I see our efforts simply as intellectual endeavors, as the taking of intellectual place. These are all matters that have very much to do with who we are. Moreover, "data" are those things we agree on for the purposes of argument. So, if Walter Burkert proves something about the Paleolithic era, it's still not data, because I don't admit anything from that era as evidence. We're not dealing with right and wrong, but with degrees of probability and with helpful analogies. Our task here is not so much to arrive at some agreement as to clarify the differences amongst our assumptions.

I am an essayist, which makes me more elusive and indirect than a writer of monographs. I tend to do my work in explicit relation to others. I tend not to speak my mind, but to speak my mind in relation to another mind. I would say that the first question that interests me is: for the purposes of academic discourse, is it possible to construct a generic theory of religion? Ritual offers a good example and testing ground for the construction of such a theory. In my terms, it's an "e.g." Sacrifice then becomes an "e.g." of ritual. And in many ways, it's not a very interesting "e.g."

I stand squarely in the rationalist tradition. I have an uncompromising faith in reason and intellection. My intellectual ancestors are the Scottish Enlightenment figures. Not surprisingly, I accord religion no privilege. It's ordinary, commonsense, and usually boring. (I often wonder what the study of religion would look like if it weren't a product of Protestant seminaries.) As I said before, there are no data as given. Data are what I choose for my argument. Neither is there a given text; it's all commentary. There is no primordium; it's all application. Everything is elaboration. So, I refuse questions of origins.

I would like to offer two examples of what I'm talking about. They're just examples, not theories. The first is language (and this does not mean that I prioritize language over action, or vice versa). Language is not representative. It always contains a point of criticism or comparison. It is governed by rules or conventions. The second example is food or cuisine. People seem to select, more or less arbitrarily, certain items out of all the possible things they could eat. They then cook these items in different ways to give variety. The culinary art is thus exegetical ingenuity, application. It makes things interesting.

I am much interested in the processes of complexity, and don't simply want to go back to some prior purport. I object to what seems to me almost a "law and gospel" argument, a dislike of the gloss as somehow secondary, and a belief that somehow or other there is one originating experience or vision that lies behind a text or ritual.

My second question has to do with the kind of texts that I have to deal with more and more. As one gets involved in the theory of religion, since most theorists of religion are romantic on the subject of origin and romantic on the subject of primitives, it's very difficult to go far without running into the problem of having to deal with ethnographic sources. And the important thing is that it is not the people the ethnographers study who are history-less. In other words, it's not the aborigine who has no history: it's the anthropologist studying the aborigine who has no history; all he can do is take a "snapshot" of that culture at "Time T" when he meets it. Anthropology is basically the process of trying to get a story out of a snapshot, and it usually doesn't work. Most important anthropological theory is built to justify that procedure. That's why functionalism had to replace evolutionism; it wasn't that we were embarrassed that mankind ended up as Victorian anthropologists, it wasn't that the political overtones of evolution embarrassed us; it was evolution as a time span, since the anthropologist cannot, while being an ethnographer, deal with a time span. He can only deal with what's going on when he happens to see it; and that he happens to see it is not unimportant, either. So of course he's going to describe society as held together, because for the instant that he looks at it— and he hasn't looked at anything in it before or anything afterward—it must, by definition, be held together or it wouldn't be there. We got into functionalism because of the necessary timelessness of the anthropologists; that means that to some degree anthropology can't answer certain kinds of questions about history.

Now I think, in fact, that in some of the work I've done, I've gone farther than most in being willing to pinpoint the time "before which," for instance, the Hainuwele story could not have been told in the form that Jensen collected it, or the time before which the Akitu festival could not have been, and so forth. So, for instance, one takes the Io myth and tries to find clues with which one can get behind what the anthropologist is doing; but there comes a point where the nature of the sources simply will not let you go any farther. In other words, my nervousness on the subject of "originating," "origins," "original" has to do in part with a stance. In another sense, it has very much to do with the nature of the reports that I, at least, am dependent on—reports designed precisely not to ask the question that's been asked, namely, the question about history, about origin.

The third thing is the question of an example. We have had three privileges conceded: sacrifice, New Year's, and initiation. Out of all the hundreds of types of ritual you could describe, those three, it seems, have been plucked up, and each has a characteristic form of data associated with it, and each seems to involve one in a characteristic stance. So here one begins to ask the question: if you really want to make your theory of ritual out of sacrifice, as opposed, say, to initiation or New Year's, or if you refuse all three, what does that tell me about what you are after? Those who favor New Year's have largely been people who really do want to emphasize the language of repetition, who want to try to get a cosmic dimension. It's not just Eliade; it's since we first started to play with New Year's scenarios; it's where the category of myth becomes terribly important. It's no accident that the myth-ritual school does its work best there. It's because that's where there are "thick," privileged texts (i.e., texts written by professional priests). Rituals surrounding New Year's are usually to be found in literate material; and then one tries by analogy, as Eliade and Lantinari and others have tried to do, to apply them to nonliterate materials, and it doesn't work. But at least if you are interested in stability, interested in repetition, interested in a kind of prioritizing of myth, then chances are you are going to build your theory on New Year's rituals. Those are the best examples you've got, and you are going to be led to that.

If you are interested, as I indicated in this paper, in sacrifice or initiation, your stance will be commensurately different: there is a tendency for those who like otherness and drama to come down on sacrifice, and those who have the notion of a long-range social project to come down on the initiation material. In one case, by and large, you are dealing again with literate sources, though very often fragmentary; in the other case, you are dealing almost entirely with ethnographic sources, which by analogy—this time going the other way—we have applied to the literate sources. So, no privilege should be granted to any block of material.

The fourth thing I want to discuss is the interest in application. It leads me to say, then, that you cannot isolate this cluster, you cannot find your single dramatic verb. We find rituals in, at the very least, paragraphs, not even sentences, and usually we find them in enormously different kinds of things, and I am interested in what principle of selectivity—if there is any, and there usually isn't—allows one to pick out of all of those sentences that make up the ritual the one particular verb as being in some way the ritual *in nuce*. And so it seems to me that one looks for the textual context, one looks for the historical context, one looks for the systemic context, in order to try to see whatever ritual you are looking at.

It's clear that if it were not for some interest other than the text that produced it, no one would have noticed the scapegoat in Leviticus 16. It's really a very uninteresting figure; we've got four animals, three of which were killed and one of which was kicked out; no one ever bothers with the other three. The text has nothing to do with sin and guilt; what we've got is pollution, and not pollution of people but pollution of a temple. We've got, then, a little fragment of something, which in fact I cannot decipher; neither can anybody else. We don't know what it has to do with; we don't know where it goes; but we have already in the text a theory: it must have something to do with the Day of Atonement. That's already a theory about it. We have the Greek translation that thinks it means to escape; we have a rabbinic fantasy that there was a demon. I don't know what it means, so I just back away from it, as I do from most biblical material, because we don't have ritual texts in the Bible. We have very poor ethnographic descriptions. You cannot perform a single biblical ritual on the basis of what is given to you in the text. If you can't perform it, then by definition it is not a ritual. The biblical texts are scattered, theoretical reconstructions of what may have happened, or on the other hand, they are what whoever wrote the text wanted you to know, as opposed to what they might know. There was no speech ever in biblical ritual, no one ever says anything in biblical ritual. Either one half of what went on has been left out, or there is not a single sentence anywhere in biblical ritual. The rabbis gleefully will supply that lacuna for you, but they don't know any more than I do on the subject.

So, one is interested, again, in selectivity: how one understands the processes of textualization; what you use—and here's where the *jeu d'esprit* comes in—what one might use as a guide to what to look for.

Take the "comedy of innocence," for instance. I really don't know of an instance where it occurs other than in a pastoral people. We thought we had one example that was really good, and that's the pygmy text, despite the fact that pygmies live in symbiosis with cattle-herding Bantus and presumably might have pastoral elements; but now that Trilles has been revealed to be a fraud, we cannot use his texts.[1] Okay, if it's pastoral, you see, then you might start thinking, "Maybe it really has more to do with the fact that you're killing a pet than with the fact that you're terribly guilty about some wild beast." Would that be more plausible? There are other details. In one ridiculous version, the Siberians are supposed to sing long love songs to the animals before they shoot them. Well, that's not, at least ethnologically, terribly plausible, but we certainly know that there are pastoral people who have enormous love lyrics that they sing to their herds. Maybe it isn't so strange to shift it and notice a

[1]See Trilles 1932; Piskaty 1957.—ED.

contextual detail that might let you place it in another kind of context. This is, at least, my instinct on how one works.

Finally, we're not going to solve today the problem of Plato's upward and downward path. We're not going to solve the issue of induction and deduction, whether one moves from what's thick and attempts to achieve some clarity, or whether one starts with where one's relatively clear and complicates it. I take it that's actually what comparison is all about and why it seems to me that comparison becomes an important object of attention. What we want is the revisionary juxtaposition of both: on the one hand, let's formulate a theory and then go and get evidence for it; on the other hand, let's be as thick as possible in the description of the evidence on which we base the theory we use.

Perhaps we should proceed like this. First, see what happens if we look at sacrifice in a domesticated scene. Do we learn anything from doing that? Second, redescribe things in a much more technical sense, try to find language like rectification or ingenuity in place of some of the other more solemn words that we use.

For me, when all is said and done, there are serious points of disagreement between me and René and Walter, two people from whom I've learned a great deal. The one overarching point of disagreement, however, is at the level of "How do you look at the world?" So I'm not sure that we do any more than clarify the fact that we disagree on that and wonder what the implications of that disagreement are. At least, I'm not prepared to convert.

It is really an issue of exegetical ingenuity. In one way or another, René and Walter are quite different on this, it seems to me, but both have at least some notion of an original, which is, then, in some sense—they are quite different in what they mean by this kind of language—concealed, displaced; something happens to it that causes it to lose its clarity, until we seem almost to "unmask" it. For me, things are surface: there simply is no depth; there simply is no original; and there is no concealment. It's all out there, it's plain, it's ordinary, it's largely uninteresting, and it's utterly—in fact, overwhelmingly, that's the problem for a scholar—accessible. The problem that I, at least, face as a scholar is what not to look at, what to refuse, what not to make relationships with, because they are just out there lying around all over the place. So I think the fundamental issue has something to do with depth and surface, or before and after, or original and secondary, or text and gloss, or revealing and concealing—however you want to put it. I sense that probably that's the point at which we have the most fundamental disagreement, and I'm not entirely sanguine that it's one that's resolvable. I think it's one that is probably clarifiable, but probably not resolvable.

WALTER BURKERT: I am prepared to go quite a way in agreement with Jonathan. For example, I do not really look on my attempt as a reconstruction of an origin or *the* origin. I once wrote that one should forbid the use of the term "origin,"[2] and I try, sometimes without success, to avoid the word in my own usage. What I am trying to find is what I would call *formative antecedents*, which of course implies the notion that the earlier is a formative power for what is later. In the context of ritual and religion, I think that for every person, what he learns—and man usually learns about ritual and religion—is not at the moment entirely clear to him. Many people spend their lives finding out what it really is. So here I find there is some difference between surface and what it may be really about, and this question is what I try to answer by exploring practical functions and the depths of history.

I agree about the interest in those really basic phenomena: sacrifice, the New Year's festival, and initiation. Perhaps I find them even more interesting than you just pretended to do. I have the impression that sacrifice is the most basic of them, and that the others somehow could be reduced to it.

But what I want to ask you now is more related to the second part of your paper. You have just told us that there is a kind of *jeu d'esprit* expressed in that part of the paper, that you are winking. So to join the game: I agree with some statements of yours—for example, "Sacrifice is an elaboration of the selective kill." I am, however, prone to agree in another way, which might be a misunderstanding of what you are really doing. From my point of view, I hail your theory as reconstructing a historical origin, because when you say sacrifice is linked to the domestication of animals, you refer to a stage about 6000 B.C. Later on, in the third millennium B.C., we have what has been called the urban revolution, the important step

---

[2]Burkert 1971: 202.—ED.

after the transition from the Paleolithic to the Neolithic, which has been called the "Neolithic revolution"; we have the development of high culture, with writing and more social differentiation than can be seen among the aborigines. In these "urban" civilizations, sacrifice is not the affair of the herdsman; rather, it's the affair of those who own the herds, of the kings and leaders of the armies and of the wealthy families. I would be very happy with this theory, and so I ask, why not go back some more millennia to Paleolithic hunting, as I do? But I feel somehow I'm misunderstanding you.

SMITH: You understand me perfectly! I just don't happen to believe my own theory! Nor would I care whether it were true or not. No, if one were to think origins are important, then precisely what I did in the second part of my paper was to propose one, and to propose one that did what I thought is no different from what you did. We just have a different evaluation of things. We both move from known to unknown, but I don't know anything about animals because we don't talk to each other, and so I don't know what they do, and that puts animals for me exactly where prehistoric man is: I can't talk with him either, and I tend to like to work on things that I can talk with, so that's why I don't go back five thousand more years. So then I simply have to say, "Okay, let me look and see what I can find out," and it is striking that I cannot find, with the dubious exception of the Ainu bear ritual, sacrifices that are not domesticated.

If that's the case, what would happen if we look at that as the originating, the "formative antecedent," sticking with your term, rather than at some hunter out in Whichitgrubtan facing some ravening beast? Would that make a difference? What would it look like? There's something playful about that. I mean, it really is accepting a strategy that is not my strategy; accepting the strategy and saying, "Okay then, what would I see if I try to look through your microscope? And how far can one build that house without it all coming crashing down?" I think it does crash down, and in the second part of the paper, I indicate that. When you see me saying that "I do not wish to strain the point," that means that I am now straining the point—making sacrifice, in fact, the ritual about ritual, which I think is probably pushing it too far. We might as well see what would happen if we pushed it that way.

On the other hand, you see, I'm not clear what that's told me. Supposing it is not hunting, supposing it's domestication: it's not clear to me that, once knowing that, I know anything more about sacrifice than I knew before. You're right that this is a historical origin theory that is probably totally wrong—what fun!

CESÁREO BANDERA: Jonathan seems to be, on the one hand, denying any "big deal" quality to sacrifice or, on the other, atomizing it into—to use Derrida's notion—an infinite "dissemination" of meaning, because it appears that's the only way now in which it can be saved. On the surface, it may seem that you don't believe in sacrifice and they do; I think that precisely the opposite is happening: the real sacrificial defender is Smith.

RENÉ GIRARD: I wanted to mention in connection with—let's use an old-fashioned word—the existential "pregnance" of ritual, a ritual that is neither a sacrifice in the narrow sense, nor a New Year's scenario, nor an initiatory rite, but that nevertheless has been bandied about enormously in the last fifty years and is obviously, in a way, a "big deal" in our modern culture. It's the potlatch. A potlatch is a marvelous example of parcelling out, because you expend the goods, destroy them one by one. At the same time, it's kind of an auction in reverse, and it's a display of human vanity, and it's something that turns back into conflict. Personally I think it's a type of ritual that goes wrong; so my question is, how would you deal with a potlatch?

SMITH: Simple answer: "René, you've got me." I really don't know what to do with it. It's an obvious one and you picked out just the elements that are obvious. If there's anything that's "parcelling out," that one's "parcelling out." It is terribly ordinary things that they're parcelling out; they do it in a context that's really not much different than haggling the whole rest of the year. It certainly has both elements of equilibrium and stability and elements of disequilibrium and digression of hostility, and all the rest.

The problem for me, and I've taught three courses where we read potlatch material, has to do with the ethnography and the category. It is terribly complicated and not clear to me what belongs in and what belongs out of the category, and I really do not have it sorted out; and particularly now that Goldman and others have re-

researched the Kwakiutl material, terribly important things are coming out. What's happened is that the opportunity to go back to Boas's notes at Columbia and see what he wrote, as opposed to what he thought he wrote twenty years later, has had the result that the Kwakiutl turn out no longer to have a potlatch. How, then, is potlatch to be related to exchange and exchange to potlatch? You're quite right; it is one of the rituals that some day I may wish to say something about. It is the one that is inherently most interesting to me, but I'm simply not ready to say anything.

FRITS STAAL: Why is it a ritual?

GIRARD: It has all the earmarks of a ritual, whatever definition of ritual you use.

SMITH: Well, again, the potlatch of the Kwakiutl may very well not be a ritual. That there are rituals of exchange I am quite convinced of, but the question is whether this one happens to be a good example. The two best examples we have—Kule on the one hand and potlatch on the other—have both been taken away from the ethnographers who first described them, and that for me now is simply a dilemma. I mean, I have to settle that, and at my usual rate of work, that's about ten more years before I can make up my mind on the ethnographic record, and for me it's terribly important that one make up one's mind on the basis of the ethnographic record.

GIRARD: One word you said really worries me. You said we don't really know what belongs in and what belongs out of the category. What is the criterion of choice going to be? I'm afraid you will keep the innocuous elements for your ritual and leave out the rivalry, the tribal nationalism gone rampant.

SMITH: If I do my job as a theorist, of course I will, and if you do your job right, you'll tell me that's what I've done, of course. I don't know what Boas claims to have seen or claims to have heard that somebody else saw. But at least we know now that there are major discrepancies between what he wrote that he heard and saw, and what he wrote twenty years later that he heard and saw. My way of working gives me the choice of whether I accept or reject this as a matter of interest. It says, simply, that you're talking about five or six years in Columbia's archives, and so on, before Smith wants to talk about potlatch, and I have not made up my mind yet whether that is the one I want to talk about.

GIRARD: I personally think it would be very interesting to read pot-latch in the context of other aspects of the Kwakiutl and other tribes around there. If you read Boas and the people who have been talk-ing about these things, you see, for instance, that even things like weddings of important people, which are rituals, have very strange aspects. Usually they are weddings between close cousins, and be-tween the two families there are battles that go on with stones and so forth. According to the text of Boas, I think that sometimes one of the slaves who is fighting for one of the two sides dies, and if that happens it's considered a very favorable omen that the marriage will last a very long time. Is this sacrificial or not, would be my question.

SMITH: I wouldn't know how you could tell on the basis of what you've told me.

GIRARD: Yes, now to me that's the essence of the sacrificial. You have again a situation that you can compare to the text of the judg-ment of Solomon. You have the doubles—you know, the brothers, the cousins who are fighting—and no decision is possible. But if there is a real death, the contract between the two people, which is the marriage, will hold; because there will be that death to sanction it, which has a decisive character, which I think is the essence of sacrifice in primitive society.

I also want to make a few general remarks about your paper, Jon-athan. In my view, the opposition Jonathan perceives between those who believe in intellectual explanations and those who do not—namely, the romantic souls who espouse the irrational, the dra-matic, and the lurid—pertinent as it may be in some instances, is not pertinent to our discussion here.

I do not regard Walter as an irrationalist. Some critics have sus-pected me of irrationalism, but I am more often criticized for an excessive trust in reason. I do not agree with this critique, of course, but I understand how it can arise. Here, I do not understand. The direction Jonathan seems to be taking is a total misunderstanding, in my opinion.

From my standpoint, the main question is: how ambitious can we be? Should we go on looking for a global theory of religion or should we not? Walter Burkert's answer, and mine, is that we should. Jonathan Smith's is that we should not.

Who has the greater faith in human reason? I do not suggest that Jonathan is the irrationalist among us, but he is terribly pessimistic about the possibilities in the field of religion. The rationalist thinkers whom he claims as his ancestors would be disturbed by his attitude. To my ears, at least, much of his talk sounds discouraging for the type of intellectual enterprise in which they believed, and in which Walter and I also believe.

I believe in a reason powerful enough to master even the violent and irrational aspects of religion, the aspects that it has been fashionable to minimize or ignore entirely with the vogue of Lévi-Straussian structuralism and other recent theories. I do not regard this minimization as the true path for the rational investigation of religious phenomena.

The most powerful incitement to limit our ambitions the way Jonathan does lies in the massive failure of theoretical anthropology thus far. Since the two world wars, especially the second, an attitude has developed that may be defined as *minimalism*. Big problems are ridiculed and only small concrete questions are entertained. If the past failures of theoretical anthropology are irreversible, this is the way of intellectual prudence, of genuine wisdom. If you deal only with small problems—a myriad of tiny problems, rather than a few big ones—you are less likely to go wrong. We must substitute a myriad of little truths for the big truths that most probably do not exist.

But can we be sure that the accumulated failures of the past really mean that we must always fail? Since there is no theoretical consensus on any essential point in the field of anthropology, Jonathan's minimalist attitude is a philosophical and theoretical choice, just as arbitrary and dogmatic as the *maximalism* of Walter and myself.

I fully agree that the ancient texts I like to quote are already interpretations; I have always regarded them as such. I simply feel they are better interpretations than what modern anthropologists have offered. They agree more with the documentary evidence as I see it. Is Genesis wrong to link human and animal sacrifice in the story of Isaac and Esau, or in the story of Abraham? Are the Brahmanas wrong? Was Sophocles an old fool when he wrote *Ajax*? He may have been, but the survivability of ancient texts compared to modern anthropological attitudes suggests the opposite conclusion. If it is ethnocentric to find religion fascinating and to look to it for essential truths about human nature, is it not ethnocentric as well to find it trivial and boring? Is this not a uniquely Western and modern trait?

Which is the more scientific attitude? No one can answer. But it cannot be irrational to believe that, diverse as they are, religious phenomena are also fundamentally one and fundamentally intelligible. I concede that my attitude is just as dogmatic as Jonathan's, but no more. And I do not believe the phenomenal evidence is on his side. The way in which he dismisses human sacrifice and associated phenomena is simply too casual.

The problem with the minimalist attitude, I feel, is that it persuades those who adopt it, if not that they eliminate all risks, at least that they take fewer and lesser risks than those who choose global intelligibility. This is a logical fallacy. The people who parcel out comparative religion into thousands of little questions, supposedly begging for trivial solutions, irresistibly remind us of what they themselves keep saying about rituals. Would the minimalist really be a kind of latter-day ritualist, with academe as a replacement for organized religion? This is what Cesáreo meant, I assume, when he said that the real defender of sacrifice here is Jonathan Smith. I agree.

Regarding the hypothesis about sacrifice and animal domestication, which I enjoyed very much, I have some questions. If domestication explains sacrifice, what will explain domestication? Or is it self-explanatory? Since domestication, in human culture, is less widespread than sacrificial practices, can we take it as a given? Why did some societies domesticate animals and others did not? Why is there no new domestication in a world that no longer practices sacrifice?

Which phenomenon demands explaining and which one can provide an explanation? It seems more rational to choose domestication as the more transparent phenomenon, because domesticated animals are still around, whereas sacrifice has disappeared. We can take domestication a little for granted, but not sacrifice. We can imagine that domestication evolved more or less "naturally" as a result of its usefulness, as if "usefulness" could be anticipated.

Animal domestication is no less mysterious than sacrifice. I agree that there must be a relationship between the two, but it could be the reverse of what Jonathan suggests. I have already written on this subject in one of my books. In the same text, I also try to reverse the ritual hunting theory that Walter defends.[3] I try to show that sacrificial practices, understood my way, could be the engine of ritual hunting in some societies and of domestication in others. Domestication as well as hunting could originate in a search for sacrificial victims. My postulate, I recall, is that rituals try to duplicate, as accurately as they can, all details and peculiarities of a unanimous victimage, which they cannot fail to understand in the light of the reconciliation it has produced, at the height of some internal brawl, or some panic, or some other form of disturbance.

The original victim is seen not as a passive victim, but as the all-powerful *agent* of both the disturbance and the return to peace. He or she, therefore, must be regarded as a supernaturally powerful outsider and, simultaneously, as an insider. If this deduction is correct, the search for substitute victims will orient a community outward, toward hunting or ritual war—but the need will be felt to bring the prospective victim inside the community, in order to make the victim an insider as well as an outsider. The combination of the two drives could account for domestication.

In the Ainu bear ritual, we have a ritual hunt and we also have something that looks like an attempt at "domesticating" the bear for a while. The bear is the object of the hunt. But a young bear is literally "adopted" by the hunters, living like a member of the community until it gets ritually killed and devoured. We have comparable rituals that have, visibly, no direct relatedness to this one, such as the ritual cannibalism of the Tupinamba in northeastern Brazil. The purpose of ritual wars was to take prisoners who were often kept alive by their captors for several years, living the life of a community member, our sources tell us, until they were ritually sacrificed and devoured. The great gap we see between "human" and "animal" sacrifice, or ritual killing, pales in the face of such ritual similarities. This gap could be the worst of all ethnocentric fallacies.

Let us ask ourselves which interesting effects will automatically

[3]"Domestication animale et chasse rituelle," in Girard 1978: 77-81.—ED.

result if, instead of human beings or bears (two species that will not be really modified by their association with a ritual community, even if allowed to live their entire lives and reproduce inside of it), the sacrificers select as their prospective victims animals that happen to be the ancestors of our sheep, of our goats, of our cows, or of our pigs. In this case, after many generations, the ritual adoption of future sacrificial victims should produce the kind of sheep, goats, cows, and pigs that we call "domesticated."

It is easy to dismiss my hypothesis on the grounds that science is the reduction of the unknown to the known. It makes more sense, we feel, to explain sacrifice as a by-product of the hunt, as Walter does, or as a by-product of domestication, as Jonathan does, than the reverse. Why? Because we think we know what it means for men to hunt animals, or to domesticate them. But do we? Why are these phenomena always interpreted religiously? That may be the major mistake of all previous theories of religion. They see religion—and, above all, ritual killing—as the mystery that should be explained by the less mysterious that surrounds it. Could not all human institutions be aspects of a single mystery dominated by sacrifice, as the Brahmanas believe? Could not sacrifice be the transformational tool of all human culture?

This sounds like a crazy idea, no doubt, but if you look at its possibilities for a transformational analysis that takes the unanimous murder as its starting point and reaches down to specific rituals, specific institutions, specific textual interpretations, you can be amazed by the results. The people who regard my global theory as preposterous while conceding that some of my concrete analyses can be illuminating simply do not realize how inseparable the one is from the others, how automatically the theory spawns the concrete analyses as soon as you make a real attempt to put it to use.

My scheme demands a radical questioning of the basis for the current perspectives, and it will not come to life unless you enter into the spirit of its revolution. Once you do, you realize that it makes sense for the very reason that it seems preposterous from the outside. It takes nothing for granted. It takes nothing as self-explanatory. Not only can you write a logically continuous genesis of the most diverse ritual and postritual institutions if you adopt my starting point, but you can retrieve a hidden rationality behind apparently outlandish and unintelligible sacrificial practices. This is a trump card that remains generally unperceived.

The "lurid story" at the entrance of my transformational scheme is responsible for the misunderstandings that surround it. Unfortunately, it cannot be eliminated. And it is more than a logical starting point: it is a kind of matrix that truly radiates in all directions to generate these transformations, as the various cultures keep interpreting the collective murder in slightly different ways.

I feel that Jonathan would certainly acknowledge my "game" as a primarily intellectual game if he decided to play it himself. It may be the wrong game to play, it may appear too complicated and risky, but it is a lot of fun, I can assure him. I suggest that he give it a try some day when he has nothing better to do, out of sheer curiosity.

JOHN LAWRENCE: I have a couple of questions for Jonathan. Perhaps I've read too much into what you said, but that would be compatible with your theory of what happens in scholarship. You have characterized here your interest in the ritual area as consisting in an interest in what other people have said about the data. And so far as you're concerned, all data are intrinsically uninteresting or equally uninteresting. They become interesting for you after someone asserts something about them that you might be interested in contesting as an interpretation. So I think you're trying to emphasize that for you, this topic is a scholarly one in which you would like to focus on the methodology of talking about it, rather than the intrinsic importance of what's talked about. Now, I perceive an important difference between your stance and René Girard's. I believe that René has the instinct or intuition that some rituals are much healthier than others, that perhaps the ritual of scapegoating, which is a ritual that survives with us today, represents a danger to the sanity or the survival of the culture, so he is interested in the scapegoating ritual because it's an issue of cultural health. For you, to be consistent with what you said earlier, your primary interest would be in the fact that he has made that statement, but not in whether any ritual has any connection with what we might call the sanity or survival of the culture. Would you ever wish to be in a position of normatively evaluating a ritual and saying, "I object to this because I feel that it threatens the continued existence of our species"?

SMITH: I have no interest in the continued existence of our species. I have a deep interest in the continuing existence of the academy. What I'm interested in is the health of academic discourse. What I'm interested in is whether it is in fact possible—and René is exactly right here, this is a very recent possibility, and so recent a possibility that it hasn't been done yet—whether it is possible to have academic discourse about religion. That's all I'm asking. As a private citizen, I have some concern for cultural survival, but the only thing that I address as I write and as I work is the health of the academy and the conditions under which responsible discourse can go on in that context. Now, it's not exactly fair to say that the only things I am interested in are things that other people have found interesting. It is certainly part of what I'm interested in, because I'm an archaeologist, too, but my archaeology is in the academy, not in the field. That really is absolutely true. I am much more interested in the origins of the theory than I am in the origins of a phenomenon—number one, because I think I can get them, and number two, because they have determined us in a way I can find rather than in a way I have to imagine. Obviously, I also say that that which I find interesting is, therefore, interesting, and so I'm not necessarily entirely dependent on what someone else says. I don't see my work as intending to have any particular commentarial function on our times. There are moments when I am willing to venture, occasionally, an observation about adequacies and inadequacies, when I'm at least prepared to note that here possibilities do not seem to have been culturally developed. But I don't know that I'd draw any deep conclusions from this. "Normative" is a very big word, and I don't know whether I quite want to do that. I'm much more inclined to frame it as an observation: "Isn't it curious?" Isn't it curious, for example, that some religions have polite ways of exiting, some religions have no ways of exiting, and other religions have odd ways of exiting? And I guess I think that a ritual is probably more adequate if someone can get out without blowing up the whole universe, but that is gossip for late at night. It is not what I understand myself to be primarily doing, which is considering how something enters and exits the academic community, which is the only community I have the slightest interest in.

ROBERT JEWETT: I'd like to talk to you a little bit more about the second, playful half of your paper, because I realize that you're not presenting your new theory of sacrifice as an exaggeration of domestication, as a formative precedent, etcetera. You don't like the term formative, quite obviously. But you do present this hypothesis, I think, although playfully. It is nevertheless susceptible of testing on the grounds of plausibility. Now, the basic logic of the position is that the selective killing in domestication is, in a sense, reified in the sacrifice system, that the sacrifice of the animal achieves a perfection. It's related to your ideal hunt. Now, I find a little logical problem following that, because killing in domestication has a clear payoff—that is, you killed the weak males, and you killed selected females. With sacrifice, you in fact reverse that. You kill precisely the strong male—the ram, very frequently, that is capable of producing a payoff. Now, there seems to be a missing link here. If sacrifice is the reification of domestication, then you would think that you would sacrifice the weakest animal—that would seem to me logically coherent—but in fact we sacrifice the strongest animal. Why this odd reversal? Is there potentially an element we need to add to your theory of domestication to explain why the best rather than the worst animal is in fact killed in the sacrifice?

SMITH: Could be. Could be that we simply have an odd characteristic inversion. Could be a number of things. I'm afraid that, frankly, I'm not interested enough in the question to worry about it, but it could be.

JEWETT: What could be? I don't quite grasp it.

SMITH: You're quite right, there could be something missing. And if there is, we may find it, or there may not be anything missing. We may simply have here an inversion, of which we have lots of examples. You're quite right. In my essay on the bear hunt, I was concerned chiefly to criticize the idea of sympathetic magic, the idea that the ritual preceding the hunt was an enactment of what the hunters hoped would happen in the succeeding hunt. On the contrary, there is no imitation in ritual.

GIRARD: The definers of "imitative" magic do not mean imitation itself; in imitative magic, you imitate the thing you would like to happen, not the thing you are actually going to do, that is, to kill the animal in the expectation—at least in the classic theory—that then what you would like will happen. I mean, the imitative magic must still be imitative of some ideal way for the animal to die, even though the people know very well they are going to do something else in order to kill the animal.

SMITH: That formulation I would adore. It's not the classical formulation, however.

GIRARD: Yes, but they are pretty weak, the classical formulations.

SMITH: Granted, granted.

GIRARD: To say there is no imitation in ritual, you know, that something is pure repetition, makes no sense.

SMITH: That ritual imitates itself is the Lévi-Straussian formulation. That it imitates something outside is the sympathetic-magic formulation. The question that interests me here is the question of perfection. Let me use Lévi-Strauss's analogy for a different purpose than he uses it for. At times, perfecting is as if there were a slow-motion camera operating: the activity is slowed down sufficiently, so that in theory you can get it perfectly right. And that's why a very important category for ritual is getting it right or wrong; in theory, at least, you can get it perfectly right. That's what I mean by the notion of perfecting. It allows you to do something that you cannot do "out there" because you do it in its own controlled environment. That's a notion of perfecting that I have—that it's slow motion.

Lévi-Strauss uses the same analogy in order to get slow motion down to identity, and that's precisely what I do not want to have happen: it is not identity; it is, indeed, extreme difference. Therefore I guess all I tried to do is to say, "Okay, let's take a look at what appears: that it is always a domesticated animal, appears; that, as far as I know, sacrifice is always by pastoralists or agriculturalists, appears. Let's look at the idea of selective killing, let's look at the notion of delayed payoffs. And again, we may ask—and this is why I'm not concerned about whether there is a link or not—is this a useful analogy?" That's what's being proposed here, an analogy: not an origin but an analogy between domestication and sacrifice. I think there will be elements that will not coalesce, or it wouldn't be an analogy. They may be significant; they may not be significant. I really don't know what to do with it. It's not important.

STAAL: I would like to say something about origins. Everybody seems to be down on origins. I must confess that I'm very much interested in origins, real origins. It is useful briefly to review why we are so down on origins. It started with de Saussure in linguistics. There had been a lot of work on Indo-European languages, diachronic philology, language change, and sound laws, but nobody had discovered that language is a system. And so at the Paris meeting of the International Congress on Linguistics around 1906, linguists adopted a rule forbidding the acceptance of any papers on the origin of language or on artificial languages. Something similar happened in anthropology; it also emphasized its synchronistic approach. Some of the things Walter has quoted show that the situation is rather different now. The New York Academy of Sciences held a large conference in 1975 on the origin and evolution of language and speech. This has a lot to do with what Jonathan said about the snapshot approach of anthropology; they tried to go beyond this. This is why much work in anthropology is unsatisfactory from my point of view as an Indologist; the snapshot approach has no historical dimension. This is also why it is important to take the Indian and Chinese evidence into account, because there is an enormous historical dimension to it that still survives, and you have not only texts but also oral traditions.

GIRARD: De Saussure himself was not like many of his followers, who were absolute fanatics. He was saying that the purpose was to have the synchronic snapshots in order to get *diachronie* and get away from vague and loose analogies. Something really amazing happened; I'm fully aware of the problem because my book *Violence and the Sacred* first appeared in 1972, when this rejection of "origins" was at its height.

For my part, I think that no science that is not looking for origins is really a science; a science that is purely classificatory and descriptive, like the structuralists have been, is just giving up. But the thing that is so strange is that they think they are very scientific at a moment when, suddenly, disciplines that have been purely synchronic are becoming spectacularly turned toward origin, in particular astrophysics; and this is true not only of astrophysics. The great question two years ago at the Stanford symposium on Disorder and Order[4] was how to get at origins from a structuralist view. You have to get from disorder to order. How is the structure created? I think this is the burning issue.

STAAL: I would like to say something about ritual and language. I agree with Rappaport's statement, in the epigraph to Jonathan's paper, about the "surface" and all that, but then I do not see how anything follows from it. However, that statement shows that ritual is not language, for language always refers to something else. Now, if we confine ourselves to the surface and to forms, it does not mean that we are behaviorists who only report sequences of events, because there is something in the succession of things that can have structure. Structure goes beyond the surface, yet it doesn't mean the same as semantics. What I'm really talking about is the difference between syntax and semantics. There's a syntax to surface phenomena, but that doesn't mean that there also has to be a semantics. Jonathan says I don't know what animals do because I cannot talk to them. To me, the position seems very different: I know what animals do, but I cannot talk to them. I know exactly what they do, and that's what I also know about ritualists. I know what they do. Now, I can also talk to them, but when I talked to them I found out that they only tell me what they do. Theologians, on the other hand, write books about ritual in which they tell us what the ritualists think, or what they think ritual is. So there's a great deal more to these questions than we have so far discussed.

GIRARD: I think there's a great ambiguity to the matter of surface and depth. It's very easy to be for surface; I'm against false depth. What we want to get away from is the idea, the idealistic language. I'll ask the question simply: is the trial of a witch in the fifteenth century to be considered a kind of ritual? It will be repeated many times. Call it sacrificial. The surface—we may have all the records, so we can read everything—the surface is right there; but any historian today reading that trial is not going to believe the surface conclusions. Even though the witch herself confesses she is guilty, a current reader would not agree with that conclusion. We disbelieve

[4]For the proceedings, see Livingston 1984.—ED.

the surface, but we do not doubt that there is a real victim on trial. In spite of the unacceptable surface, there is something true in the text. My whole point about myth and ritual is that we should be able to reach that same level of sophistication in the reading of mythology. I have a depth reading of the Oedipus myth, because I say we cannot take seriously the parricide and incest; the truth is that Oedipus was a scapegoat. I read the Oedipus myth exactly as you, everybody here, would read the witch trial.

STAAL: I do agree with you and understand what you say, but there is one problem: you are not talking about what I call ritual. You're talking mostly about myth.

GIRARD: Ah, because we read ritual only in a world where ritual is breaking down. So the witch-hunt, I say, is quasi-ritual that can be read more easily because it's a ritual that is breaking down ritual; so I don't say it is perfectly comparable to the Oedipus myth—it's different. It's more easily readable. Even the people who do it don't believe as much, but at the same time, the analogy is such that I think today the time has come to perform on mythology the operation that people in the seventeenth and eighteenth centuries were able to perform on the witch-hunt. I think the greatest feat of interpretation in the Western world was what happened when the English pastors decided that the witch-hunt laws had to go. It seems to me that today the problem of mythology is the same.

There is a great resistance; but my thesis is scientific, not because it can be demonstrated, but because, since it is the same thesis that we have when we read the accounts of a witch-hunt, fifty years from now it will either be equally banal and no one will talk about it, because as soon as we read the Oedipus myth we will realize that the same thing is going on in this myth as in an eighteenth-century witch-hunt text, or it will be forgotten. There will be no in-between; there will be none of that attitude of our literary critics who say, "All interpretations are good, he's a little bit good, and so is this one." Either the Oedipus myth is a "witch-hunt text" with an incredible surface that conceals a credible depth, like the accounts of the Salem trials, or it is not. There you have an either/or that you have to decide. I feel that it's a very interesting dilemma today. What strikes me about the historical text of the witch trials is that, in the text,

there are certain things that we know are certainly wrong, like certain types of accusations: she killed the neighbor's cow, she gave the
plague to my son. When we see those untrue accusations, we know
that the conclusion, "She's a witch; and she was put on a pyre" is,
nevertheless, true. In other words, the more false certain things are
in the text, the more true they are. We do not dare do that sort of
thing with any other text. Why? We see it's very paradoxical. In
other words, certain themes do not get into a text innocently. If you
read, for instance, a newspaper report of a lynching in the South in
1933, when you see certain telltale signs in the text, you will know;
but a historian a thousand years from now—he may not know. The
truth will lie only in a novel written by someone named William
Faulkner. Then the sound historians will say that we should not believe the novel; we have the press, we have all the documents. In
fact, however, it is only the novel that puts together all the signs.

STAAL: Now, I agree that those things could be very interesting, and
that you have to consider interesting interpretations. The question
is, to my mind: what does this have to do with ritual?

GIRARD: It has to do with religion. Primitive religion seems to be
mixed up in that; and, you know, the rituals nineteenth-century anthropologists used to call most primitive were the ones that most
resembled the mob lynching of a victim in a fit of anger. If you take
accounts of the massacres of the Jews during the fourteenth century,
you have the same kind of text; you have the same clues. You know
it's true.

STAAL: But what's happening there, according to you, is entirely
different from what I call ritual. We have to go back, I think, to
Jonathan's notion of paradigms, of what people had in mind as a
paradigm. If you start with the paradigm of ritual as a sacrifice and
you look at certain elements of sacrifice, they seem to resemble certain things that you are talking about, but if you don't start with
that notion, you never need make that link.

GIRARD: But if there is that resemblance, you have to start with
that. Resemblance seems to give you a hold.

STAAL: I would like to talk about some of the other things that one
can start with, and then move in an entirely different direction.

Now, you say ritual has something to do with religion. That is fine, but I do not accept the view that ritual is necessarily a part of religion. On the contrary, I see a lot of ritual in places where there doesn't seem to be any religion.

GIRARD: The academic ritual.

STAAL: Yes. As one would expect, the Indians have most of the paradigms that you enumerated. They have initiation rituals and rituals of sacrifice. They don't have, incidentally, a New Year's ritual, but they have full- and new-moon rituals, fourth-monthly ritual, and plenty of that sort of thing. But those are functional and really not very interesting rituals. When I talk about ritual, I realize increasingly that I have a very different paradigm in mind from yours— rituals that do not belong to the class of rituals that I just mentioned. These latter rituals are performed in order to get something or for someone to reach a certain place. A good example of the rituals I am interested in is one that is called "The Sixteenth." The name does not indicate anything important about it. Rituals such as "The Sixteenth"—which is a very mysterious ritual about which an enormous amount has been written in the Brahmana literature— such rituals consist almost entirely of what I call purely ritual sequences, which have to be performed according to very precise rules and to which no clear implication of function can be attached. It is not clear that anyone is initiated. It is not clear that they perform a service. People have said that such rituals are the creations of intellectual priests who merely wanted to make things more and more complex, but this is exactly the opposite of what I believe. I believe that the purest rituals are those in which the pure ritual form is not attached to anything else, for instance, anything having to do with society. Those pure rituals show what is really ritualistic about ritual, namely, a certain obsessiveness with rules, a certain repetitiveness, a *morcellement*, and many other things that Lévi-Strauss has never even touched on.

GIRARD: Consider this example from your own field, the story of Manou. It is directed against human sacrifice. Two Brahmans arrive to sacrifice for him, and the Asuras are really angry because Manou is making too much noise with his pots and pans. And they say, "Manou, we have come to sacrifice for you," and they destroy the pots and pans; after that, they come back and say, "Manou, your bull is making too much noise," and they sacrifice the bull. When they come again, Manou says, "I have nothing left." "You have your wife," they say, and they decide to sacrifice her. While they are preparing the huge altar—they take one year to build it—Indra looks down and says, "These rascal Asuras, the demons, are going to get poor Manou to sacrifice his wife; I'm going to show them up." And he comes down to Manou and says, "Manou, I'm a Brahman, and I'm going to sacrifice for you," and Manou says, "I have absolutely nothing to sacrifice; I have only my wife left, and these two Brahmans are sacrificing her." So Indra says, "Yes, but these Brahmans are your guests, therefore they belong to you, and so I shall sacrifice them." And immediately the demons leave. This reintroduces revenge into the process of sacrifice.

STAAL: The trouble about it is this: they have nothing to do with the ritual, these texts. These texts were written by people who, just like us, propound theories, who want to explain something. The ritualists do not know about those theories. They don't accept them if they are told about them. If they are asked about them, they say, "I don't know. I know how to *do* this." These are the people we should go to if we want to study ritual. The authors of the Brahmanas, on the other hand, come up with the same kind of theories that some modern scholars have come up with—theories that bear little relation to the ritual as it is being performed.

GIRARD: I feel that excluding these great texts would be a little bit like studying the history of nineteenth- and twentieth-century literature statistically, bad books and good books together.

STAAL: No, it's very different, because to study those texts is to study mythology, but to study ritual is to study something different.

GIRARD: I wouldn't call it mythology; I would call it the interpretation of ritual.

STAAL: That's what mythology is! Sometimes it is a satire of ritual, sometimes it is amusing.

GIRARD: That means, don't go too far with sacrifice.

STAAL: What I'm saying is this: that the Brahmanas are not a source for our knowledge of ancient Indian ritual. They have always been studied because people have been fascinated by those stories, and I wouldn't want to prohibit people from studying interesting stories; but we should not think that they throw light upon ritual, because they don't. They don't explain why the rituals are performed and why the ritualists do these extraordinary and strange things.

GIRARD: Yes, but you would admit that they throw light on the antisacrificial era that followed—interiorization in the Upanishads, and so on.

STAAL: For the historical understanding of Indian religion, if there is one, and of Indian philosophy, they are certainly important.

BANDERA: I don't really have a question. I want to make an observation. There is no need to find out what ritual is saying; so ultimately we have something in which obsessive repetition and minute distinction have to be observed, minute observation of details that must be repeated in a certain sequence, and not in any other way. Is that correct?

STAAL: Yes, that is a large part of it, although it may not be minute; it may go on for twelve years.

BANDERA: "Minute" in the sense that it is extremely important that it be done in the right way.

STAAL: Yes, it doesn't have to be accompanied by pangs of conscience, though, as Freud said. It doesn't have to be obsessive; it may or may not be, but it has to be done carefully and according to the rules.

BANDERA: There is already something in the ritual itself, in the performance of the ritual, that in a sense tries to negate a global interpretation of the ritual, the meaning of the ritual that will come later in the myth. In a sense, ritual is somehow denying ahead of time that such a global interpretation is possible. The important thing is that you don't lump all things together and come up with a big theory, but that you separate things and put them in the proper order; and you have, ultimately, a very clear, repetitive structure. I simply wanted to make the observation that that resembles the extraordinary efforts of the structuralists to do, in academic rituals, exactly the same thing: "let's talk about meaning; let's talk about—you know—how many pieces you can cut a text into, and how many things you can do with it." There is, nevertheless, a difference, and the difference is that for the structuralist there would be, perhaps, a thousand different ways of arranging the material, whereas a primitive ritual has sequence, and the sequencing is considered sacred. Nevertheless, this sort of structuralism *avant la lettre* sounds very interesting to me, and it goes in the direction of what I said a moment ago to Jonathan. In a very deep sense, he is far closer to ritualistic sacrificial mentalities than either one of his conversation partners, especially René Girard.

SMITH: I want to push your structural remark, although I don't really associate myself with all that. You're quite right in theory; there are a thousand ways of assembling things, but it's only at that level. When the structuralists go to work, factoring all the topographies and all of that, there turns out not to be an infinity of ways of doing it. In fact, one of the things that I can't quite understand is how they derive so much necessity for the particular way of ordering things in any particular instance they're looking at.

STAAL: I give you a myth, not from the Brahmanas, but from the grammarian Patanjali. Indra wanted to learn Sanskrit, and so he asked the teacher of the gods, Brhaspati, "Could you please teach me Sanskrit?" And so Brhaspati started enumerating the forms of Sanskrit, but he could not reach the end, because there are infinitely many forms of language; therefore, says Patanjali, we need rules that generalize, and exceptions; i.e. grammar. And then he makes a most interesting remark: "just like the performance of protracted rituals." In rituals, there are also infinitely or indefinitely many things to do; and this is because some of the ritual rules are recursive, in the sense that you can apply them to their own output. That applies to the rules of grammar, just as it applies to the rules of ritual. The Indians studied such rules in a synchronistic science of language, namely, in the grammar of Patanjali and in a synchronistic science of ritual that no other culture has produced as far as I know. The object of that science is to map the paradigm or prototype of ritual.

BURKERT: To what extent is ritual communication? In my paper, I talk very much about communication; in his part on ritual, Jonathan Smith does not even mention the concept; Frits Staal has told me this is an old-fashioned concept, that I'm slow in changing fashions. My favorite examples would, of course, be from the field of sacrifice and initiation and the New Year's festival, communicating the reverse of order, the reestablishment of order, and bringing in all the parts of the community and especially the authority of the king. Another example: in Catholic Bavaria, the greatest festival of the year is the *Fronleichnam*, the great procession with the Corpus Christi, and the whole community takes part. There are altars all along the processional way, and thus the space of the city is marked out. The Catholic inhabitants of the city take part, and of course it shows they are on this side, and the Protestants who may be in the city on the other. So it's very much a demonstration and a form of communication concerning who belongs where and how they are all related to their God.

In my sense, this is ritual because it is a fixed action pattern that can be described, and they repeat it—with variations, of course—as in a New Year's festival. Your paradigms seem to be of a different character. I think for Jonathan it is mainly rabbinic; for Frits it is the brahmanic tradition. But both are special cases, because you have there groups of people who really spend their lives meditating on ritual or doing ritual, and they keep their own identity just by this, in my view, nearly obsessive concentration on ritual. I am looking at more humane kinds of ritual that are communicative and are understandable to a certain degree, though perhaps not totally understandable.

Just a note on purification: if you say it's all surface, I think the notion "to purify by blood" cannot be understood, because on the surface it is nonsense; you do not clean up, you just make a mess with blood.

SMITH: Well, that's a good sense of surface, but let me go back to your example, because it's a very good one—your Bavarian example. I guess my formulation of those phenomena would include something more about ritual and a phrase that says something about "among other things," and so forth. I have no doubt that ritual does an awful lot of things. The question (and it's a question of choice, a question of theory and all) is: what does one focus on as being the best clue to what is "ritual" about the ritual, as opposed to all the other things the ritual might be doing just as well? I have no doubt that your example shows ritual as communication.

It seems to me, however, that what is ritualistic about that ritual, at least as I pick up on the tail of something I know absolutely nothing about (and therefore have a tremendous exegetical advantage), is the altars all over the city, and I presume you'd better go to them in the right order. You'd better not start here. You'd better start there and go here, and I take it that if at any point somebody went in the other direction, you'd either stone him or decide he's a Protestant, or he would create a story about how an angel appeared and told him to start heading in that direction. So what I would pick out as being the most "ritual" thing about that ritual is that everyone is moving from here to here to here, that they're carrying something on a tree in that way, and so forth. This is not to question that there are many, many things going on; it is only to ask the question again quite narrowly: if we're trying to decide what is ritualistic about ritual (and remember that I don't like the idea that glossing and so forth is just secondary and to be easily cut out), should we not focus on that multiplicity of altars and the order in which you move from the one to the other? I wouldn't pay any attention to why they told me they did it that way. That already is starting the other kinds of processes in motion.

MATEI CALINESCU: My impression is this. Jonathan, you obviously have strong opinions, yet you proclaim the principle of no privilege. How do you reconcile these two? You privilege the surface and deprivilege the depth. Your whole paper consisted of very strong value judgments. I know that the intellectual fashion is against depth and for the surface (deconstructive methods of Derrida, etc.), not, however, according to the principle of "no privilege," but rather according to the principle of "privilege the second term" (that is, in the case of model and imitation, you privilege the imitation, the imitation is the conditional possibility of the original, etcetera). But still you grant privilege, so I would say your principle of "no privilege" is purely utopian.

SMITH: No, it's probably a truly wicked thing! I liked everything you said until the last sentence. I'm not holding out for fake objectivity. For me, privilege is a funny kind of word. It doesn't have anything to do with strong opinions or anything like that; those I think you have to display, you have to argue for them where you can argue for them. It has to do with, it seems to me, a kind of mythology.

Let me go back to something that was said earlier. I can buy every point of your description of science, René, if you would allow me to substitute the word explanation for the word origin. You're doing something when you hold the word origin that makes it special, makes it carry an awful lot with it. And that's what I mean when I talk about things that are privileged. It doesn't mean strong, it doesn't mean no passion, no argument. When I say that if you look at that ritual there, you should look at the moving from the place to the place and not listen to what the people doing it say, those arguments will have to stand or fall on the grounds I give them. Talk of privilege is about presuppositions that we hold because of who we are, presuppositions that we see as self-evident. I understand "roots and origins" to be that kind of presupposition. It's not just a linguistic notion; it's the notion that religion was formed at some point in time, and that an understanding of that point in time is a privileged understanding. That's a very queer view of religion. I know of very few religions that find it necessary to tell you about that. So it's that kind of privilege that's troubling me more than if you want strength of position, but those positions will have to stand and fall on their merits.

Four

RENATO ROSALDO

Anthropological Commentary

I APOLOGIZE for speaking without having heard the discussion. I really wish I could have; I read the papers with a great deal of interest. I gathered that people had hoped to hear an anthropologist deliver authoritative remarks because all three of the papers invoke anthropology. I'm not going to do that—it would be foolhardy to try—but I will react to the papers.

My general sense in reading the papers' discussions about what happened in the Paleolithic age and earlier is like that of the farmer from Vermont: it might have been that way, and then again it might not. I see no reason to believe or disbelieve the origin stories on sacrifice in the papers. My own bias would be to encourage people to continue to do just what they're doing, but perhaps less innocently. Certainly people should check the evidence to make sure they are not saying something wildly inappropriate to the evidence. For the origin stories in the papers, there really isn't much evidence that's going to be decisive one way or the other.

I would suggest that, in much the way that one would read Freud's *Totem and Taboo*, these origin stories can be a useful exercise. This is especially so if, on the one hand, it is an exercise in conceptual clarification. If, for example, one posits a story about the primal murder, then one can understand the Oedipus complex more clearly. It could thus be used as a theoretical exercise to clarify concepts. It can be a useful exercise just as, for instance, I would read Ursula K. Le Guin's *The Word for World Is Forest* to clarify the nature of colonialism and its role in ecological destruction. I used Le Guin's book in teaching because imaginative literature can encompass so many issues in a brief span, in a way that you couldn't if you were constrained by talking about Manila in 1903. As an imaginative exercise it's enormously clarifying.

There could be a second use to which imaginative origin stories could be put. They could also be a way of talking about what people performing a sacrifice imagine to have been the primal incident. So that one's theory could say that if a certain primal incident exists in the ritual participants' imaginations, the act of sacrifice should be understood in a way that one wouldn't otherwise. That's a very different kind of enterprise from conceptual clarification. If I were going to study sacrifice, I'd ask ritual participants to talk about the imagined primal incident. I would ask participants whether they imagine that a primal incident, the really real, underlies the act of sacrifice. Is the sacrifice, in this sense, a reenactment?

Let me talk about how plausible the versions of sacrifice in the papers seem to me as an anthropologist. Maybe I'll begin with the question raised in one of the papers about whether or not cannibalism is real. My comment is a good news–bad news story. The good news is that there's no doubt in the mind of any anthropologist of repute that cannibalism is real. That is not a point for debate. W. Arens's book, *The Man-Eating Myth: Anthropology and Anthropophagy* (1979), for all its publicity, should have been about the overreporting of cannibalism and the extent to which cannibalism corresponds with Western myths about the primitive "other." I've done some work on a closely related subject. I've spent three years in northern Luzon living with a group who are headhunters. Their headhunting is vastly exaggerated and overreported, but they do headhunt; there's no question about that.

Despite lurid overreporting, there is in fact cannibalism in the world. There are many, many reliable reports. Perhaps people don't trust sailors' reports. I don't know why we should disbelieve a sailor any more than we disbelieve an anthropologist. Sailors say they've seen it firsthand, and they give a lot of circumstantial detail. The thing that's absolutely decisive is that in New Guinea there is a disease that's only transmitted through human flesh. It results from the custom of eating the human brain. If anyone remains unconvinced, in the *New York Review of Books*, Marshall Sahlins has gone over the evidence on cannibalism (Sahlins 1978-79). I'm glad to say that an anthropologist can authoritatively say that cannibalism is real, even if overreported and exaggerated in lurid ways that correspond to our own mythologies.

Another thing that I'd say as an anthropologist is that, with respect to some of Girard's work, I'm very uneasy. In anthropology, we've been through structural functionalism, and if we draw on it, we do so with the wisdom of hindsight. One must be cautious in phrasing the notion of terribly threatening chaos that is a trigger for scapegoating. If one starts with chaos and then deduces instances of scapegoating, as if that were the real energetics of the system, one will run into a lot of analytical trouble. It's just very hard to scale the degrees of social chaos, social disorganization, disruption, disturbance, and so on.

What do you mean by chaos? Navaho witchcraft is the classical example in anthropology. McCarthyism is the classical example in sociology. The Industrial Revolution is the classical example in historical sociology. Could we say, to take Navaho witchcraft as an example, that chaos is indicated by gossip about witches or by witchcraft killings? And are gossip and killings both "disturbances" of the same kind? One way out of that impasse would be to talk about the subjective experience of chaos. Then you don't need a hydraulic model where disturbance and witchcraft co-vary. Instead, you can say that when there is a perception on the part of some group that there's impending chaos, a sacrificial process begins. Such a rephrasing would enable one to keep the theoretical apparatus pretty much intact. This was one area that, as an anthropologist, made me uneasy. Maybe with such a revision you wouldn't get nearly so embroiled in the enormous empirical difficulties of analyzing degrees of disturbance and chaos.

A third and last thing that made me uneasy was the emphasis some of you put on guilt and horror about killing. No matter how many instances from within a Western tradition are piled up about this, whether one is reading Dostoyevski, or looking at actual sacrifice, or whatever, the notion of guilt as a primary term seems terribly embedded within the Western tradition. It seems the least plausible term that one could import to the Neolithic. As anthropologists, we come to Western tradition as one case and then look at Bantu as another case, so that we find the Western case to be only one example among many. For the preponderant number of examples, guilt wouldn't emerge as a key term. As I read information about sacrifice in most societies, the term guilt makes me uneasy, at least for any universal claims.

Some of Smith's remarks about domestication seemed quite cogent to me. It seemed that his was a consistent use of the term sacrifice, but one could imagine other, looser definitions. I would hope for a kind of limbering up of theories with more valences and possibilities. It seemed that the initial paper by Mack was trying to advocate something like getting away from a monolithic definition of sacrifice.

My own sense of headhunting is that it's very like sacrifice. It's not like sacrifice in a strict sense, but when its relation to feuding is attenuated, it is ritualized, and the victim is depersonalized in such a way that he or she is almost like a domesticated animal. Headhunting has to be considered from the position of more than one subject. The papers that I read didn't take on the issue of "Whose perspective are we looking at as we're interpreting?" It seemed to me that for the young men, a position very like Girard's is quite appropriate. The sense of mimesis or rivalry applies. It's adolescent turmoil and a tremendous sense of envy or rivalry. The young men want to become like older men. In this particular case, the young men want to take only one head in their lifetime. They want to wear red-hornbill earrings like the older men. Adult males have the greatest entitlement in this society, and these young men are just burning with envy. They'll weep, they carry on, they want to take a head, they want to be just like the other men. I think that Girard's theory would be enormously suggestive from their point of view.

Where I get uneasy is that I would want to look very closely at the idiom in which envy is expressed. It would be a little bit like the study of power, another trendy term these days, since Foucault and everybody else is interested in power. When I get right down to it, I need to know exactly the idiom that's being deployed in using power, so that I can notice that idiom when somebody with enormous power says, "Well, I just want to be loved." What you have to study is not the concept of power, but what it means for somebody to say, "I just want to be loved," how in practice they go about getting love and giving gifts, and so on. If you keep to the abstract notion of power, you are too far from the idiom that's actually deployed. I think you lose something because you don't understand that the guy is just trying to be loved. You're very puzzled about why he is so generous in a particular way when he has other avenues of consolidating power. Not that he doesn't consolidate power through generosity, but it's just that you see why he's chosen that tack. So with that qualification, I find Girard's terms quite useful.

But what is the position of the person in the system of sacrifice? For older men in headhunting societies, these terms of emulation and rivalry don't apply at all. Instead, what is typically going on for the older man is that he no longer needs to take a head. He's already taken a head. It's a once-in-a-lifetime thing. The older men are not full of adolescent turmoil. The young men are the constant adolescents, always ready to hit the road and go headhunting, at least by their own stereotype. The older men are not. They're much more cautious and prudent. They say, "The time is right" or "The time is not right." The thing that really gets them going is devastating personal loss. If a spouse dies suddenly, a parent dies prematurely, or somebody close to them dies, they become enraged. Among other things, there's rage in loss. One of our stereotypes is that you suffer devastating loss and you get unhappy. That's just not the case. Among the other states that one's in is rage. What these people say is that they need a place to carry their anger. So it's the anger that grows out of loss that impels to go headhunting.

Now, this view has enormous appeal. Why do people do something like headhunting? What better motive force than something that puts them in a state of rage? It turns out that in many, many cases—I haven't done a systematic job, but I've read fairly widely on this—one of the things that happens after a successful headhunting raid is that mourning prohibitions are lifted. The moral of the story is that one has to consider the social position of the people involved in the sacrificial enactment. It's quite a different sort of process for young men and for older men.

Finally, I think there is one other thing that could be questioned, and that is whether or not ritual really does encapsulate the deep wisdom of a culture. René Girard assumes that a ritual is like a coherent but cryptic text that has to be unlocked. One could have a rather different view of things. In funeral rites, for example, one could ask whether the ritual encapsulates the deep wisdom of the

culture about death, about mourning, about loss. In many instances, the ritual enables people to go on: it's something like a
crossroads; it's a catalyst that facilitates the process of mourning.
There can be many other sorts of processes going on within a single
ritual. One view holds that ritual is a highly condensed, highly coherent kind of act that's cryptic but contains, in a microcosmic way,
a wider process. Another, quite different view holds that ritual pre-
cipitates certain kinds of processes without encapsulating them. It
is more a crossroads at which a number of processes intersect
(mourning and coming of age, for example) than an encapsulation
of these processes in their totality.

Now, I wouldn't advocate either of these views as universal, but
one should consider both possibilities and gain analytical flexibility
by asking when one, the other, or yet another view obtains. That
would be another place where loosening up concepts and not insist-
ing on a monolithic view could be productive.

Discussion

WALTER BURKERT: Just one question: you said that the concept of guilt is too much a Western one to be generalized. On the other hand, you have said that these headhunting people need somehow to dehumanize their victim, that is to say, they must have some kind of moral justification for what they are doing. So what is the difference? How would you describe this, if not as guilt, this kind of moral justification that others could say is a strategy to avoid guilt, to avoid feeling guilty? How would you put this in relation to the concept of guilt?

RENATO ROSALDO: Well, I think that the idiom the Ilongot use is much more one of kinship. They say, for example, "We don't want to think of this person as being like one of our kin or one of our brethren." They are making an effort to push the person outside the group. They describe the victim, for instance, as the spot where the person urinated, in a dehumanizing way. They no doubt have trouble killing their fellow humans, so there is an effort to treat them as nonhuman.

It's just that the Western apparatus of guilt is not there. Instead, their idea is to say of victims that "they're not like my brothers." What happens when a Westerner comes across such practices is that you ask about how somebody could get to this position of dehumanizing the victim. One of the things that we inevitably do as Westerners is draw on our Western imagination. We say, "If I were to think such a thing, I would do so through a notion of guilt." But I never heard them using that idiom. One uses Western categories and deploys the idiom of guilt too much, so that it takes on an exaggerated importance. It's an idiom that is very easy for us to elaborate, but very hard for most other cultures to elaborate. It's not that it's totally absent, just that it's not at all central.

BURKERT: They need a form of excuse, so to speak?

ROSALDO: Well, yes, I suppose so, but I think there is a gap between an excuse and a very elaborate notion of guilt.

BURTON MACK: Excuse is okay with you?

ROSALDO: Well, it's okay with me only if it's not so charged and loaded and elaborated. An excuse to me is a fairly cursory thing, you know, something like saying casually, "Sorry about that."

BURKERT: In relation to those hunting customs, too, you could use the word excuse for what hunters do when they kill their animal.

ROSALDO: Well, the thing is that they say, "Sorry I have to take your life." That's very different from what I think of when I say, "Sorry, fellow, but I've gotta live too." They do this in ritual forms. As I was reading through your work, I looked at the centrality and elaboration of the term guilt. It just didn't ring true for most cultures; it seemed too central, too verbally elaborated. It would be like taking the notion of excuse and running with it. I think that the headhunters I lived among take the notion of excuse and mean just that and no more than that.

BURKERT: Is it a difference of intensification?

ROSALDO: Yes, and elaboration.

BURKERT: Or are things totally different?

ROSALDO: In the end, it's quite different in just how central it is, how elaborated it will be as an idiom, how consequential it will be in the sacrifice. As I read the very elaborated notions of guilt, they appeared to be enormously consequential in ritual and in other terms, whereas the excuse, in the sense of simply bumping into somebody and saying, "I'm sorry," and going on about my day, is not enormously consequential. By consequential I mean: does it lead to a lot of other symbolic and actual actions? It isn't consequential in that sense. It's about as consequential as bumping into somebody and saying, "I'm sorry." I don't dwell on that. I don't think about it the rest of the day. I don't do atonement at the end of the day. I don't darken my face and wear a hair shirt. I just forget about it. That's the way with hunters I've seen hunt. It just doesn't seem to ramify through the rest of what they do. That's where my discomfort with the formulation lies.

FRITS STAAL: I feel unhappy about the concept of guilt in relation to other cultures, but I feel much unhappier with your concept of excuse, especially when you say the headhunters take only one head during their life, which turns a young man into an old man. That's certainly a very consequential transition.

ROSALDO: You could flip it around and say, "So it's not the excuse that's leading to this. Then what should be the central term?"

STAAL: It need not be guilt, I think.

ROSALDO: That's right, but what is the central term?

RENÉ GIRARD: It seems to me that Freud is pertinent here, for when we say "reify" or "dehumanize in order not to feel guilt," we are very close to something that Freud called fetishization.

ROSALDO: My sense in this particular system is that the dehumanization that goes on is not the most important thing. Freud can always catch you because he says it's the most trivial detail that can be most important. I would see the elaboration of an idiom of anger as the most important thing. These headhunters, in a way that's quite unfamiliar to us, see anger as a source of vitality and energy. It's enactment that is a key thing in this particular system. They don't deny their anger; rather, it is for them enormously productive. Anger is the sort of thing that gets one up in the morning. Their notions of anger would be my starting point, rather than guilt or excuse.

GIRARD: I like the reference to anger, but anger is a Western concept, just as Walter's notion of guilt is. Is it a matter of some Western concepts being limited and others being universal? Another question: when you say "primal murder" and so forth, are you referring to my paper?

ROSALDO: I was referring at that moment to the Freudian idea of the primal crime. Your papers seemed to assume that there must have been an actual incident that sacrifice reenacts.

GIRARD: Even though I admire *Totem and Taboo* more than most anthropologists do, the notion of a single primal crime is alien to my thinking. The evidence gathered by Freud is relevant, I think, but in my view it points to the innumerable instances of unanimous violence that unified or reunified specific human groups before their specific forms of mythology and ritual could be derived from it. Each instance can be called "original" in a relative sense. Or perhaps I should say "initial" in the sense that it must happen before the ritual imitation and mythological interpretation that it triggers, because it provides them with a model. It is not original or primal in an absolute sense.

So the notion of one primal murder is not part of my theory; but if you have a witch-hunt or a plague that gives rise to a text in which mythological accusations similar to that of the Oedipus myth occur, then you can say that the pattern has a historical basis and origin. I agree completely with you that the degree of disturbance cannot be measured, and that all we can talk about is the subjective, the system of representation of the people involved in those events; but I would say that we could use the term primary murder if that murder then gave rise to mythological themes.

ROSALDO: Very much so, but I think that the primary murder I'm most concerned with is the one that supposedly took place in the Paleolithic or earlier.

GIRARD: Yes, the connotations of primal, primary origin, taken in a certain sense, refer back to the type of thinking from which I want to dissociate myself. There was no explicit or implicit reference to Freud's "primal murder" in my paper. All references were to my own views.

ROSALDO: I was referring to the *Totem and Taboo* story of origin.

GIRARD: One word about "chaos" in my work. I agree one hundred percent that chaos is subjective. I agree that no objective measurement of a societal disturbance can be derived from this subjective fear. Othello's jealousy is a good illustration: "When I love thee not, Chaos is come again." Othello's experience would remain primarily subjective even if he had a real cause to be jealous, and he has none. The chaos in his heart does not necessarily mean chaos everywhere. And yet Desdemona really dies. Subjective as it is, the feeling of chaos can nevertheless generate objective events, such as the murder of Desdemona.

When communities describe in terms of chaos epidemics of plague or the other scourges, real or imaginary, by which they feel threatened, they are likely to resort to victimage, or scapegoating. One observation leads to another. Hundreds of myths, we all know, begin with a so-called original chaos and continue with some form of violence, often described as unanimous, directed against a single victim or several victims.

The human mind is naturally curious and cannot help wondering if the same relationship that we have between subjective chaos and objective victimage in *Othello*, or in medieval persecution, might not obtain in traditional religion, since we have the same thematic sequence in all cases. *Othello* is fiction, but medieval persecutions are real. If you are willing to envisage the possibility of real persecution as a real origin in the medieval examples, why not envisage the possibility of the same real origin in the case of mythology and rituals? Are they the poetical work of another Shakespeare, or are they the work of real persecutors? That is the question.

This is not the "original murder" of *Totem and Taboo*, and it is not some other origin story in the style of Rousseau or anyone else. And I will repeat once more that it is not the Frazerian scapegoat, either. Nine times out of ten, my idea is wrongly assimilated to one of these better-known ideas: (1) Freud's primal murder, (2) some other origin story that remains undefined, or (3) the Frazerian scapegoat. It seems impossible to dispel these misconceptions. An origin story is, by definition, unique. The phenomena I am interested in are, by definition, countless, and they turn into stories only in societies where they surface as myths. In the modern world, they are revealed as collective persecution because, as a society, we no longer buy the perspective of the persecutors, which is always a kind of myth.

One word, if I may, about the exploitation of the "lurid." We agreed earlier that it should be avoided. We might have added that there is also a danger, today, of exaggerating this exploitation, in order to whitewash the genuinely lurid in primitive religion, for the sake of castigating Western sins against non-Western societies. Renato Rosaldo has obviously not succumbed to this danger, since he maintains that cannibalism and headhunting really exist, in the face of all those who are tempted to deny their existence.

I am glad to hear a respected field anthropologist guarantee the reality of the phenomenon. This is quite different from the opinion voiced by Jonathan Smith in footnote twelve of his paper. Jonathan did not take human sacrifice into account, he says, any more than "other modes of the ritual killing of humans (headhunting, cannibalism, 'sacral regicide,' etc.)," for the following reason: "The evidence for these practices is frequently less certain than for animal sacrifice—often being more illustrative of intercultural polemics than cultural facts." His entire thesis depends on this negative justification for the exclusion of all phenomena that involve the sacrifice of human beings. Jonathan himself does not say that the evidence is nonexistent. He says it is less certain.

I think anthropology is always exposed to a double threat. In the past, it occasionally became an instrument of colonial imperialism, of the Western illusion of superiority. Today, the opposite danger threatens. It can turn into a game of "Trivial Pursuit." It can also turn into an unscientific celebration of the primitive and a monotonous indictment of the white devils.

The new dangers are just as ideological as the old ones. It takes no courage at all to denounce the old ones—everybody does it—but it does take some courage to denounce the new ones, because they are extremely popular and you run the risk of being alone. The new ideological fallacies are often well intentioned, but they can also hide a more subtle form of condescension toward the non-Western world.

The idea that violence is primarily a Western phenomenon cannot even be refuted, because it is simply too absurd and is never expressed directly, but it silently permeates much contemporary writing. The fact that an earlier anthropology was dominated by the opposite absurdity explains some of the current excesses, but it does not justify them.

The respect for cultural singularities is essential, but it is not correctly understood if it paralyzes theoretical thinking. If all universal notions are to be condemned as "monolithic," anthropology will never become a science, and its interest is quite limited. The search for maximum flexibility and "loose" definitions is legitimate in purely descriptive work, but description cannot be the sum total of anthropology. If the search for a tightening of definitions and for intellectual tools applicable to more than one culture is discouraged *a priori*, the current practice can only lead to intellectual sterility. Even in literary studies, the search for universals has never ceased.

I admire Renato Rosaldo's work precisely because it does not let the trends to which I am alluding get in the way of the facts when the facts contradict the trends. I feel, however, that his uneasiness about what Walter Burkert is doing, or what I am doing, is a little colored by these same trends. When I hear Renato speak on specific anthropological facts, I see no contradiction between his fieldwork and my own views. He told us not only that headhunting exists, but that, first, it is very much *like sacrifice*; I do not have to tell you that I agree. And, second, that mimetic rivalry fits the mood of the young headhunters; I do not have to tell you that I agree. And, finally, that old men hunt heads as a result not of mimetic rivalry, but of "a devastating loss." They do not "get unhappy" in the sense that "one of our [Western] stereotypes" demands, but they may get into a state of "rage."

This "rage" triggers a reaction that is not unusual, even though it assumes the culturally specific form of headhunting. How is headhunting justified? Let us listen again to Renato: "What these people say is that they need a place to carry their anger. So it's the anger that grows out of loss that impels them to go headhunting."

This violent displacement of violence on an objectively irrelevant victim is exactly what I mean by scapegoating: nothing less and nothing more. I do not mean Leviticus 16, but the standard modern meaning of the word scapegoat. I said it many times already, and this spectacular example of sacrificial scapegoating provides me with an excellent illustration of what I mean. Headhunting is not a collective deed, to be sure, but it is sanctioned, I suppose, by the approval of the entire group.

If headhunting is really motivated either by mimetic rivalry or by this type of scapegoating, and if, as a kind of institution, it is "like sacrifice," can we avoid the inference that a close relationship may exist between sacrifice and the mimetic-rivalry-plus-scapegoating scheme that I propose?

LANGDON ELSBREE: But why a head for the older men? They're cautious; they don't have to prove themselves again. They could spear fish, kill a bear, or go out and chop a tree. There are many possibilities. In that system of explanation, is there some concealed notion of an exchange going on? Why does it have to be a human head?

ROSALDO: It's funny you should say that, because that's where I started. I'd read a lot of anthropology before meeting the Ilongots during my fieldwork. I thought about Lévi-Strauss and Edmund Leach and decided, for bookish reasons, that exchange must be at the root of this. When Ilongots said, "I headhunt because I need a place to carry my anger," I would say to them, "Do you believe that one death cancels another?" I asked about exchange because I thought it would explain things. These people would say to me, "Well, I guess somebody might think that." Since *I* had just thought so, they were right. But then they said, "But *we* don't think that." They saw headhunting as a way of venting their anger. There was no notion of reciprocity and exchange.

Perhaps it's like trying to have an exchange theory of pleasure. With pleasure, the goal of the act is pleasure itself. You don't necessarily have a notion of exchange. I think that it's very like that for the older Ilongot men. The older men participate in the act, but they don't do what's called "taking a head." They'll often hold the victim so that a younger man can take the head. I've never seen this, but I've heard many reports of people learning of the death of somebody they've loved very much, being devastated by it, picking up a long knife, and just chopping up everything in sight, just hacking it to pieces. When it's culturally available that one can go headhunting, that's the ultimate place to carry one's rage and anger. If it's not culturally available, then you hack up the furniture.

ELSBREE: Can you tell from the story or from a gloss on the rituals why that would be the ultimate? Why the human heads?

ROSALDO: They feel it's the ultimate act of violence and anger. Their sense is that it's cathartic. What they do with the head is simply throw it away. They talk about themselves, in doing that, as letting go of something. It's not like our stereotype in much of the literature: acquiring soul-stuff.

In the tropical forest, there is a forest canopy with very little underbrush. These trees often have many vines on them. They speak of themselves as being like a tree burdened with vines until they go raiding. They feel that they are encumbered by anger that's built up, that's pent up in them. They are trying to get rid of the "vines." Their ritual is a kind of peculiar sacrifice. I've been troubled by the family resemblance problem, because it's very like sacrifice but not exactly like sacrifice in a strict sense. In the ritual attitude, it's probably more like sacrifice than one would imagine at first. The Ilongots feel that there is nothing else quite like headhunting. They hunt animals several times a week, but that's just not the same. They don't have a very elaborate explanation of why it's a greater act of violence to kill a human being than a wild pig; but I don't need a very elaborate explanation for the difference they see.

STAAL: It doesn't have much to do with machos proving themselves, then?

ROSALDO: No, it really doesn't. That's the great shock in living with headhunters; they are not very macho. They do a lot of child care, and they are in fact very gentle. Hunting is a job you can do at night, and then during the day you're kind of groggy, so you take care of the kids while the kids' mother is out in the fields. I was very struck in the Philippines that Roman Catholic lowlanders were much more macho. I did once see acculturated members of this tribe displaying bravado, but most Ilongots did very little of that kind of thing.

GIRARD: Let me be provocative vis-à-vis anthropologists. Can we really consider that a culture in which it would be normal to take out one's anger in headhunting, rather than going to play golf or poker, should be regarded with equanimity? Why should we not adopt the older view and say that these people should be Westernized?

ROSALDO: And give up the bad habit?

GIRARD: Well, why not consider headhunting a bad habit? I really consider headhunting a bad habit, personally.

ROSALDO: Let me tell you what I have to say about that. I am not here as an advocate of headhunting. I feel that it's a bad habit.

GIRARD: You feel it's a bad habit?

ROSALDO: It's a very bad habit. I was there for a year before I realized that they did take heads. I thought they had stopped immediately after the Second World War. Because when missionaries in the area told me that my companions had recently gone headhunting, I said, "Look, I've heard you guys take heads still." They said, "No! How could you possibly think this of me? I held your wife's hand on the trail. I carried you across this bridge. I fed you. I've looked after you. How could you think that I would do such a thing?" I said, "You're absolutely right. I'm sorry I brought it up. So, tell me about how you used to take heads." It turned out that after I had been there a year, something cracked. We were going to a place, and a man said, "That's where I took a head." Pretty soon everybody, with much embarrassed giggling, started to tell their headhunting stories. Within about three weeks, I realized that every man there above the age of eighteen had taken a head.

ROBERT HAMERTON-KELLY: Why did they cover it up? Did they feel guilt?

ROSALDO: No, it's against the law.

HAMERTON-KELLY: Oh, they're just afraid of the gendarmes.

ROSALDO: Yes, they have been imprisoned for it.

GIRARD: What you say is very impressive, because you have just come from headhunting country; you know what you're talking about. I fear, however, that nine out of ten modern anthropologists would try to play down the incidence of such practices.

ROSALDO: Now, there is one thing I'd like to say about the bad habit. Let me begin by saying that I've written a book on these people. The book is meant to show that headhunting has stopped many times, and that it's not a unitary thing.

When I suddenly discovered that everybody took heads, that all the nice people who held my hand and fed me had taken heads, I felt completely disoriented. You can't imagine what a devastating experience it was. It confounds your categories, to say the least. Well, it did a lot more confounding than that with me. My categories were the least of the problem. The way I came to terms with their bad habit of headhunting started when I was classified 1-A for the draft. I told my companions, "I've got to fight in Vietnam." (It turned out I didn't, but I had just been classified 1-A.) They said, "Well, obviously you should stay here with us." I said, "Stay here with you?" They said, "No soldiers could come here and get you; you'll be fine." I said, "I thought you guys were into headhunting. Don't you think I should go off to fight the war?" They said, "War? Soldiers sell their bodies." They were more horrified at the news that I might become a soldier than I was at the news that they took heads.

You should keep in mind that in three weeks of June 1945, they lost one-third of their population. Imagine what a catastrophe that was. The Japanese were forced to retreat into that area. The Ilongots had seen the Second World War up close. They said that what had appalled them morally was not the loss of population; that devastated them in quite another way. What appalled them morally and was utterly beyond their comprehension was the fact that one guy would get up there and tell his brothers, as they would put it, to move into the line of fire. And they said, "I could never ask my brother to sell his body." They said, "That's unspeakable; how can a human being do that?" They were just horrified when they saw the soldiers come out of a protected area and move into the line of fire because one person was telling them to do that. It's hard to describe how morally appalled they were by this. It was just unthinkable to them that anybody could do that. And then I realized that I lived in a society with its own bad habits. Headhunting is a bad habit, there's no doubt about it.

BURKERT: How interesting. It's one of the most appalling phenomena that, in our society, structures of authority and of command can make men do nearly anything; but I was thinking of a simpler stage, namely, the concept of aggression. I understand that in Ilongot society every man who wishes to be respected must kill another person. So I would say that this is a society that teaches aggression in its most dangerous form: accomplished murder. And in your second level of headhunting, these older men who had suffered a loss—this looks like a model case of the frustration-aggression hypothesis.

ROSALDO: It's a part of the process of mourning. It's not frustration; it's loss that they're reacting to.

BURKERT: Are loss and frustration not very closely related? My question was, why do you avoid speaking about aggression? There, I would say, is a society that has really made aggression in a special form the very foundation of prestige and order.

ROSALDO: This is again from one of the papers, and you will recognize it, but it's a society that has a tradition. My view of tradition is that it is something people receive and remold, and receive and remold, and so on. It's not inert. They have in fact given up headhunting at various times during this century. It's a society that cultivates the notion that can be loosely translated as "anger." What anger is, is a subject for a book itself. In fact, the book on that quite complicated concept has been written by Michelle Rosaldo.[1] It's a society that has many forms of cultivating something like anger. Their concept of anger has many vectors that we wouldn't expect it to have. It has a tradition that emphasizes anger, but it's never quite as we'd imagine it. I mean, it's anger in very specific contexts, so as we were saying before, there's not a lot of bravado, not a lot of male display. It doesn't mean that you're displaying aggression all over the place all of the time. Either you're a mature person or you're not, in that society. Either you're an adult or you're a child. I guess that's more the way to put it. But it's really not that that differentiates the degrees of prestige and influence. What differentiates more is the capacity to orate and be persuasive. There is very little leverage for people; it's a classic Rousseau-type situation. If you don't like the way somebody is pushing you around, you move away. So there are real limits to the authority somebody can exercise. So a term like prestige, unless very carefully stripped of a lot of its baggage, is quite misleading, because prestige suggests enormous differentiation within an adult population.

[1] *Knowledge and Passion: Ilongot Ideas of Self and Social Life* (Cambridge, Eng., 1980).—ED.

References

References

d'Aquili, E. G., C. D. Laughlin, and J. McManus. 1979. *The Spectrum of Ritual: A Biogenetic Structural Analysis.* New York.

Ardrey, R. 1976. *The Hunting Hypothesis.* London.

Baudy, G. J. 1983. "Hierarchie oder die Verteilung des Fleisches," in B. Gladigow and H. G. Kippenberg, ed., *Neue Ansätze in der Religionswissenschaft* 131-74. Munich.

Baumann, H. 1950. "Nyama, die Rachemacht," *Paideuma* 4: 191-230.

Bernays, J. 1866. *Theophrastos' Schrift über Frömmigkeit.* Berlin.

Burkert, W. 1966. "Greek Tragedy and Sacrificial Ritual," *Greek, Roman, and Byzantine Studies* 7: 87-121.

———. 1971. "Review of R. Stiglitz, *Die grossen Göttinnen Arkadiens,* Wien, 1967," *Anzeiger für die Altertumwissenschaft* 24: 200-202.

———. 1972a. *Homo Necans: Interpretationen altgriechischer Opferriten und Mythen.* Berlin.

———. 1972b. *Lore and Science in Ancient Pythagoreanism.* Cambridge, Mass.

———. 1974. "Die Absurdität der Gewalt und das Ende der Tragödie: Euripides' Orestes," *Antike und Abendland* 20: 97-109.

———. 1979. *Structure and History in Greek Mythology and Ritual.* Berkeley, Calif.

———. 1981. "Glaube und Verhalten: Zeichengehalt und Wirkungsmacht von Opferritualen," in *Le Sacrifice dans l'antiquité: Entretiens sur l'antiquité classique* 27: 91-125.

———. 1983. *Homo Necans: The Anthropology of Ancient Greek Sacrificial Ritual and Myth.* Tr. Peter Bing. Berkeley, Calif.

Burridge, K. 1969. *New Heaven and New Earth: A Study of Millenarian Activities.* New York.

———. 1970. *Mambu: A Study of Melanesian Cargo Movements and Their Social and Ideological Background.* New York.

Calame, C. 1973. "Essai d'une analyse sémantique de rituels grecs," *Études de Lettres* 6: 53-82.

Campbell, J. 1959 (1969). *The Masks of God: Primitive Mythology.* New York.

Carthy, J. D., and F. J. Ebling, eds. 1964. *The Natural History of Aggression*. New York.

Colman, A. M., ed. 1982. *Cooperation and Competition in Humans and Animals*. Wokingham, Eng.

Dart, R. 1953. "The Predatory Transition from Ape to Man," *International Anthropological and Linguistic Review* 1: 201-19.

Davies, N. 1981. *Human Sacrifice in History and Today*. London.

Dawkins, R. 1976. *The Selfish Gene*. Oxford.

Detienne, M. 1979. *Dionysus Slain*. Baltimore. Originally published in 1977 as *Dionysos mis à mort* (Paris).

Detienne, M., and J. P. Vernant. 1979. *La Cuisine du sacrifice en pays grec*. Paris.

Diener, P., and E. E. Robbin. 1978. "Ecology, Evolution, and the Search for Cultural Origins: The Question of Islamic Pig Prohibition," *Current Anthropology* 19: 493-509.

Douglas, M. 1957. "Animals in Lele Religious Symbolism," *Africa* 27: 46-58.

Edwards, S. W. 1978. "Nonutilitarian Activities in the Lower Paleolithic: A Look at the Two Kinds of Evidence," *Current Anthropology* 19: 135-37.

Eliade, M. 1967. *From Primitives to Zen: A Thematic Sourcebook on the History of Religions*. New York.

———. 1969. *The Quest: History and Meaning in Religion*. Chicago.

Fossey, D. 1981. "The Imperiled Mountain Gorilla," *National Geographic* 159: 501-23.

Franz, L. 1937. *Religion und Kunst der Vorzeit*. Prague.

Frazer, J. G. 1922 (1963). *The Golden Bough: A Study in Magic and Religion*. One-volume abridged ed. New York.

Freeman, D. 1964. "Human Aggression in Anthropological Perspective," in J. D. Carthy and F. J. Ebling, eds., *The Natural History of Aggression* 109-19. New York.

Freud, S. 1907 (1924). "Obsessive Acts and Religious Practices," in Vol. 2 of J. Riviere, ed., *Sigmund Freud, M.D., LL.D.: Collected Papers* 25-35. London.

Friedrich, A. 1941-43. "Die Forschung über das frühzeitliche Jägertum," *Paideuma* 2: 20-43.

Galdikas, B. M. F. 1980. "Living with the Great Orange Apes," *National Geographic* 157: 830-53.

Galdikas, B. M. F., and G. Teleki. 1981. "Variations in the Subsistence Activities of Female and Male Pongids: New Perspectives on the Origins of Hominid Labor Division," *Current Anthropology* 22: 241-56.

Gay, V. 1975. "Psychopathology and Ritual," *The Psychoanalytic Review* 62: 493-507.

———. 1979. *Freud on Ritual: Reconstruction and Critique*. Missoula, Mont.

Girard, R. 1965. *Deceit, Desire, and the Novel.* Baltimore, Md. Originally published in 1961 as *Mensonge romantique et vérité romanesque* (Paris).
————. 1977. *Violence and the Sacred.* Baltimore, Md. Originally published in 1972 as *La Violence et le sacré* (Paris).
————. 1978. *Des Choses cachées depuis la fondation du monde.* With J. M. Oughourlian and G. Lefort. Paris.
————. 1982. *Le Bouc émissaire.* Paris.
Goldschmidt, W. R. 1966. *Comparative Functionalism: An Essay in Anthropological Theory.* Berkeley, Calif.
Goodall, J. 1977. "Infant Killing and Cannibalism in Free-Living Chimpanzees," *Folia Primatologica* 28: 259-82.
Gruppe, O. 1921. *Geschichte der klassischen Mythologie und Religionsgeschichte.* Leipzig.
Haken, H. 1978. *Synergetics: An Introduction.* 2d ed. Berlin.
————. 1981. *Erfolgsgeheimnisse der Natur: Synergetik: Die Lehre vom Zusammenwirken.* Stuttgart.
Hallowell, A. I. 1926. "Bear Ceremonialism in the Northern Hemisphere," *American Anthropologist* 28: 1-175.
Harding, R. S. O, and G. Teleki, eds. 1981. *Omnivorous Primates: Gathering and Hunting in Human Evolution.* New York.
Harrison, J. E. 1921. *Epilegomena to the Study of Greek Religion.* Cambridge, Eng.
Henrichs, A. 1972. *Die Phoinikika des Lollianos: Fragmente eines neuen griechischen Romans.* Bonn.
Herrenschmidt, O. 1978. "A qui profite le crime? Cherchez le sacrifiant: Un désir fatalement meurtrier," *L'Homme* 18: 7-18.
Hofstadter, D. R. 1983a. "Virus-like Sentences and Self-replicating Structures," *Scientific American* 248.1: 14-19.
————. 1983b. "Computer Tournaments of the Prisoner's Dilemma Suggest How Cooperation Evolves," *Scientific American* 248.5: 14-20.
Hubert, H., and M. Mauss. 1964. *Sacrifice: Its Nature and Function.* Chicago. Originally published in 1899 as "Essai sur la nature et la fonction sociale du sacrifice," *L'Année Sociologique* (Paris).
Isaac, E. 1962. "On the Domestication of Cattle," *Science* 137: 195-204.
————. 1963. "Myths, Cults and Livestock Breeding," *Diogenes* 41: 70-93.
————. 1970. *Geography of Domestication.* Englewood Cliffs, N.J.
Isaac, G. L. 1978a. "Food Sharing and Human Evolution," *Journal of Anthropological Research* 34: 311-25.
————. 1978b. "The Food-Sharing Behavior of Protohuman Hominids," *Scientific American* 238: 90-108.
Jensen, A. E. 1939. *Hainuwele: Volkserzählungen von der Molukken-Inseln Ceram.* Frankfurt am Main.
————. 1963. *Myth and Cult Among Primitive Peoples.* Tr. Marianna Tax Choldin and Wolfgang Weissleder. Chicago. Originally published in

1951 as *Mythos und Kult bei Naturvölkern: religionswissenschaftliche Betrachtungen* (Wiesbaden).

Johnson, R. N. 1972. *Aggression in Man and Animal*. Philadelphia.

Kindaichi, K. 1949. "The Concepts Behind the Ainu Bear Festival," *Southwestern Journal of Anthropology* 5: 345-50.

Kitagawa, J. M. 1961. "Ainu Bear Festival (Iyomante)," *History of Religions* 1: 95-151.

Koby, F. E. 1951. "L'Ours des cavernes et les paléolithiques," *L'Anthropologie* 55: 304-8.

Koch-Gründberg, T. [1908-]1910. *Zwei Jahren unter den Indianern: Reisen in Nordwest-Brasilien, 1903-1905*. 2 vols. Berlin.

Konner, M. 1982. *The Tangled Wing: Biological Constraints on the Human Spirit*. New York.

Koppers, W. 1933. "Der Bärenkult in ethnologischer und prähistorischer Beleuchtung," *Palaeobiologica* 6: 47-64.

Kruntz, G. S. 1980. "Sapienization and Speech," *Current Anthropology* 21: 773-92.

Lancaster, J. B. 1978. "Carrying and Sharing in Human Evolution," *Human Nature* 1: 82-89.

Leach, E. R. 1964. "Anthropological Aspects of Language: Animal Categories and Verbal Abuse," in E. H. Lenneberg, ed., *New Directions in the Study of Language*. Cambridge, Mass.

Lee, R. B., and I. DeVore, eds. 1968. *Man the Hunter*. Chicago.

Leroi-Gourhan, A. 1971. *Les Religions de la préhistoire: Paléolithique*. 2d ed. Paris.

Lévi-Strauss, C. 1963. *Totemism*. Tr. Rodney Needham. Boston.

———. 1966. *The Savage Mind*. Chicago. Originally published in 1962 as *La Pensée sauvage* (Paris).

———. 1981. *The Naked Man*. Tr. J. and D. Weightman. New York. Originally published in 1971 as *L'Homme nu* (Paris).

Lieberman, P. 1972. "On the Evolution of Human Language," *Proceedings of the 7th International Congress of Phonetic Sciences* 258-72. Leiden.

———. 1975. *On the Origins of Language*. New York.

———. 1976. "Interactive Models for Evolution: Neural Mechanisms, Anatomy, and Behavior," *Annals of the New York Academy of Sciences*. 280: *Origins and Evolution of Language and Speech* 660-72.

Lieberman, P., E. S. Crelin, and D. H. Klatt. 1972. "Phonetic Ability and Related Anatomy of the Newborn and Adult Human, Neanderthal Man, and the Chimpanzee," *American Anthropologist* 74: 287-307.

Livingston, P., ed. 1984. *Disorder and Order: Proceedings of the Stanford International Symposium, September 14-16, 1981*. Stanford Literary Studies 1. Saratoga, Calif.: Anma Libri.

Lorenz, K. 1966. *On Aggression*. New York. Originally published in 1963 as *Das sogenannte Böse: Zur Naturgeschichte der Aggression*.

Lot-Falck, E. 1953. *Les Rites de chasse chez les peuples sibériens*. Paris.

Lumsden, C. J., and E. O. Wilson. 1980. *Genes, Mind and Culture*. Cambridge, Mass.

Malinowski, B. 1948. *Magic, Science, and Religion*. New York.

Maringer, J. 1960. *The Gods of Prehistoric Man*. New York.

———. 1968. "Die Opfer des paläolithischen Menschen," *Anthropica: Gedenkschrift zum 100. Geburtstag von P. Wilhelm Schmidt* 249-71. Vienna.

Marshall, L. 1976. *The !Kung of Nyae Nyae*. Cambridge, Mass.

Mauss, M. 1967. *The Gift: Forms and Functions of Exchange in Archaic Societies*. New York. Originally published in 1925 as *Essai sur le don, forme archaïque de l'échange* (Paris).

Meggitt, M. J. 1957. "Notes on the Vegetable Foods of the Walbiri of Central Australia," *Oceania* 28: 143-45.

Mellaart, J. 1967. *Çatal Hüyük: A Neolithic Town in Anatolia*. London.

Meuli, K. 1946. "Griechische Opferbräuche," *Phyllobolia: Festschrift Peter Von der Mühll* 185-288. Basel. Reprinted in 1975 in K. Meuli, *Gesammelte Schriften* 2: 907-1021. Basel.

Milgrom, Jacob. 1970. "The Function of the Hatta't Sacrifice" (in Hebrew), *Tarbiz* 40: 1-8.

———. 1976. "Sacrifice and Offerings, OT," *The Interpreter's Dictionary of the Bible*, supplementary vol. Nashville, Tenn.

Morris, D. 1967. *The Naked Ape: A Zoologist's Study of the Human Animal*. New York.

Moyer, K. E. 1968. "Kinds of Aggression and Their Physiological Basis," *Communications in Behavioral Biology* 2: 65-87.

Müller-Karpe, H. 1966. *Handbuch der Vorgeschichte*. Munich.

Narr, K. J. 1952. "Das höhere Jägertum: Jüngere Jagd- und Sammelstufe," in F. Valjavec, ed., *Historia Mundi* 1: 502-22. Bern.

di Nola, A. 1972. "Demythicization in Certain Primitive Cultures," *History of Religions* 12: 1-27.

Piskaty, L. K. 1957. "Ist das Pygmäenwerk von Herrn Trilles eine zuverlässige Quelle?," *Anthropos* 52: 33-48.

Pohlhausen, H. 1953. "Zum Motive der Rentierversenkug," *Anthropos* 48: 987-90.

Pötscher, W. 1964. *Theophrastos Peri Eusebeias*. Leiden.

Rappaport, R. A. 1971. "Ritual, Sanctity, and Cybernetics," *American Anthropologist* 73: 59-76.

———. 1979. *Ecology, Meaning and Religion*. Richmond, Calif.

Reichel-Dolmatoff, G. 1971. *Amazonian Cosmos: The Sexual and Religious Symbolism of the Tukano Indians*. Chicago. Originally published in 1963 as *Desana: Le Symbolisme universel des Indiens Tukano de Vaupés* (Paris).

Reik, T. 1931. *Ritual: Psychoanalytic Studies*. New York. Originally published in 1928 as *Das Ritual: Psychoanalytische Studien* (Leipzig).

Robinson, J. M., ed. 1977. *The Nag Hammadi Library in English*. New York.

Rosaldo, R. 1980. *Ilongot Headhunting, 1885-1974: A Study in Society and History.* Stanford, Calif.

Ross, E. B. 1978. "Food Taboos, Diet, and Hunting Strategy: The Adaptation to Animals in Amazon Cultural Ecology," *Current Anthropology* 19: 1-16.

Russell, C., and W. M. Russell. 1979. "The Natural History of Violence," *Journal of Medical Ethics* 5: 108-17.

Sahlins, M. 1978-79. "Culture as Protein and Profit," *New York Review of Books*, Nov. 23, 1978, March 22, 1979, June 28, 1979.

Scheff, T. J. 1977. "The Distancing of Emotion in Ritual," *Current Anthropology* 18: 483-90.

Silk, J. B. 1978. "Patterns of Food Sharing Among Mother and Infant Chimpanzees at Gome National Park, Tanzania," *Folia Primatologica* 29: 129-41.

Smith, J. Z. 1970. "The Influence of Symbols on Social Change: A Place on Which to Stand," *Worship* 44: 457-75. (Reprinted in Smith 1978a: 129-46.)

———. 1971. "*Adde Parvum Parvo Magnus Acervus Erit*," *History of Religions* 11: 67-90. (Reprinted in Smith 1978a: 240-64.)

———. 1974. "Animals and Plants in Myth and Legend," *Encyclopædia Britannica*, 15th ed., 1: 911-18.

———. 1976. "A Pearl of Great Price and a Cargo of Yams: A Study in Situational Incongruity," *History of Religions* 16: 1-19. (Reprinted in Smith 1982a: 90-101.)

———. 1978a. *Map Is Not Territory: Studies in the History of Religion.* Leiden.

———. 1978b. "Map Is Not Territory," in Smith 1978a: 289-309.

———. 1980. "The Bare Facts of Ritual," *History of Religions* 20: 112-27. (Reprinted in Smith 1982a: 53-65.)

———. 1982a. *Imagining Religion: From Babylon to Jonestown.* Chicago.

———. 1982b. "In Comparison a Magic Dwells," in Smith 1982a: 19-35.

———. 1982c. "Sacred Persistence," in Smith 1982a: 36-52.

———. 1983. "No Need to Travel to the Indies: Judaism and the Study of Religion," in J. Neusner, ed., *Take Judaism, For Example* 215-26. Chicago.

Smith, W. J. 1979. "Ritual and the Ethology of Communication," in E. G. d'Aquili et al., *The Spectrum of Ritual: A Biogenetic Structural Analysis* 51-79. New York.

Staal, F. 1979. "Ritual Syntax," in *Sanskrit and Indian Studies: Festschrift Ingalls* 119-42. Dordrecht.

———. 1980. "The Meaninglessness of Ritual," *Numen* 26: 2-22.

———. 1982. "Ritual, Grammar, and the Origins of Science in India," *Journal of Indian Philosophy* 10: 3-35.

Stone, L. 1981. *The Past and the Present.* Boston.

Storr, A. 1968. *Human Aggression.* New York.

Tambiah, S. J. 1969. "Animals Are Good to Think and Good to Prohibit," *Ethnology* 8: 423-59.

Teleki, G. 1973a. *The Predatory Behavior of Wild Chimpanzees.* Lewisburg, Pa.

———. 1973b. "The Omnivorous Chimpanzee," *Scientific American* 228.1: 32-42.

Trilles, R. P. 1933. *Les Pygmées de la forêt équatoriale.* Paris.

Turner, V. 1967. *The Forest of Symbols: Aspects of Ndembu Ritual.* Ithaca, N.Y.

———. 1968 (1981). *The Drums of Affliction: A Study of Religious Processes Among the Ndembu of Zambia.* Ithaca, N.Y.

———. 1969. *The Ritual Process: Structure and Anti-Structure.* Chicago.

Tuzin, D. F. 1980. *The Voice of the Tambaran.* Berkeley, Calif.

Ucko, P. J., and G. W. Dimbleby, eds. 1969. *The Domestication and Exploitation of Plants and Animals.* Chicago.

van Baal, J. 1976. "Offering, Sacrifice and Gift," *Numen* 23: 161-78.

———. 1981. *Man's Quest for Partnership: The Anthropological Foundations of Ethics and Religion.* Assen, The Netherlands.

van Gennep, A. 1960. *Rites of Passage.* Chicago.

Warren, P. 1981. "Minoan Crete and Ecstatic Religion," in R. Hägg and N. Marinatos, eds., *Sanctuaries and Cults in the Aegean Bronze Age* 155-66. Stockholm.

Washburn, S. L., and C. S. Lancaster. 1968. "The Evolution of Hunting," in R. B. Lee and I. DeVore, eds., *Man the Hunter* 293-303. Chicago.

Watenabe, H. 1968. "Hunting as an Occupation of Males," in R. B. Lee and I. DeVore, eds., *Man the Hunter* 74-77. Chicago.

Widengren, G. 1969. *Religionsphänomenologie.* Berlin.

Wilson, E. O. 1975. *Sociobiology: The New Synthesis.* Cambridge, Mass.

———. 1978. *On Human Nature.* Cambridge, Mass.

Wilson, P. J. 1975. "The Promising Primate," *Man* n.s. 10: 5-20.

Wolpoff, M. H. 1982. "Ramapithecus and Hominid Origins," *Current Anthropology* 23: 501-10.

Wreschner, E. E. 1980. "Red Ochre and Human Evolution: A Case for Discussion," *Current Anthropology* 21: 631-44.

Wu Rukang and Lin Shenglong. 1983. "Peking Man," *Scientific American* 248.6: 78-86.

Young, J. Z., ed. 1982. *The Emergence of Man: A Joint Symposium.* London.

Index

Index

Accidental (the), disjunction between the Sacred and, 45–50 passim
Aeschylus, 126
Aggression: cycles of violence, murder, and, 8–9; hunting and, 24–27; theories of, 30f, 151, 159, 169–70, 173f, 256; mimetic rivalries and, 124–25. *See also* Collective murders; Hunting; Killing; Sacrifice; Violence
Agrarian societies, sacrifice in, 198–202
Ainu (the), 186–87, 203, 219
Aliens, *see* Strangers
Altruism, 157
Anatolia, 167
Ancestors: sacred, 98–99; religious ritual and, 156, 158–59
Anger, headhunting and, 243, 247, 251–53, 256
Animals: theories about hunting and sacrifice of, 22–32, 44–49, 53–61 passim, 65, 67, 107, 162–87 passim; in myths, 86; dominance patterns among, 123–29 passim; rituals of, 151; intraspecific killing by, 163–66 passim, 171; sacrifice of, 166–67, 186–87, 197–203, 205, 213–14, 218–24 passim. *See also specific kinds of animals by name*
Anthropological perspectives: scapegoating and, 73–77 passim, 97, 103–11 passim, 117, 129; on cannibalism, 175–76; failures of theoretical, 193, 207–8, 217–18; time questions and,

207–8; on origin stories, sacrifice, religion, and ritual, 239–56
Anxiety, in ritual, sacrifice, 173, 178
Apes, *see* Chimpanzees
Ardrey, Robert, 164n
Arens, W., 240
Aristotle, 124
Awe, *see under* Religion
Aztec myth, 173

Bacchae, The (Euripides), 102, 172
Baldur, 135
Bandera, Cesáreo, 187, 214, 231–32
Bavaria, 233
Bears, 44–48, 49, 186–87, 202–3
Berger, Peter, 39
Bible (Judeo-Christian): sacrifice, guilt, victim, in, 22; scapegoat in, 73; importance of, 107–8, 115–18, 141–45; redemptive violence in, 139–40; lack of ritual texts in, 210
Blindness, in myths, 104–5
Boas, Franz, 215
Bones, *see* Paleolithic evidence
Brahmanas, 217, 220, 229–31
Brahmans, 188
Brazil, 219
Burkert, Walter, 3ff, 22–32, 52–69 passim, 108, 118–19, 121, 137–38, 210–11, 232–33, 245f, 255f
Burridge, Kenelm, 42
Butler, Terrell, 145, 184